Economic Justice and Liberty

This new book reopens the debate on theories of justice between utilitarian theorists and scholars from other camps. John Rawls' 1971 publication of *A Theory of Justice* put forward a devastating challenge to the long-established dominance of utilitarianism within political and moral philosophy, and until now no satisfactory and comprehensive utilitarian reply has yet been put forward.

By expounding John Stuart Mill's system of knowledge and by reconstructing his utilitarianism, Huei-chun Su offers a fresh and comprehensive analysis of Mill's moral philosophy and sheds new light on the reconciliation of Mill's idea of justice with both his utilitarianism and his theory of liberty. More than a study of Mill, this book uses a systematic framework to draw a comparison between Mill's theory of justice and those of John Rawls, Amartya Sen and Friedrich von Hayek. It hence establishes common ground between different schools of thought in the fields of economics and philosophy, and enables more effective dialogue.

This book will be indispensable both to those interested in Mill's moral philosophy and to those seeking a solid theoretical basis for analysing the idea of justice, as well as to anyone with an interest in economic philosophy, the history of economic thought and intellectual history more generally.

Huei-chun Su is an Honorary Research Associate at the Bentham Project, University College London, UK.

Routledge studies in the history of economics

1 **Economics as Literature**
Willie Henderson

2 **Socialism and Marginalism in Economics 1870–1930**
Edited by Ian Steedman

3 **Hayek's Political Economy**
The socio-economics of order
Steve Fleetwood

4 **On the Origins of Classical Economics**
Distribution and value from William Petty to Adam Smith
Tony Aspromourgos

5 **The Economics of Joan Robinson**
Edited by Maria Cristina Marcuzzo, Luigi Pasinetti and Alesandro Roncaglia

6 **The Evolutionist Economics of Léon Walras**
Albert Jolink

7 **Keynes and the 'Classics'**
A study in language, epistemology and mistaken identities
Michel Verdon

8 **The History of Game Theory, Vol 1**
From the beginnings to 1945
Robert W. Dimand and Mary Ann Dimand

9 **The Economics of W. S. Jevons**
Sandra Peart

10 **Gandhi's Economic Thought**
Ajit K. Dasgupta

11 **Equilibrium and Economic Theory**
Edited by Giovanni Caravale

12 **Austrian Economics in Debate**
Edited by Willem Keizer, Bert Tieben and Rudy van Zijp

13 **Ancient Economic Thought**
Edited by B. B. Price

14 **The Political Economy of Social Credit and Guild Socialism**
Frances Hutchinson and Brian Burkitt

15 **Economic Careers**
Economics and economists in Britain 1930–1970
Keith Tribe

16 **Understanding 'Classical' Economics**
Studies in the long-period theory
Heinz Kurz and Neri Salvadori

17 **History of Environmental Economic Thought**
E. Kula

18 **Economic Thought in Communist and Post-Communist Europe**
Edited by Hans-Jürgen Wagener

19 **Studies in the History of French Political Economy**
From Bodin to Walras
Edited by Gilbert Faccarello

20 **The Economics of John Rae**
Edited by O. F. Hamouda, C. Lee and D. Mair

21 **Keynes and the Neoclassical Synthesis**
Einsteinian versus Newtonian macroeconomics
Teodoro Dario Togati

22 **Historical Perspectives on Macroeconomics**
Sixty years after the 'General Theory'
Edited by Philippe Fontaine and Albert Jolink

23 **The Founding of Institutional Economics**
The leisure class and sovereignty
Edited by Warren J. Samuels

24 **Evolution of Austrian Economics**
From Menger to Lachmann
Sandye Gloria

25 **Marx's Concept of Money**
The God of Commodities
Anitra Nelson

26 **The Economics of James Steuart**
Edited by Ramón Tortajada

27 **The Development of Economics in Europe since 1945**
Edited by A. W. Bob Coats

28 **The Canon in the History of Economics**
Critical essays
Edited by Michalis Psalidopoulos

29 **Money and Growth**
Selected papers of Allyn Abbott Young
Edited by Perry G. Mehrling and Roger J. Sandilands

30 **The Social Economics of Jean-Baptiste Say**
Markets and virtue
Evelyn L. Forget

31 **The Foundations of Laissez-Faire**
The economics of Pierre de Boisguilbert
Gilbert Faccarello

32 **John Ruskin's Political Economy**
Willie Henderson

33 **Contributions to the History of Economic Thought**
Essays in honour of R. D. C. Black
Edited by Antoin E. Murphy and Renee Prendergast

34 **Towards an Unknown Marx**
A commentary on the manuscripts of 1861–63
Enrique Dussel

35 **Economics and Interdisciplinary Exchange**
Edited by Guido Erreygers

36 **Economics as the Art of Thought**
Essays in memory of G. L. S. Shackle
Edited by Stephen F. Frowen and Peter Earl

37 **The Decline of Ricardian Economics**
Politics and economics in post-Ricardian theory
Susan Pashkoff

38 **Piero Sraffa**
His life, thought and cultural heritage
Alessandro Roncaglia

39 **Equilibrium and Disequilibrium in Economic Theory**
The Marshall–Walras divide
Michel de Vroey

40 **The German Historical School**
The historical and ethical approach to economics
Edited by Yuichi Shionoya

41 **Reflections on the Classical Canon in Economics**
Essays in honour of Samuel Hollander
Edited by Sandra Peart and Evelyn Forget

42 **Piero Sraffa's Political Economy**
A centenary estimate
Edited by Terenzio Cozzi and Roberto Marchionatti

43 **The Contribution of Joseph Schumpeter to Economics**
Economic development and institutional change
Richard Arena and Cecile Dangel

44 **On the Development of Long-run Neo-Classical Theory**
Tom Kompas

45 **F. A. Hayek as a Political Economist**
Economic analysis and values
Edited by Jack Birner, Pierre Garrouste and Thierry Aimar

46 **Pareto, Economics and Society**
The mechanical analogy
Michael McLure

47 **The Cambridge Controversies in Capital Theory**
A study in the logic of theory development
Jack Birner

48 **Economics Broadly Considered**
Essays in honour of Warren J. Samuels
Edited by Steven G. Medema, Jeff Biddle and John B. Davis

49 **Physicians and Political Economy**
Six studies of the work of doctor-economists
Edited by Peter Groenewegen

50 **The Spread of Political Economy and the Professionalisation of Economists**
Economic societies in Europe, America and Japan in the nineteenth century
Massimo Augello and Marco Guidi

51 **Historians of Economics and Economic Thought**
The construction of disciplinary memory
Steven G. Medema and Warren J. Samuels

52 **Competing Economic Theories**
Essays in memory of Giovanni Caravale
Sergio Nisticò and Domenico Tosato

53 **Economic Thought and Policy in Less Developed Europe**
The nineteenth century
Edited by Michalis Psalidopoulos and Maria-Eugenia Almedia Mata

54 **Family Fictions and Family Facts**
Harriet Martineau, Adolphe Quetelet and the population question in England 1798–1859
Brian Cooper

55 **Eighteenth-Century Economics**
Peter Groenewegen

56 **The Rise of Political Economy in the Scottish Enlightenment**
Edited by Tatsuya Sakamoto and Hideo Tanaka

57 **Classics and Moderns in Economics, Volume I**
Essays on nineteenth- and twentieth-century economic thought
Peter Groenewegen

58 **Classics and Moderns in Economics, Volume II**
Essays on nineteenth- and twentieth-century economic thought
Peter Groenewegen

59 **Marshall's Evolutionary Economics**
Tiziano Raffaelli

60 **Money, Time and Rationality in Max Weber**
Austrian connections
Stephen D. Parsons

61 **Classical Macroeconomics**
Some modern variations and distortions
James C. W. Ahiakpor

62 **The Historical School of Economics in England and Japan**
Tamotsu Nishizawa

63 **Classical Economics and Modern Theory**
Studies in long-period analysis
Heinz D. Kurz and Neri Salvadori

64 **A Bibliography of Female Economic Thought to 1940**
Kirsten K. Madden, Janet A. Sietz and Michele Pujol

65 **Economics, Economists and Expectations**
From microfoundations to macroeconomics
Warren Young, Robert Leeson and William Darity Jnr.

66 **The Political Economy of Public Finance in Britain, 1767–1873**
Takuo Dome

67 **Essays in the History of Economics**
Warren J. Samuels, Willie Henderson, Kirk D. Johnson and Marianne Johnson

68 **History and Political Economy**
Essays in honour of P. D. Groenewegen
Edited by Tony Aspromourgos and John Lodewijks

69 **The Tradition of Free Trade**
Lars Magnusson

70 **Evolution of the Market Process**
Austrian and Swedish economics
Edited by Michel Bellet, Sandye Gloria-Palermo and Abdallah Zouache

71 **Consumption as an Investment**
The fear of goods from Hesiod to Adam Smith
Cosimo Perrotta

72 **Jean-Baptiste Say and the Classical Canon in Economics**
The British connection in French classicism
Samuel Hollander

73 **Knut Wicksell on Poverty**
No place is too exalted
Knut Wicksell

74 **Economists in Cambridge**
A study through their correspondence 1907–1946
Edited by M. C. Marcuzzo and A. Rosselli

75 **The Experiment in the History of Economics**
Edited by Philippe Fontaine and Robert Leonard

76 **At the Origins of Mathematical Economics**
The economics of A. N. Isnard (1748–1803)
Richard van den Berg

77 **Money and Exchange**
Folktales and reality
Sasan Fayazmanesh

78 **Economic Development and Social Change**
Historical roots and modern perspectives
George Stathakis and Gianni Vaggi

79 **Ethical Codes and Income Distribution**
A study of John Bates Clark and Thorstein Veblen
Guglielmo Forges Davanzati

80 **Evaluating Adam Smith**
Creating the wealth of nations
Willie Henderson

81 **Civil Happiness**
Economics and human flourishing in historical perspective
Luigino Bruni

82 **New Voices on Adam Smith**
Edited by Leonidas Montes and Eric Schliesser

83 **Making Chicago Price Theory**
Milton Friedman–George Stigler correspondence, 1945–1957
Edited by J. Daniel Hammond and Claire H. Hammond

84 **William Stanley Jevons and the Cutting Edge of Economics**
Bert Mosselmans

85 **A History of Econometrics in France**
From nature to models
Philippe Le Gall

86 **Money and Markets**
A doctrinal approach
Edited by Alberto Giacomin and Maria Cristina Marcuzzo

87 **Considerations on the Fundamental Principles of Pure Political Economy**
Vilfredo Pareto (Edited by Roberto Marchionatti and Fiorenzo Mornati)

88 **The Years of High Econometrics**
A short history of the generation that reinvented economics
Francisco Louçã

89 **David Hume's Political Economy**
Edited by Carl Wennerlind and Margaret Schabas

90 **Interpreting Classical Economics**
Studies in long-period analysis
Heinz D. Kurz and Neri Salvadori

91 **Keynes's Vision**
Why the great depression did not return
John Philip Jones

92 **Monetary Theory in Retrospect**
The selected essays of Filippo Cesarano
Filippo Cesarano

93 **Keynes's Theoretical Development**
From the tract to the general theory
Toshiaki Hirai

94 **Leading Contemporary Economists**
Economics at the cutting edge
Edited by Steven Pressman

95 **The Science of Wealth**
Adam Smith and the framing of political economy
Tony Aspromourgos

96 **Capital, Time and Transitional Dynamics**
Edited by Harald Hagemann and Roberto Scazzieri

97 **New Essays on Pareto's Economic Theory**
Edited by Luigino Bruni and Aldo Montesano

98 **Frank Knight and the Chicago School in American Economics**
Ross B. Emmett

99 **A History of Economic Theory**
Essays in honour of Takashi Negishi
Edited by Aiko Ikeo and Heinz D. Kurz

100 Open Economics
Economics in relation to other disciplines
Edited by Richard Arena, Sheila Dow and Matthias Klaes

101 Rosa Luxemburg and the Critique of Political Economy
Edited by Riccardo Bellofiore

102 Problems and Methods of Econometrics
The Poincaré lectures of Ragnar Frisch 1933
Edited by Olav Bjerkholt and Ariane Dupont-Keiffer

103 Criticisms of Classical Political Economy
Menger, Austrian economics and the German historical school
Gilles Campagnolo

104 A History of Entrepreneurship
Robert F. Hébert and Albert N. Link

105 Keynes on Monetary Policy, Finance and Uncertainty
Liquidity preference theory and the global financial crisis
Jorg Bibow

106 Kalecki's Principle of Increasing Risk and Keynesian Economics
Tracy Mott

107 Economic Theory and Economic Thought
Essays in honour of Ian Steedman
John Vint, J Stanley Metcalfe, Heinz D. Kurz, Neri Salvadori and Paul Samuelson

108 Political Economy, Public Policy and Monetary Economics
Ludwig von Mises and the Austrian tradition
Richard M. Ebeling

109 Keynes and the British Humanist Tradition
The moral purpose of the market
David R. Andrews

110 Political Economy and Industrialism
Banks in Saint-Simonian economic thought
Gilles Jacoud

111 Studies in Social Economics
Léon Walras
Translated by Jan van Daal and Donald A. Walker

112 The Making of the Classical Theory of Economic Growth
Anthony Brewer

113 The Origins of David Hume's Economics
Willie Henderson

114 Production, Distribution and Trade
Edited by Adriano Birolo, Duncan Foley, Heinz D. Kurz, Bertram Schefold and Ian Steedman

115 The Essential Writings of Thorstein Veblen
Edited by Charles Camic and Geoffrey Hodgson

116 Adam Smith and the Economy of the Passions
Jan Horst Keppler

117 **The Analysis of Linear Economic Systems**
Father Maurice Potron's pioneering works
Translated by Christian Bidard and Guido Erreygers

118 **A Dynamic Approach to Economic Theory**
Lectures by Ragnar Frisch at Yale University
Edited by Olav Bjerkholt and Duo Qin

119 **Henry A. Abbati: Keynes' Forgotten Precursor**
Selected writings
Serena Di Gaspare

120 **Generations of Economists**
David Collard

121 **Hayek, Mill and the Liberal Tradition**
Edited by Andrew Farrant

122 **Marshall, Marshallians and Industrial Economics**
Edited by Tiziano Raffaelli

123 **Austrian and German Economic Thought**
Kiichiro Yagi

124 **The Evolution of Economic Theory**
Edited by Volker Caspari

125 **Thomas Tooke and the Monetary Thought of Classical Economics**
Matthew Smith

126 **Political Economy and Liberalism in France**
The contributions of Frédéric Bastiat
Robert Leroux

127 **Stalin's Economist**
The economic contributions of Jenö Varga
André Mommen

128 **E.E. Slutsky as Economist and Mathematician**
Crossing the limits of knowledge
Vincent Barnett

129 **Keynes, Sraffa, and the Criticism of Neoclassical Theory**
Essays in honour of Heinz Kurz
Neri Salvadori and Christian Gehrke

130 **Crises and Cycles in Economic Dictionaries and Encyclopaedias**
Edited by Daniele Bensomi

131 **General Equilibrium Analysis**
A century after Walras
Edited by Pascal Bridel

132 **Sraffa and Modern Economics, Volume I**
Edited by Roberto Ciccone, Christian Gehrke and Gary Mongiovi

133 **Sraffa and Modern Economics, Volume II**
Edited by Roberto Ciccone, Christian Gehrke and Gary Mongiovi

134 **The Minor Marshallians and Alfred Marshall**
An evaluation
Peter Groenewegen

135 **Fighting Market Failure**
Collected essays in the Cambridge tradition of economics
Maria Cristina Marcuzzo

136 The Economic Reader
Edited by Massimo M. Augello and Marco E. L. Guido

137 Classical Political Economy and Modern Theory
Essays in honour of Heinz Kurz
Neri Salvadori and Christian Gehrke

138 The Ideas of Ronald H. Coase
Lawrence W. C. Lai

139 Anticipating the Wealth of Nations
Edited by Maren Jonasson and Petri Hyttinen, with an Introduction by Lars Magnusson

140 Innovation, Knowledge and Growth
Edited by Heinz D. Kurz

141 A History of Homo Economicus
The nature of the moral in economic theory
William Dixon and David Wilson

142 The Division of Labour in Economics
A history
Guang-Zhen Sun

143 Keynes and Modern Economics
Edited by Ryuzo Kuroki

144 Macroeconomics and the History of Economic Thought
Festschrift in honour of Harald Hagemann
Edited by Hagen M. Krämer, Heinz D. Kurz and Hans-Michael Trautwein

145 French Liberalism in the 19th Century
An anthology
Edited by Robert Leroux

146 Subjectivisim and Objectivism in the History of Economic Thought
Edited by Yukihiro Ikeda and Kiichiro Yagi

147 The Rhetoric of the Right
Language change and the spread of the market
David George

148 The Theory of Value and Distribution in Economics
Discussions between Pierangelo Garegnani and Paul Samuelson
Edited by Heinz Kurz

149 An Economic History of Ireland Since Independence
Andy Bielenberg

150 Reinterpreting the Keynesian Revolution
Robert Cord

151 Money and Banking in Jean-Baptiste Say's Economic Thought
Gilles Jacoud

152 Jean-Baptiste Say
Revolutionary, entrepreneur, economist
Evert Schoorl

153 Essays on Classical and Marxian Political Economy
Samuel Hollander

154 **Marxist Political Economy**
Essays in retrieval: selected works of Geoff Pilling
Edited by Doria Pilling

155 **Interdisciplinary Economics**
Kenneth E. Boulding's engagement in the sciences
Edited by Wilfred Dolfsma and Stefan Kesting

156 **Keynes and Friedman on Laissez-Faire and Planning**
'Where to draw the line?'
Sylvie Rivot

157 **Economic Justice and Liberty**
The social philosophy in John Stuart Mill's utilitarianism
Huei-chun Su

Economic Justice and Liberty

The social philosophy in John Stuart Mill's utilitarianism

Huei-chun Su

Routledge
Taylor & Francis Group
LONDON AND NEW YORK

First published 2013
by Routledge
2 Park Square, Milton Park, Abingdon, Oxon OX14 4RN

Simultaneously published in the USA and Canada
by Routledge
711 Third Avenue, New York, NY 10017

Routledge is an imprint of the Taylor & Francis Group, an informa business

British Library Cataloguing in Publication Data
A catalogue record for this book is available from the British Library

Library of Congress Cataloging in Publication Data
Su, Huei-chun.
Economic justice and liberty: the social philosophy in John Stuart Mill's Utilitarianism/Huei-chun Su.
pages cm
1. Mill, John Stuart, 1806–1873. Utilitarianism. 2. Utilitarianism.
3. Distributive justice. 4. Liberty. I. Title.
B1603.U873S82 2013
171′.5–dc23 2013001784

ISBN: 978-0-415-69275-5 (hbk)
ISBN: 978-0-203-74311-9 (ebk)

Typeset in Times New Roman
by Wearset Ltd, Boldon, Tyne and Wear

Contents

Acknowledgements xvii
A note on texts and references xix

Introduction 1

PART I
Scientific foundation of Mill's philosophy 7

1 Epistemological and psychological foundations of Mill's utilitarian moral philosophy 9

PART II
Utilitarianism and theory of justice 27

2 Mill's utilitarianism as a system of moral philosophy 29

3 Mill's utilitarianism as a theory of morality 50

4 Reconstructing Mill's theory of justice 74

5 Economic justice, liberty and utilitarianism 99

PART III
Dialogues – justice and liberty in focus 111

6 Rawls versus Mill: deontological versus teleological theory of justice 113

7 Sen versus Mill: equal capability versus equal claim to happiness 136

8 Hayek versus Mill: equality before the law versus equal real freedom for all 156

Conclusions: prospect – the continuing relevance of Mill's utilitarianism today 168

Notes 188
Bibliography 198
Index 207

Acknowledgements

I would like to express my deepest gratitude to my Ph.D. supervisor Professor John Maloney, who was an invaluable mentor as well as an excellent teacher while I was pursuing my Ph.D. at the University of Exeter in the UK. On numerous occasions John provided his most encouraging support, assisting me without hesitation in pursuing my studies and my career. Years after I left Exeter, his help and support has never stopped. He provided valuable comments on a series of drafts of this book.

I am also grateful to many people who have been kind enough to read and comment on the manuscript in its later stages. I would like to thank Professor Henry West, Dr Andy Hamilton, Dr Roger Crisp, Dr Michael Quinn, Mr John Gent, Mr Richard Davies and Dr Christopher Macleod for their detailed and valuable comments on parts of the manuscript. I also received assistance with my research on Mill from Professor Fred Rosen, Professor Philip Schofield, Professor David Colander, Professor Wendy Donner, Dr David Chilosi, Professor Ben Fine, Professor María Alejandra Carrasco, Professor Sumitra Shah, Dr Georgios Varouxakis, Professor Jonathan Riley and Professor Ricardo Crespo. I owe a special debt of gratitude to Professor Philip Schofield, whose support during the later stages of the book and my appointment as an Honorary Research Associate at the Bentham Project at University College London was indispensable for completing this work.

My gratitude also goes to Professor Sandra Peart and Professor Robert Dimand for their help and encouragements since the early stages of my research on Mill and the history of economic thought. I appreciate very much the encouragement from Professor Peter Boettke, Professor Steve Horwitz and Professor Emily Chamlee-Wright, whose recognition of my work helped me appreciate the true meaning of liberal thought and learn to be open-minded to different schools of thought. This attitude has an important impact on this work. The Mellon Prize Research Grants awarded by the Centre for History and Economics at the University of Cambridge provided me an invaluable opportunity to be a visiting student at Cambridge and to improve my Ph.D. research, part of which is presented in this book. The support and friendship of my ex-colleagues at the London School of Economics was certainly unforgettable. The lively and intriguing discussion my students brought into the class made the teaching there most enjoyable and was also beneficial to my research. A portion of Chapter 9 appeared as 'Is Social Justice For or Against Liberty? On the Philosophical Foundations of Mill and Hayek's Theory of Liberty' in *Review of Austrian Economics* 22 (December 2009).

I am indebted to Professor Chen Ting-an, Professor Huang Shi-Sin, Professor Ju Tze-Ming and Professor Yen Chueh-An, my teachers back home, for their long-time encouragement. For decades they have been writing and speaking for the people of Taiwan. Their influence on my firm belief in social justice is beyond doubt. A special gratitude goes to Mr Lin Shin-Hong, the first person to introduce me to John Stuart Mill as a great man and a great philosopher. He also provided constructive comments on the book.

The support from dott. Renato Caretta and Mrs Michela Marin, my parents-in-law, was crucial during the writing of this book. The constant support from my beloved parents Mr Su Ming-Shan and Mrs Hsu Chiu-Hsia was essential to make this book possible. Last but not least a big hug and a kiss to my dear husband Ottone Caretta and my lovely son Cornelio for supporting my dreams and for bearing my endless absence from family time.

Huei-chun Su
December 2012, Oxford

A note on texts and references

All references to Mill's writings in this book are to the *Collected Works of John Stuart Mill*, Toronto University Press, by volume and page number. The list below indicates the titles of specific items cited in this book and the volumes and page numbers they appear in the *Collected Works*. For the convenience of searching, the volume and page numbers come before the title in the list. The number in '()' indicates the year in which the work was first published and the number in '[ ]' indicates the year in which the edition of work cited in this book was published. In the case where there is only the year for the first publication, the year for citation is the same. In the case of Mill's correspondences, the year refers to the year when the letter was written.

CW, I: 1–290, Autobiography (1873)
CW, II: 1–429, Principles of Political Economy, Books I–II (1844) [1871]
CW, III: 455–971, Principles of Political Economy, Books III–V (1844) [1871]
CW, IV: 309–339, On the Definition of Political Economy; and on the Method of Investigation Proper to It (1836) [1844]
CW, V: 631–668, Thornton on Labour and Its Claims (1869)
CW, V: 703–753, Chapters on Socialism (1879)
CW, VIII: 833–952, A System of Logic, Ratiocinative and Inductive, Book VI (1843) [1872]
CW, X: 3–18, Remarks on Bentham's Philosophy (1833)
CW, X: 19–29, Blakey's History of Moral Science (1835)
CW, X: 31–74, Sedgwick's Discourse (1835) [1867]
CW, X: 75–115, Bentham (1838) [1867]
CW, X: 117–163, Coleridge (1840) [1867]
CW, X: 165–201, Whewell on Moral Philosophy (1852) [1867]
CW, X: 203–259, Utilitarianism (1861) [1871]
CW, X: 261–368, Auguste Comte and Positivism (1865) [1866]
CW, XV: 644–650, Letter to William George Ward (1859)
CW, XVIII: 117–147, Civilization (1836)
CW, XVIII: 213–310, On Liberty (1859) [1869]
CW, XIX: 579–613, Centralisation (1862)
CW, XX: 317–363, Vindication of the French Revolution of February 1848 (1849)

CW, XXI: 51–60, Austin's Lectures on Jurisprudence (1832)
CW, XXI: 259–340, Subjection of Women (1869)
CW, XXXI: 93–253, James Mill's Analysis of the Phenomena of the Human Mind (1869)

Introduction

Utilitarianism has been an influential but controversial philosophy since its modern inception by Jeremy Bentham (1748–1832). The misgivings about utilitarianism as the foundation of morals and legislation are particularly grave when justice is under consideration. Its status in political and moral philosophy was further undermined by John Rawls's *A Theory of Justice* in 1971. Despite controversies over his methodology, Rawls's challenges to utilitarianism are devastating: they almost pronounced the obituaries for utilitarian theories of justice, since it seems that no satisfactory and comprehensive utilitarian reply has yet been put forward.

Indeed, while writing *A Theory of Justice*, Rawls had a large aim in mind: he intended to offer an alternative account of justice to the dominant utilitarianism by generalizing and carrying the traditional theory of social contract to a higher order of abstraction. What led him to attempt this ambitious project, as he explains clearly in the preface of his book, was his belief that those who criticized such great utilitarians as David Hume, Adam Smith, Bentham and John Stuart Mill, often did so on a much narrower front: the critics failed to construct a workable and systematic moral conception to oppose these great utilitarians. The extensive theory of distributive justice systematically constructed by Rawls was a shattering blow to the credibility of utilitarian account of justice.

This book, despite being largely inspired by Rawls' aim, does not intend to present a definitive work on social justice. Instead, it aims to reopen a constructive debate on theories of justice between utilitarian theorists and scholars from other camps.

Why Mill?

'It is a rule both of justice and of good sense', as Mill puts it, 'to grapple not with the absurdist, but with the most reasonable form of a wrong opinion' (Mill, *CW, VIII*: 880). For that reason, this study chooses Mill as the core of its reply to the most fatal challenge to utilitarianism, that it is doomed to be an unjust and illiberal philosophy through its ultimate aim of maximizing total utility.

Since Rawls forcefully argued that utilitarianism violates ideas of distributive justice and equal liberty, his view has been repeatedly affirmed by many political philosophers, ethical theorists and economists. Amartya Sen's criticisms of utilitarianism, in line with Rawls's, have a particularly significant influence in the field of economics. The economists who show inclination for philosophical conversation seem to be persuaded by a standard criticism that utilitarianism ignores the issues of distributive justice, liberty, and rights, a theme presented in several of Sen's influential books, including *Utilitarianism and Beyond*, a book co-edited with Bernard Williams, *On Ethics and Economics*, and *Development as Freedom*. However, it is intriguing to note that in spite of their criticisms of utilitarianism, neither Rawls nor Sen has ever initiated vigorous attacks against Mill. Rawls is clearly aware that Mill's utilitarianism is not subject to most of his charges against utilitarianism and even believes that Mill would agree with his view regarding equal liberty. Sen hardly if ever directly argues against Mill's utilitarianism and he actually delightedly admits the influence of Mill on his thinking, in particular the idea of personal liberty. The special treatment of Mill by these two influential leading opponents of utilitarianism suggests that his utilitarianism deserves a scrupulous treatment separate from other variants.

It is Mill's ideal that

> the great end of social improvement should be to fit mankind by cultivation, for a state of society combining the greatest personal freedom with that just distribution of the fruit of labour, which the present laws of property do not profess to aim at.
>
> (Mill, *CW, II*: xciii)

This claim does not imply that Mill's utilitarianism can provide a sound philosophical foundation consistently to support his ideal. However, it offers a good starting point to explore the social philosophy on which Mill's ideal is based. Our provisional contention is that Mill's utilitarianism does not clash with justice or liberty. The major assumption underlying this contention is that Mill's principle of utility is not a direct criterion of rightness and justice. It must be stressed that this assumption is not a new proposition. It can be traced back at least to the revisionary view of Mill which emerged in the 1970s. In the last few decades more Mill scholars have accepted it. However, this view has not yet been widely accepted because there is still no comprehensive and rigorous theoretical framework for explaining it systematically and coherently. This author intends to undertake such a theoretical reconstruction.

Main arguments of this book

The central assertion of this research is that Mill's utilitarianism can effectively support equal rights to individual liberty and distributive justice. In addition to the main thesis, it also explores three other important issues. First, by reconstructing the system of Mill's utilitarianism as a three-level moral system, this research attempts to disentangle the puzzling relationships between expediency, rightness and justice in moral theory. Second, it attempts to bridge the gap Mill left between the first principle of morality and moral rules in practice, by introducing a new method of moral reasoning, so that Mill's utilitarianism can help to regenerate modern utilitarianism. Lastly, this research aims at demonstrating that different attitudes of theorists towards political and economic institutions are largely affected by their concepts of happiness, justice and liberty as well as the different views on the priorities between these three ideas, and therefore are ultimately determined by their epistemological approach and their understanding of human nature.

Organization of this book

In addition to the introductory and concluding chapters, this book comprises three parts: Part I is an exploration of epistemological and psychological foundations of Mill's moral philosophy; Part II is an investigation and reconstruction of Mill's utilitarianism, with an examination of his ideas of economic justice and liberty within the reconstructed framework; Part III is a defence of Mill's theory of justice by replying to the criticisms of the utilitarian theory of justice made by John Rawls and Amartya Sen as well as the criticisms of the idea of social justice made by Friedrich Hayek.

Part I

Part I contains one chapter that deals with the scientific foundations of Mill's moral philosophy. Chapter 1 demonstrates how Mill bases his utilitarian moral philosophy on scientific theories. The first part of Chapter 1 investigates the epistemological and psychological foundations of Mill's moral philosophy. The second part focuses on some of Mill's propositions of human nature and how these affect his moral philosophy.

Part II

Part II concerns Mill's theory of justice as part of his moral theory, and his moral theory as part of his utilitarian moral philosophy. As the introductory chapter of Part II, Chapter 2 investigates the status of Mill's utilitarianism as a general philosophy, a perspective broader than that of morality. By elucidating some elementary concepts in Mill's moral philosophy, it clarifies the structural relationship between the realms of expediency, morality and justice in Mill's utilitarianism. The second part of Chapter 2 discusses how well the act- and rule-utilitarian framework can represent Mill's utilitarianism by examining some of the most influential interpretations made by well-known scholars. The last part of this chapter reconstructs Mill's utilitarianism as a three-level structure and builds a framework for utilitarian moral reasoning, so that his general theory of justice and theory of economic justice in particular can be examined in a comprehensive and analytical manner in the later chapters.

In contrast to Chapter 2, which focuses on the formal structure of Mill's moral philosophy, Chapter 3 deals more directly with the substantive content of his theory of morality. It starts with reinterpreting some of its key notions, including moral wrong, sentiments of justice and moral obligations. By placing Mill's *Utilitarianism* in context, the first part of Chapter 3 rereads his arguments from a non-traditional perspective and reaches several new interpretations. The second part of Chapter 3 discusses the relationship between the right and the good in Mill's philosophy. It does not aim to address the questions inherent in teleology regarding the relationship between the right and the good or to defend Mill's position fully. Rather, it only aims to clarify the argumentation strategy he adopts in *Utilitarianism*, which has not been fully appreciated by scholars. The last part of Chapter 3 explores Mill's idea of happiness, utility and pleasure, in particular his distinction of higher and lower pleasures.

Chapter 4 demonstrates how to apply the theoretical structure discussed in Chapters 2 and 3 to analyse Mill's theory of justice. The first part investigates Mill's idea of justice in general by scrutinizing the relationship between justice and equality at three different levels. It also discusses the differences between three closely connected ideas – social justice, economic justice, and distributive justice. The second part focuses on Mill's theory of economic justice by exploring his arguments for different principles of justice in different economic affairs.

Chapter 5 demonstrates a central assertion of this project, that Mill's utilitarianism can effectively and consistently support equal rights to individual liberty and distributive justice. Mill's social philosophy requires distributive justice as the premise of equal liberty, because he believes that before the means of subsistence have been assured, liberty is a vacuous concept. Thus Mill's utilitarian account of social justice aims at real freedom for all.

Part III

Part III defends Mill's theory of justice against the criticisms of Rawls, Sen and Hayek. It argues that Mill's theory of justice, if not superior to, is at least as promising as those of Rawls, Sen and Hayek in securing individual liberty. It also demonstrates that Mill's theory of justice shares similarities with Rawls's two principles of justice, and Sen's capability approach.

Chapter 6 first examines Rawls's writings on Mill. In order to explain the characteristics he attributes to Mill's utilitarianism, the first part briefly reviews the transition of the notion of utility and maximizing total utility from the late nineteenth century to the mid-twentieth century. It then argues that Rawls's understanding of Mill, despite being sympathetic, is inaccurate and hence several of his criticisms are not applicable. The second part of Chapter 6 compares Mill's theory of justice and Rawls's. It first argues that it is mistaken to compare Mill's principle of utility with Rawls's two principles of justice because they are not counterparts. It then identifies the principles of justice in Mill's utilitarianism which can be seen as the counterpart to Rawls's two principles of justice. The third part of Chapter 6 examines the relationship between justice and liberty in Rawls's theory and argues that for him, justice is to ensure everyone equal prospects of life. The fourth part demonstrates the similarities between Mill and Rawls by showing how their theories of distributive justice converge in social institutions at the level of practice. Lastly, the chapter suggests that in some aspects Rawls's deontological theory of justice is not superior to Mill's teleological theory of justice.

Chapter 7 contrasts Mill's utilitarianism with Sen's capability approach. It starts with Sen's criticisms of utilitarianism and then gives a brief summary of his capability approach in order to contrast Mill's and Sen's theories. The second section of Chapter 7 argues that Mill's utilitarianism cannot be characterized by welfarism, sum-ranking or narrowly defined consequntialism, the three components Sen attributed to utilitarianism in general. In reply to Sen's criticisms, this section focuses on why Mill's utilitarianism cannot be characterized as welfarism by exploring his idea of happiness. In so doing, it also shows the similarities between Mill's conception of happiness and Sen's concept of well-being. The next section examines the relationship between justice and liberty in Sen's theory. It argues that for him, justice is for real substantive freedom for all. Thus Sen's and Mill's idea of justice shares an important feature: that poverty is one of the biggest threats to individual liberty and hence a major obstacle to happiness or well-being. Last, this chapter argues that as a system of moral philosophy Sen's capability approach encounters at least two challenges. The challenges are likely to be resolved, but Sen's capability approach in its current form does not seem to have a clear approach to address them. However, there is built-in mechanism in his utilitarianism which enables Mill to resolve the same problems in a more systematic manner.

Chapter 8 attempts to answer Hayek's attack on Mill's idea of justice. Hayek, one of the most influential liberal thinkers in the twentieth century, argues strongly against Mill's notion of social justice and believes that its pursuit confers absolute power on the state and hence threatens individual liberty. The inevitable tension between social justice and individual liberty alleged by Hayek is the central theme of his theory of liberty, shared by many liberals and most neo-liberals after him. Whether Mill's theory can successfully reply to Hayek's challenge thus has relevance to today's global political and economic order, which is largely led by the neo-liberal thinking. Chapter 8 starts with Hayek's discussion of justice and social justice and his charge that Mill fosters a socialist mentality. It then assesses his reading of Mill and argues that Mill is immune from Hayek's attack because his criticisms are targeted on a straw man rather than the real Mill. The third part of Chapter 8 analyses why in Hayek's view social justice suppresses individual liberty while for Mill it protects it. The analysis suggests that the difference in the concept of individual liberty results from a different understanding of human nature. The chapter ends by arguing that Mill's theory of justice is superior to Hayek's from both theoretical and practical perspectives.

Based on the reinterpretation and reconstruction of Mill's utilitarianism presented in Part I to Part III, the concluding chapter attempts to illustrate the continuing relevance of Mill's utilitarianism today. It demonstrates that his system of knowledge allows a dynamic and forward-looking process that advances his moral philosophy. Two streams of recent scientific studies are particular relevant to Mill's philosophy: first, the latest neuroscientific evidence supports the psychological foundation of his moral theory; moreover, empirical investigations in the science of happiness in recent years also support his theory of happiness and pleasure. Mill's utilitarian philosophy, consciously built on the science of man, is promising to provide a set of consistent and comprehensive logic and moral principles to bridge the gap between the science and the politics of happiness, a hotly debated issue in several Western countries. The last part of the concluding chapter explains why Mill's utilitarianism is a promising philosophy to rebuild a happy, just and liberal society when extremely unequal income and wealth distribution seriously threaten happiness, justice and liberty today – the three grand values for which human beings have fought throughout history.

How to read Mill

The last remark in this introductory chapter is a declaration of how Mill's work has been approached by this author when writing this book. Perhaps the best way to present this approach is to identify the opposite manner by quoting Mill's words:

> This is a reading age; and precisely because it is so reading an age, any book which is the result of profound meditation, is perhaps less likely to be duly and profitably read than at a former period. The world reads too much, and too quickly, to read well [...] The world, in consequence, gorges itself with intellectual food of all qualities, and in order to swallow the more, bolts it. Nothing is now read slowly, or twice over.
>
> (Mill, *CW, XXI*: 53)

More than 170 years after this passage was written, this vivid description remains true. Admittedly, in an era of explosion in information like today, it is necessary to read quickly in order to read more so that we can cope with the abundant information surrounding us. It is also true that in a world stuffed with various books it does not cause much loss to read through most books in haste. Yet for Mill's work this is not the case. It will be a great loss if we read Mill's work without the patience to appreciate his thought. This author intends to demonstrate this by presenting this book as a result of reading Mill carefully and thoroughly.

Part I

Scientific foundation of Mill's philosophy

1 Epistemological and psychological foundations of Mill's utilitarian moral philosophy

Before Mill, David Hume (1711–1776) had attempted to ground his moral theory on the science of the human mind. Both his *A Treatise of Human Nature* and *An Enquiry Concerning Human Understanding* essentially provide the scientific foundation for his moral theory. Like Hume, Mill also builds his system of moral philosophy on the basis of moral sciences. It follows that a thorough understanding and full evaluation of Mill's utilitarian moral theory requires a careful examination of the relationship between his moral theory and his theory of human beings. This chapter will investigate the scientific foundation of Mill's moral philosophy.

Epistemology and utilitarian morality

The most effective approach to understanding the epistemological foundation of Mill's moral theory is to contextualize his work by recognizing the intellectual landscape against which he defends the utilitarian moral philosophy. This approach is particularly helpful, given that the main opponents of utilitarianism in philosophy have shifted from the intuitionism school in the nineteenth and early-twentieth century to contractarianism, of which John Rawls is a representative, in the mid-twentieth century. In *Utilitarianism*, Mill argues against intuitionism and the a priori school at the most abstract level regarding the *final* judgement on moral questions and the *origin* of moral sentiments, which for him are the essentially epistemological issues.

Ethical intuitionism developed as a reaction to the Enlightenment in the eighteenth century, and reached its apogee in Britain in the nineteenth century. In Mill's view, as a consequence of the reaction of the nineteenth century against the eighteenth, the apotheosis of Reason had been replaced by Instinct: 'we call everything instinct which we find in ourselves and for which we cannot trace any rational foundation' (Mill *CW, XXI*: 263). With the endorsement of important philosophers, such as Adam Sedgwick (1785–1873), William Hamilton (1788–1856), and William Whewell (1794–1866), ethical intuitionism had become the most influential approach to ethical theories in Mill's time. Meanwhile, on the other side of the Channel, Kant's moral theory also became noticeably influential. In spite of some important differences, these two schools echoed each other's a priori view of morality, namely, human beings have a priori moral knowledge about what is right and wrong.

Strictly speaking, British intuitionists and German transcendentalists had different views about the origins of moral judgement. The former believed that human beings perceive moral properties through peculiar faculties called moral *senses*;[1] for the later, it is pure *reason* that tells us what is right and wrong. Nevertheless, both schools share a similar view of the objectivity of morality: moral properties of actions or states of affairs are objective knowledge, knowable prior to rather than learnt from experience.

Despite Mill's criticisms of the intuitionist and Kantian moral theory, it is important to note that what distinguishes Mill's moral theory from the other two is not the content of moral rules. In fact, they would have many shared views on which moral rules should be obeyed in practice. For instance, they all agree that it is a general moral rule that human beings ought to promote others' happiness, and that keeping promises, not lying, and not stealing are proper moral rules. It is the *origin* of moral obligation and the *first* principle of morality that are the main divergences between the moral philosophy of Mill and those of the intuitionists and Kant.

Mill considers the lack of a first principle a serious problem inherent in ethical intuitionism. This problem, to borrow the distinction within intuitionism made by Bernard Williams, is one of the characteristics of 'methodological intuitionism', in contrast to 'epistemological intuitionism'.[2] Indeed, Mill stresses this problem of the a priori moral theory in both the *System of Logic* and *Utilitarianism*. Nevertheless, it seems that for Mill 'epistemological intuitionism' will cause a far more serious problem than methodological intuitionism. In Mill's view, the chance of appealing directly to a first principle is in fact very low because there is often agreement on various secondary ends among people, despite their differing in ultimate standards (Mill, *CW, X*: 110–111). In contrast, he considers the a priori view of morality as 'an instrument devised for consecrating all deep-seated prejudices', which had hindered the improvement of English society in the eighteenth century (Mill, *CW, I*: 233). As Ryan comments, the intuitionist view seems to Mill to be 'a doctrine designed to foster conservatism, for it assured people that anything they believed deeply enough must be true' (Ryan, 1974, p. 60).

Far from being a purely philosophical debate, the argument between intuitionism and the empiricism conducted by utilitarian philosophy is 'full of practical consequences' (Mill, *CW, I*: 233, 269; *CW, X*: 73). The practical consequences which deeply concerned Mill are the threats to the progress of the human mind which may result from the a priori view of moral judgements and moral feelings. If it were true that 'man has a sense given him to determine what is right and wrong', Mill worries, 'his moral judgments and feelings cannot be susceptible of any improvement' (Mill, *CW, X*: 73–74).

The barriers to progress in nineteenth-century England have to be traced to the epistemological foundation of the a priori view of morality:

> The notion that truths external to the mind may be known by intuition or consciousness, independently of observation and experience, is, I am persuaded, in these times, the great intellectual support of false doctrines and bad institutions. By the aid of this theory, every inveterate belief and every intense feeling, of which the origin is not remembered, is enabled to dispense with the obligation of justifying itself by reason, and is erected into its own all-sufficient voucher and justification.
>
> (Mill, *CW, I*: 233)

Moreover, Mill believes that 'the chief strength of this false philosophy in morals, politics, and religion, lies in the appeal which it is accustomed to make to the evidence of mathematics and of the cognate branches of physical science' (Mill, *CW, I*: 233). It follows that if he intends to expel the a priori view of knowledge from morals, he has first to deal with the epistemological foundation of mathematics and physical science. This idea of demolishing the a priori view of morality led Mill to his writing of the *System of Logic*, where he encounters intuitive philosophers on the epistemological ground.[3]

For Mill, epistemology is the starting-point of every consistent scheme of philosophy, including moral philosophy. It deals with two fundamental questions: 'the sources of human knowledge' and 'the objects which the mind is capable of knowing' (Mill, *CW, X*: 125). On the first issue, Mill believes that experience is the only material of knowledge: 'All knowledge consists of generalizations from experience [...] There is no knowledge *a priori*; no truths cognizable by the mind's inward light' (Mill, *CW, X*: 125). On the second issue, he believes that nothing can be the object of our knowledge 'except our experience and what can be inferred from our experience by the analogies of experience itself' (Mill, *CW, X*: 128–129).

It is Mill's view that the sources of our knowledge in moral science and in natural science are the same. Although the subject matter is very different – one refers to human phenomena, the other to natural phenomena – sensation and the mind's consciousness of its own acts are the sole materials of human knowledge (Mill, *CW, X*: 125). In other words, experience is the source of moral knowledge: a priori moral knowledge is impossible.

The psychological foundation of utilitarianism

Laws of mind

In Mill's time, it was still debatable whether psychology was a science. It was once widely accepted that states of mind were merely the products of bodily processes: it would follow therefore that there is no science of psychology, only one of physiology. Mill disputes this view. He believes that observation and experiment have made it incontestable that some states of mind, instead of being the direct results of the body, are the results of other states of mind, and that there exist uniformities of succession among states of mind (Mill, *CW, VIII*:

851). Therefore, psychology is 'a distinct and separate science of mind', that studies the laws between these states of mind (Mill, *CW, VIII*: 851).

Mill confines the subject of psychology to the 'uniformities of succession', that is, the laws 'according to which one mental state succeeds another, is caused by, or at least, is caused to follow, another' (Mill, *CW, VIII*: 852). Of these laws, there are two most general ones. The first is:

> whenever any state of consciousness has once been excited in us, no matter by what cause [...] a state of consciousness resembling the former, but inferior in intensity, is capable of being reproduced in us, without the presence of any such cause as excited it at first.
>
> (Mill, *CW, VIII*: 852)

In short, 'every mental impression has its idea', as Mill writes, using the language of Hume (Mill, *CW, VIII*: 852).

The second general law, which is particularly significant for our present discussion, is that 'these ideas, or secondary mental states, are excited by our impressions, or by other ideas, according to certain laws which are called Laws of Association' (Mill, *CW, VIII*: 852). Among them, Mill summarizes the three most elementary laws of ideas: first, 'similar ideas tend to excite one another'; second, 'when two impressions have been frequently experienced (or even thought of) either simultaneously or in immediate succession, then whenever one of these impressions, or the idea of it, recurs, it tends to excite the idea of the other'; third, 'greater intensity in either or both of the impressions, is equivalent, in rendering them excitable by one another, to a greater frequency of conjunction' (Mill, *CW, VIII*: 852). Further, he maintains that complex laws of thought and feeling must be generated from these simple or elementary laws of mind (Mill, *CW, VIII*: 853).

Mill's psychology adopts most of his father's views. In the psychological analyses of James Mill, the laws of the phenomena of mind are analogous to mechanical laws. But Mill claims that they are sometimes analogous to chemical laws: 'When many impressions or ideas are operating in the mind together, there sometimes takes place a process of a similar kind to chemical combination' (Mill, *CW, VIII*: 853). He uses an example to demonstrate the case of 'mental chemistry':

> When impressions have been so often experienced in conjunction, that each of them calls up readily and instantaneously the ideas of the whole group, those ideas sometimes melt and coalesce into one another, and appear not several ideas, but one; in the same manner as, when the seven prismatic colours are presented to the eye in rapid succession, the sensation produced is that of white. But as in this last case it is correct to say that the seven colours when they rapidly follow one another *generate* white, but not that they actually *are* white; so it appears to me that the Complex Idea, formed by the blending together of several simpler ones, should, when it really

appears simple, (that is, when the separate elements are not consciously distinguishable in it), be said to *result from*, or *be generated by*, the simple ideas, not to *consist* of them.

(Mill, *CW, VIII*: 853–854; emphases original)

Such a view of the formulation of complex ideas distinguishes Mill's psychology from that of Bentham and James Mill and, as Wilson comments, gives him a powerful tool to explain the nature of moral sentiments and to support utilitarian moral theory (Wilson, 1998, pp. 215–216). Mill uses it to analyse moral feelings, which are not the result of any peculiar law of our nature but can be explained by the same laws on which all our other complex ideas and feelings depend.

The origin of moral sentiments

The issue of the origin of moral sentiments is different from that of the standard of moral obligation. These two questions, though closely connected, are distinct. The *standard* or *test* of moral obligation is about 'what rule we *ought* to obey and why'; the *origin* of our moral sentiments is about 'how our feelings of approbation and disapprobation *actually* originate' (Mill, *CW, X*: 26; emphases original).[4] The former is a matter of art; the latter, a matter of science. It is important to remember that the focus of this chapter is not the criterion of morality, which is a matter of norm, but the origin of moral sentiments, which is a matter of fact.

Mill's moral theory is in the British empiricist tradition in the sense that, for him, 'moral' is a property which cannot be found in objects or by reason. Nevertheless, Mill's views of moral sentiments is clearly different from that of his predecessors in this tradition. A brief discussion of Hume, Bentham and James Mill's views on moral sentiment can help us in appreciating the distinctive features of Mill's theory.

Hume has a significant place in the history of moral theory. In Book III of *A Treatise of Human Nature* and *An Enquiry concerning the Principles of Morals*, he argues that morality is not an objective property existing in the object, but a subjective property existing in the human mind. This view has become a distinguishing mark of British empiricism. Hume seems to believe that the perception of moral qualities takes place through distinct faculties, namely, moral senses (Hume, 1975, Appendix I). Nevertheless, there is still an important distinction between Hume and the intuitionists. Despite believing that moral sentiments are excited by the particular structure and fabric of the human mind, Hume does not claim that the faculties of sentiments inform us of an objective moral property existing in the object we observe. Rather, the sentiments generated by human faculties are subjective feelings of approbation or disapprobation and it is these feelings that determine what moral qualities are. That is to say, morals originate in natural *feelings*. It has to be remembered that this does not mean that rightness or wrongness is simply determined by these subjective feelings. Rather, it suggests that 'moral feelings are feelings of a special kind (a distinctive kind of pleasure and pain) which we entertain about certain characters, actions and states of affairs' (Scarre, 1996, p. 58). In other words, moral judgement does not express objective reality existing outside the human mind, nor does it ascribe objective moral qualities to things. How moral standards are formed in relation to these natural feelings is another question.[5]

According to Mill's reading, Bentham, unlike Hume, does not appreciate the existence of the feeling of moral approbation or disapprobation (Mill, *CW, X*: 95). While criticizing the theory of moral sense, natural right and conscience as a mere cover for dogmatism, Bentham did not offer metaphysical grounds for his own moral doctrine. Mill complains that this neglect of the foundations of moral doctrine in fact leaves plenty of space for those who are acquainted with the moral doctrines either of the Reid and Stewart school, or of the German metaphysicians, to easily answer Bentham's critiques of the intuitionist view of moral sense. Mill worries that if the metaphysical explanation which Bentham can provide for the utilitarian doctrine is attributing the love of pleasures and the aversion of pains to 'nature', the a priori school of morality can likewise claim that our moral sentiments are 'as much part of the original constitution of man's nature as the desire of happiness and the fear of suffering' (Mill, *CW, X*, pp. 5–6).

In contrast to Bentham, James Mill elaborates on the origin of moral distinctions and the formation of moral sentiments in his psychological analysis. In the notes Mill made for the new edition of his father's *Analysis of the Phenomena of the Human Mind*, he summarizes James Mill's theory of moral sentiments as follows:

> the *foundation* of the moral feeling is the adoption of the pleasures and pains of others as our own [...] The moral feeling rests upon this identification of the feelings of others with our own, but is not the same thing with it. To constitute the moral feeling, not only must the good of others have become in itself a pleasure to us, and their suffering a pain, but this pleasure or pain must be associated with our own acts as producing it, and must in this manner have become a motive, prompting us to the one sort of acts, and restraining us from the other sort.
>
> (Mill, *CW, XXXI*: 232–233, emphasis original)

Mill inherited most of his father's theory of moral sentiments. He also holds firmly that moral feelings and sentiments, like other sentiments, are accounted for by the laws of association. This view is sometimes called ethical naturalism because it holds that the moral feeling originates from our natural feelings (for instance, Berger, 1984, p. 9; Raphael, 1994, pp. 17–18). It is important to note, however, that naturalism in this sense does not imply that the natural feeling is the standard or test of the morality.

To hold the view that the moral sentiments are simply the results of associations, both James Mill and John Mill have to demonstrate the existence of a causal relationship between the causes and moral sentiments as the effects and to distinguish the case of moral sentiments from other ordinary cases.[6] In other words, they have to be able to show that feelings, when they are moral feelings, are not simply likings or dislikings. It is James Mill's observation that there are actions as beneficial as any others, yet they do not excite the moral sentiment of approbation if 'the spontaneous motives to those beneficial acts are in general sufficient'; for example, 'to eat when we are hungry or to do a service for which we are to be amply paid' (Mill, *CW, XXXI*: 240). Similarly, there are actions of very harmful character, but they may not become objects of moral reprobation if the natural deterrents are sufficient for preventing those acts, for instance, in general, 'acts destructive of one's own life or property' (Mill, *CW, XXXI*: 240).

Mill rejects his father's explanation of why in some cases but not others moral sentiment will be provoked. For James Mill, the origin of moral sentiments is the need to encourage those beneficial acts which will not be produced due to the insufficiency of the spontaneous motives and the need for checking those hurtful acts which will not be prevented due to the insufficiency of the natural deterrents. In Mill's view, such an explanation seems to 'explain everything about the moral feelings, except the feelings themselves' (Mill, *CW, XXXI*: 240). It explains praise and blame, reward and punishment, and 'every other distinction which we make in our behaviour between what we desire to encourage, and what we are anxious to check' (Mill, *CW, XXXI*: 240). They are the expression of the feelings of approbation and disapprobation, but not the feelings themselves:

> we may give expression to the feeling without really having it, in the belief that our praise or blame will have a salutary effect; but no anticipation of salutary effects from our feeling will ever avail to give us the feeling itself.
>
> (Mill, *CW, XXXI*: 240)

Finding his father's reasons inadequate, Mill proposes another explanation of why the feeling of moral approbation is usually absent in the case of actions for which there are sufficient motives:

> These actions are done, and are seen to be done, by everybody alike. The pleasant associations derived from their usefulness merge, therefore, in our feelings towards human life and towards our fellow-creatures generally, and do not give rise to any special association of pleasure with given individuals.
>
> (Mill, *CW, XXXI*, pp. 240–241)

In contrast, in the case where moral approbation is present, there must be some elements

> when we find that a certain person does beneficial acts which the general experience of life did not warrant us in counting upon – acts which would not have been done by everybody, or even by most people, in his place; we

> associate the pleasure which the benefit gives us, with the character and disposition of that individual, and with the act, conceived as proceeding from that specially beneficent disposition.
>
> (Mill, *CW, XXXI*, p. 241)

'Pleasure', 'beneficial act', and 'unusually beneficent disposition of the agent' are the three indispensable elements in this judgement of an act to be moral based on association, differentiating it from a likeable act.

Moreover, it should be noted that the moral feeling here is one in a broad sense. It covers not only the feelings of obligation, but also the feelings towards all properties which can be named virtue. Although the feelings of obligation and the feelings of virtues are both called 'moral' feelings, this class of feelings called moral in fact 'embraces several varieties, materially different in their character' (Mill, *CW, XXXI*: 241). Mill considers that the feeling of duty or obligation is 'a very different state of mind from mere liking for the action and good will to the agent' and that a complete association theory of the moral sentiments must be able to show the difference (Mill, *CW, XXXI*: 241). Yet he found that his father's association theory may account for the feeling of mere liking for the action and good will to the agent, but not for the feeling of duty. Mill considers that this deficiency was also the challenge of their moral doctrine, given that it is based on their psychology of association. The problem, Mill told the reader, as examined in the last chapter of *Utilitarianism*, is 'the connexion between Justice and Utility' (Mill, *CW, XXXI*: 241). Mill's discussion of the moral feeling of duty or obligation and the sentiment of justice will be scrutinized in Chapter 2.

Mill's discussion of moral sentiments has two significant implications for his moral philosophy. First, it announces the possibility of the improvement of the human mind and therefore morality. Further, it demonstrates the possibility that utilitarian doctrine is a workable moral doctrine with the assistance of education. Before exploring Mill's views regarding how the moral sentiments can be cultivated, we will first examine his theory of human nature.

Human nature and the motives of human conduct

For Mill, the theory of human life is the fundamental theory of moral science and moral philosophy. On Mill's view, the field of human nature and life can never be studied too much. On the contrary, he believes that the study of human nature and life should cover as many perspectives as possible, including moral and aesthetic parts. (Mill, *CW, X*: 94) Despite recognizing its importance, Mill did not produce a single complete discourse on human nature. So in order to understand his concept of human nature thoroughly, it is necessary to gather views scattered in different places of his works.

Here we focus on his essays 'Remarks on Bentham's Philosophy' (1833) and 'Bentham' (1838) because some of Mill's most important propositions on human nature can be found in these two essays, in which he makes critical comments on Bentham's concept of man. Another important reason for us to study Mill's account of human nature in this way is that for a long time his concept of man has been overshadowed by Bentham's, which has been taken as representative of the utilitarian account of man. By studying Mill's criticisms, we will also learn the difficulties of Bentham's account of human nature for the utilitarian moral theory. Attention will be focused on how two concerns distinguish Mill's moral theory from Bentham's: first, the diversity in motives of human conduct; second, the status of self-regarding interest and sympathy in Mill's concept of human nature.

Bentham begins his *An Introduction to the Principles of Morals and Legislation* by claiming that 'Nature has placed mankind under the governance of two sovereign masters, pain and pleasure [...] They govern us in all we do, in all we say, in all we think' (Bentham, 1970, p. 11). Similarly to Bentham, James Mill also holds that every voluntary act is produced by a motive and that a motive is an idea of pleasure or pain contemplated as effects of our action. As a result of the influence of Bentham and James Mill, the following two claims become the features of utilitarian views of human nature: first, 'persons always act from a desire for pleasure; all voluntary acts are sought only as a means to the end of pleasure'; and second, 'persons always seek their own pleasure or good in all their voluntary acts' (Berger, 1984, p. 12). The first claim is often labelled 'psychological hedonism', the second 'psychological egoism' (Berger, 1984, p. 13). Sometimes it is maintained that psychological hedonism is a specific form of psychological egoism.[7] In effect however they are two different theories, even though there is a close link between them. Bentham may accept psychological hedonism, but not psychological egoism. Mill clearly rejects both, even though these two views are sometimes ascribed to him, as Crisp notices (Crisp, 1997, pp. 88–89).

That the actions of sentient beings are wholly determined by pleasure and pain is the fundamental principle of Bentham's theory. This view of human nature can be categorized as psychological hedonism, but not egoism. Based on it, Bentham creates a *motive* and an *interest* corresponding to each pleasure or pain (Mill, *CW, X*: 12–13). There are various possible motives of human conduct on Bentham's list, yet conscience and many others are left out.[8] For Mill, it is a fact that people sometimes act for the sake of conscience without contemplating pleasure or pain as consequences, even though this is a result of constant associations with pleasure or pain. Yet Bentham rejects the notion of conscience as a natural call for action. Moreover, in Mill's view, Bentham's list of motives omits not only conscience, but also the sense of honour, the sense of personal dignity, and the love of beauty. It is Mill's view that Bentham fails to recognize the possibility of pursuing 'spiritual perfection' for its own sake.

The inclusion of conscience and other possible motives of human conduct is one of the most crucial differences between Mill and Bentham's concept of man. It has significance in Mill's moral theory, which has been long neglected in the literature. For Mill, it is only when people act solely for the sake of these motives, without the deliberation of interests, that they are considered to be virtuous.[9] If Mill's reading is correct, Bentham's view of motives virtually makes it impossible for humans to be virtuous, in the very meaning of the word. Moreover, it leaves little space for improvement of the moral state of human beings.[10]

In addition to connecting each motive with pleasure or pain, it is also Bentham's view that human actions always obey their interests. This assertion is one of the most important axioms of his philosophy. In Mill's opinion, this axiom says no more than the 'very trivial proposition' that all persons do what they feel themselves most disposed to do (Mill, *CW, X*: 13). However, this common-sense proposition, after being presented by Bentham with philosophical expressions, became unclear. It caused serious confusion about Bentham's theory of human nature, confusion mainly caused by the term 'interest'.

Mill maintains that Bentham by no means intended to impute universal selfishness to mankind by asserting that human actions are always obedient to their own interests. He notices that Bentham does include sympathy among his list of possible springs to action:

> Man is conceived by Bentham as a being susceptible of pleasures and pains, and governed in all his conduct partly by the different modifications of self-interest, and the passions commonly classed as selfish, partly by sympathies, or occasionally antipathies, towards other beings.
>
> (Mill, *CW, X*: 94)

To Mill, the real challenge of Bentham's theory is that he categorizes sympathy with the group of 'interests'. Even though Bentham distinguishes two kinds of interests – the self-regarding and social – the everyday meaning of the word 'interests' is usually associated with the former but not the latter. Mill therefore complains that Bentham's grouping sympathy with interests is confusing. As a result, Bentham's proposition that 'a man's selfish interest would prompt him to a particular course of action' eventually became 'a man will act as the selfish interest prompts' (Mill, *CW, X*: 14). Bentham himself seems to be the victim of this confusion of language and a strong tendency to egoism consequently appears in Bentham's words:

> In *every* human breast (rare and short-lived ebullitions, the result of some extraordinarily strong stimulus or excitement, excepted) self-regarding interest is predominant over social interest; each person's own individual interest over the interests of all other persons taken together.
>
> (Bentham, *Book of Fallacies*, cited by Mill, *CW, X*: 14)

Certainly, Bentham does not ignore the importance of other-regarding interests in human actions. However, it is also true that in his understanding of human behaviour, self-regarding interests are dominant. Hence it is fair to say that in Bentham's mind human beings are predominantly selfish.

It is often debated whether Bentham subscribes to psychological egoism. If psychological egoism means 'each person will prefer their own interest to that of others', Bentham seems to be a psychological egoist. On the other hand, if psychological egoism means 'all motives are self-regarding', then it is clear that he does not hold this view. Bentham's statement that 'the only interests which a man at all times and upon all occasions is sure to find *adequate* motives for consulting, are his own' cannot be used to suggest that he thinks that human beings will never have other-regarding motives (Bentham, 1970, p. 284, emphasis original). Such a suggestion apparently ignores the sentences immediately following the statement:

> Notwithstanding this, there are no occasions in which a man has not some motives for consulting the happiness of other men. In the first place, he has, on all occasions, the purely social motive of sympathy or benevolence: in the next place, he has, on most occasions, the semi-social motives of love of amity and love of reputation.
>
> (Bentham, 1970, p. 284)

Unlike Bentham, who places sympathy in the category of self-interest, Mill treats sympathy as a part of human nature distinct from self-love or selfishness. Human beings are inclined to sympathize with other sentient beings no less than to consider their own interests. In Mill's view, sympathy, other-regarding interests, or even conscience can be the potential leading factor in human decision-making. Some people may still argue that when we think of the pleasure of others, we ultimately think of our own pleasure. For Mill, this reasoning is invalid. According to Mill's idea of motivation, if we do not consider our own pleasure or interest at the moment when the decision is made, the action cannot be considered the result of a self-interested motive.[11] However, as Berger comments, it is not an easy task to argue that sympathy alone is sufficient to be a motive, given that sympathizing with other sentient beings cannot be separated from our mental experience of pleasures and pains (Berger, 1984, p. 20). Yet Berger's quotation of Mill clearly disputes the claim that our being sympathetic towards others is motivated by contemplating *our own pleasure*:

> It is [...] obvious that the pleasure or pain with which we contemplate the pleasure or pain felt by somebody else, is itself a pleasure or pain of our own. But if it be meant that in such cases the pleasure or pain is *consciously* referred to self, I take this to be a mistake. By the acts or other signs exhibited by another person, the idea of a pleasure (which is a pleasurable idea) or the idea of a pain (which is a painful idea) are recalled, sometimes with considerable intensity, but in association with the other person as feeling them, not with one's self as feeling them.
>
> (Mill, *CW, XXXI*: 219, emphasis added)

It is worth mentioning that Adam Smith has a similar view of sympathy. He does not think self-love can account for sympathy either. Smith's vivid illustration adequately explains why sympathy cannot be reduced to self-love:

> Sympathy [. . .] cannot, in any sense, be regarded as a selfish principle. When I sympathize with your sorrow or your indignation, it may be pretended, indeed, that my emotion is founded in self-love, because it arises from bringing your case home to myself, from putting myself in your situation, and thence conceiving what I should feel in the like circumstances. But though sympathy is very properly said to arise from an imaginary change of situations with the person principally concerned, yet this imaginary change is not supposed to happen to me in my own person and character, but in that of the person with whom I sympathize. When I condole with you for the loss of your only son, in order to enter into your grief I do not consider what I, a person of such a character and profession, should suffer, if I had a son, and if that son was unfortunately to die: but I consider what I should suffer if I was really you, and I not only change circumstances with you, but I change persons and characters. My grief, therefore, is entirely upon your account, and not in the least upon my own. It is not, therefore, in the least selfish. How can that be regarded as a selfish passion, which does not arise even from the imagination of any thing that has befallen, or that relates to myself, in my own proper person and character, but which is entirely occupied about what relates to you?
>
> (Smith, 2002, p. 374)

This view of sympathy as a motive independent from the consideration of self-interest has particular significance to modern economic analyses of human actions. In the last two decades, many economists have incorporated sympathy in their models to explain cooperative personal exchange in experimental situations.[12] In these experiments, there seems to be no clear distinction between sympathy and reciprocity: gift, assistance, and favours are out of sympathy; 'reciprocal altruism' is generated by sympathy. However, it is arguable whether the concept of reciprocity, the origin of exchange, can be attributed to the concept of sympathy, because sympathy may be aroused without any expectation of return in the future or even without any contemplation of the agent's own pleasures or pains at all. For instance, we show sympathy to strangers or those who are unlikely to have any relationship with us in the future. When we watch a tragic movie most people will feel pity for the characters; when we see a dog being ill-treated, most people will sympathize with it. Yet we do not expect any similar affections in return either by those who we feel sorry for or any other unknown beings. If these economic experiments fail to recognize that sympathy can be a genuine motive of benevolent conduct, it is very likely that their outcomes will suffer from the mistaken conflation of reciprocity and sympathy. The probable vicious effect of blurring reciprocity and sympathy should not be overlooked. Associating expectations of reciprocity with sympathy may be harmful to the cultivation of moral sentiment, since it tends to deny the possibility of sympathy being the basis of virtuous generous behaviour. By the very meaning of virtuous behaviour, expectation of return should not be the reason for the action, or at least not play the major role in the process of decision-making.

Happiness as the end of all human conduct

The claim that human beings desire nothing but happiness is a foundation of Mill's utilitarian moral philosophy. This claim encountered challenges because it is an apparent fact that people do desire things other than happiness. Mill recognizes this and considers it to be true that sometimes people act without considering pleasure or pain as consequence of their actions. Nevertheless, he believes it is also true that a motive to an act consists of the *association* of pleasure with the act. His associationist psychology underlies his view that happiness is the sole end of all human conduct.

Following his father, Mill does not consider many things such as wealth, power, and dignity as pleasures *in their own nature*. Instead, they are only *causes* of pleasurable sensations or of relief from pain (Mill, *CW, XXXI*: 220, 231). It is by association that these things become *pleasurable in themselves*, and the objects of desire. Once they become so, they are a part of happiness. Otherwise, they are desired only as a means of happiness. Moreover, the fact that things are not by their nature sources of pleasure does not imply that they are less desired. Through the multitude and variety of the pleasurable ideas associated with them, wealth, power, and dignity 'become pleasures of greater constancy and even intensity than any of the primitive pleasures of our constitution' (Mill, *CW, XXXI*: 220).

For the above theory to be considered true there is still one challenge to be answered. If money, among other things, is not a pleasure in its own nature but as a result of association, then the pleasurable idea of money must resemble the pleasures which have been attached to other things. However, the pleasure of acquiring money usually appears to be strong and distinct from pleasure from other sources. This is a phenomenon that could not be explained by James Mill's psychology, but can be explained by Mill's, with its view of mental chemistry. Mill demonstrates how mental association works as if the human mind experiences a *chemical* change:

> When a complex feeling is generated out of elements very numerous and various, and in a corresponding degree indeterminate and vague, but so blended together by a close association, the effect of a long series of experiences, as to have become inseparable, the resulting feeling always seems not only very unlike any one of the elements composing it, but very unlike the sum of those elements. The pleasure of acquiring, or of consciously possessing, a sum of money (supposed not to be desired for application to some specific purpose), is a feeling, to our consciousness, very different from the pleasure of protection against hunger and cold, the pleasure of ease and rest from labour, the pleasure of receiving consideration from our fellow-creatures, and the other miscellaneous pleasures, the association with which is admitted to be the real and only source of the pleasure of possessing money.
>
> (Mill, *CW, XXXI*: 239)

In addition to wealth, power and dignity, the above analysis is also applicable to other goods such as virtue, knowledge, etc. In fact, virtue is one of the examples which Mill uses to demonstrate how it comes to be something desired for its own sake while there was no original desire of it (Mill, CW, X: 236–237). If the above analysis is correct, then he has proved his claim that happiness is the end of all human conduct to be truth as a fact.

Human character and utilitarian moral philosophy

Both human nature and human character are crucial concepts in Mill's science of man and his moral philosophy. Nevertheless, human character plays a particularly significant role in his utilitarian moral theory. Although Mill has not offered a clear definition for either human character or human nature, his description of selfishness serves well as the starting point for differentiating these two concepts:

> The deep-rooted selfishness which forms the general character of the existing state of society, is so deeply rooted, only because the whole course of existing institutions tends to foster it; modern institutions in some respects more than ancient, since the occasions on which the individual is called on to do anything for the public without receiving its pay, are far less frequent in modern life, than the smaller commonwealths of antiquity.
>
> (Mill, *CW, I*: 241)

This passage implies that selfishness, the prevailing state of mind among most English people in Mill's time, is not a pure reflection of human nature, for it was largely fostered by social institutions. In other words, Mill considers that selfishness is part of human nature, but its dominance is not. For him, the disposition of being selfish represents a type of human *character*, which is the outgrowth of human nature, but not human nature itself. Mill's distinction of human character from human nature announces the malleability of human mind, which can be cultivated in such a way that selfishness is less effective. To reach this goal, it is necessary to understand how human character is formulated on the ground of human nature.

Ethology and political ethology as the scientific foundation of moral philosophy

In spite of its importance psychology, as an experimental science, has serious limitations in explaining the phenomena of the human mind in reaction to numerous circumstances, Mill believes.[13] Therefore, he considers it necessary to construct a science of human nature which studies the universal laws by which 'the whole of the phenomena of human action and feeling are produced' (Mill, *CW, VIII*: 864). Ethology is such a science, studying the laws of the formation of character, which eventually result from the general laws of mind. The laws of the formation of character have to be obtained by deduction from the general laws of mind 'by supposing any given set of circumstances, and then considering what, according to the laws of mind, will be the influence of those circumstances on the formation of character' (Mill, *CW, VIII*: 869). Mill believes that this deductive method endows ethology with a true scientific character and hence ethology may be called 'the Exact Science of Human Nature' (Mill, *CW, VIII*: 870). Nevertheless, it has to be noted that the propositions of ethology are strictly hypothetical. They do not affirm facts, but tendencies only: '[t]hey must not assert that something will always or certainly happen, but only that such and such will be the effect of a given cause, so far as it operates uncounteracted' (Mill, *CW, VIII*: 870). It follows that the main function of ethology is not for predicting, but for informing us what we can do if we hope to make certain kinds of results happen.

In addition to individual character, Mill stresses the national or collective character. The laws of national or collective character are 'by far the most important class of sociological laws' (Mill, *CW, VIII*: 905). For Mill, the collective character which is formed by any state of social circumstances is the element of all the other social phenomena (Mill, *CW, VIII*: 905). Moreover, the interaction between collective character and social circumstances is like a dynamic circle:

> the character, that is, the opinions, feelings, and habits of the people, though greatly the results of the state of society which precedes them, are also greatly the causes of the state of society which follows them; and are the power by which all those of the circumstances of society which are artificial – laws and customs, for instance – are altogether moulded: customs evidently, laws no less really, either by the direct influence of public sentiment upon the ruling powers, or by the effect which the state of national opinion and feeling has in determining the form of government, and shaping the character of the governors.
>
> (Mill, *CW, VIII*: 905)

In Mill's view, a better understanding of the diversities of individual and national character is crucial to the development of the other moral sciences. Although the omission of ethological considerations is no defect for each separate branch of social inquiry at the stage of being a hypothetical science, it will vitiate the sciences 'in their practical application as branches of a comprehensive social science' (Mill, *CW, VIII*: 905–906). Since it is necessary to undertake the inquiry of social phenomena by breaking up into several branches for the purpose of employing scientific methodology, a highly cultivated ethology becomes indispensable. Mill demonstrates how ethology may improve the scientific quality of human studies by using the discipline of political economy as an example. In the nineteenth century, it was commonly assumed by English political economists that an intensity of competition is a general mercantile fact and that businessmen will always care about their pecuniary gain more than their ease. However, Mill suggests that these assumptions were true only in Great Britain and the United States: in Continental Europe it was very common that other motives often outweigh 'the desire of money-getting, even in the operations which have money-getting for their direct object' (Mill, *CW, VIII*: 906). If the assumptions are different from the real circumstances, then the conclusions, deductively derived from hypothetical assumptions, need to be modified by taking real circumstances into account. Mill considers that this can only be achieved properly by a well-established political ethology.

Moreover, the relationship between social character and social environment is not static, but dynamic. In addition to being an effect of social institutions, social character is an important cause in determining the change of social institutions. Social character, based on human nature, is moulded by the structure of society. The dominant character traits will in their turn become the forces shaping the social process. This dynamic relationship indicates the necessity of understanding the formulation of human character for the reform of social institutions.

Characters and the cultivation of moral sentiments

From Mill's definition of ethology, we can infer that a character is a certain disposition of the human mind. It represents the totality of a person's 'mental states, and our mental capacities and susceptibilities, [which] are modified, either for a time or permanently, by everything which happens to us in life' (Mill, *CW, VIII*: 863). In contrast to human nature, the innate properties of human beings, human character is the outgrowth of human nature formed 'under the circumstances in which mankind have happened to be placed' (Mill, *CW, VIII*: 862). Essentially, character is formed by a person's experiences. It is changeable by insight and new kinds of experiences.

In Mill's view a comprehensive moral theory should not overlook the influence of human character on human behaviour. Although the consideration of character will not change the judgement of the rightness or wrongness of the actions, it has significance in the improvement of the moral state of the human mind in the long term. Mill believes that every action must presuppose a certain state of mind. In other words, some types of character are more inclined to cause certain types of actions. Moreover, the consequences of every action will in turn influence the characters. This dynamic relationship between character and the consequences of action caused by the character is an important feature of Mill's moral theory, and was overlooked by Bentham and many other utilitarians. The neglect may not have caused problems on the judgement of rightness or wrongness, but it makes their utilitarianism a far less progressive moral theory, because virtuous characters are less likely to be encouraged and hence the moral state of the human mind will be less likely improved.

Furthermore, unless we accept that it is possible for character to play a greater role than rationality in most human actions, the chances of human beings improving their moral state will be very low.[14] By definition, a virtuous person is one who has a constant tendency to do good things without contemplating their own interests before taking the action. That is to say, they respect the interest of others not for instrumental reasons but for its own sake. A person, unless having a confirmed character, cannot be expected to act morally. Mill believes that character can, and has to, be directed to a preferable virtuous state through education and sound social institutions. Moreover, cultivating such a virtuous character is not merely an ideal, far beyond human capacities. On the contrary, Mill considers that a virtuous character can be firmly grounded in sympathy and social feelings, which are the universal sentiments in human nature.

It is worth emphasizing here that sympathy is not the same thing as moral sentiment, despite being its basis. Mill also considers sympathy as a quite different feeling from that of morality. Sympathy is an innate part of human nature; yet moral sentiments are not an 'original' part of mankind's constitution (Berger, 1984, p. 23). Nevertheless sympathy, this unselfish part of human nature, is inclined to associate with the feeling of morality and offers a stable foundation for morality. Unlike self-love, sympathy is a much weaker part in human nature, and hence has to be carefully nurtured and developed (Berger, 1984, pp. 21–22).

In addition to sympathy, fellow-feeling is another important psychological characteristic of human nature which offers a stable foundation for moral feelings. In Mill's view, human beings have a natural desire 'to be in unity with our fellow creatures' (Mill, *CW, X*: 231). This desire, according to Berger's interpretation, is manifested in such forms as 'the love of glory, the love of praise, the love of admiration, the love of respect and deference' as well as 'the fear of shame, the dread of ill repute, or of being disliked or hated' (Berger, 1984, p. 22). The desire to be in accord with our fellows is so strong that it becomes one of the most promising sources for the cultivation of moral sentiments:

> Through all departments of human affairs, regard for the sentiments of our fellow-creatures is in one shape or other, in nearly all characters, the pervading motive. And we ought to note that this motive is naturally strongest in the most sensitive natures, which are the most promising material for the formation of great virtues.
>
> (Mill, *CW, X*: 60)[15]

Similar to sympathy, fellow feeling or social feeling itself is not a moral feeling. It was Mill's view that feelings become 'moral' only when they arise from, and are in conformity with, a regard for the general utility (Berger, 1984, p. 26). From our experience of social life, the feeling of being part of society will gradually grow and we will recognize the need to take account of others' interests. Consequently, our own feelings become 'more and more identified with the feelings of others' and then the moral feelings will be formed (Donner, 1991, p. 115). In other words, despite being a much stronger natural impulse than sympathy, fellow feeling needs 'direction and encouragement' for the cultivation of moral sentiments (Donner, 1991, p. 115). 'Direction' is an issue that needs to be dealt with cautiously, since this natural feeling may also be improperly used as a tool to suppress dissenting views. For Mill, social feelings are the natural basis of sentiment for utilitarian morality; if the general happiness is recognized as the ethical standard the cultivation of moral sentiments can be more effectively based on social feelings.

Part II

Utilitarianism and theory of justice

2 Mill's utilitarianism as a system of moral philosophy

Despite Mill's effort of expelling intuitionism from ethical thinking, as discussed in the previous chapter, the influence of intuitionism remained predominant in the English-speaking world during the early decades of the twentieth century.[1] One of the reasons that accounted for the unpopularity of utilitarianism as a moral theory at the time was the belief that utilitarianism was a moral doctrine which is ready to allow exceptions to general accepted rules, a view largely due to the enormous influence of G. E. Moore. Such exceptions caused misgivings because they justify conduct which struck our common consciousness as immoral from the intuitionist point of view. This problem was deemed as the chief defect of utilitarianism by Roy F. Harrod (1900–1978), who published a paper 'Utilitarianism revised' in 1936 in order to restore a fairer view of utilitarianism.[2] Harrod differentiated the crude utilitarian maxim from the more refined one, which recognizes moral obligations by 'applying the process of generalization in all relevant cases, that is in all cases where the consequences of n similar acts exceed n times the consequences of any one' (Harrod 1936, p. 148). In other words, when considering the consequence of an act, what should be taken into account by a utilitarian is not the consequence of one individual act, but the consequence of one type of action being generally performed in similar circumstances. Later this view was denoted as 'rule-utilitarianism' in contrast to the traditional 'act-utilitarianism' by Richard Brandt.[3] Ever since, 'act-utilitarianism' and 'rule-utilitarianism' have become the basic vocabularies of the literature on moral theories in the twentieth century.

A vast literature has also developed to examine whether Mill is an act-utilitarian or rule-utilitarian. A book on Mill's moral theory might be considered incomplete if it does not discuss the difference between act-utilitarianism and rule-utilitarianism or use this distinction to approach Mill's moral theory. The enormous literature on the act- and rule-utilitarian interpretation of Mill may give modern readers the impression that Mill's utilitarianism is either act- or rule-utilitarianism, but how well do these two concepts characterize Mill's moral system? Before we attempt to answer this question, we should notice that both act- and rule-utilitarianism are concerned the form of utilitarianism as a theory of morality which is devoted to determining the moral standard of right and wrong *actions*. It is important to bear in mind that moral theory in this sense is only part of Mill's broad concept of utilitarianism as a system of moral philosophy.[4] In order to understand Mill's moral theory correctly, it is essential to examine it within the architecture of his moral philosophy.

In this chapter, we will first scrutinize the formal structure of Mill's moral philosophy. This will allow us to appreciate the role and stature of the principle of utility as the first principle in his moral philosophy. We then examine whether Mill's moral theory could be classified as act- or rule-utilitarianism. Lastly, we attempt to reconstruct a framework of Millian utilitarian moral reasoning.

The architecture of Mill's moral philosophy

It is well known that Mill divides his system of knowledge into two parts: science and art. In contrast to the famous distinction per se, the *interrelationship* between science and art in Mill's theory has received far less attention. The field of science and that of art are closely linked and complement each other. An art, in order to be an art, has to be grounded in a scientific knowledge of the properties of the subject-matter; otherwise, it would not be philosophy (Mill, *CW, IV*: 312). According to Mill, art cannot exist alone without science as its theoretical foundation. The reverse is also true. The art and the science have their own distinct functions. Through a series of interactions between art and science, a desirable end defined by the art will be provided by the science with a theorem by which the end could be produced, and the theorem will finally be converted into a rule or precept of art (Mill, *CW, VIII:* 944).

Science and art are like two pillars in the architecture of Mill's system of knowledge. There is a matching interrelation between these two piers: each art has its corresponding sciences.[5] For instance ethics, being a moral art, corresponds to the science of man, including psychology and ethology (Mill, *CW, VIII*: Book 6, Chapters 4 and 5). The art of government, another example of moral art, corresponds to such sciences as political economy and politics in addition to psychology and ethology (Mill, *CW, IV*: 320–321). Furthermore, there is a hierarchical structure inside each pillar. For example, in the pillar of science, psychology and ethology are the most fundamental sciences; the construction of other sciences has to be based on them. Similarly, the pillar of art is also of a hierarchical structure: there is a body of doctrine to which 'all other arts are subordinate' and its principles determine 'whether the special aim of any particular art is worthy and desirable, and what is its place in the scale of desirable things' (Mill, *CW, VIII*: 949). This body of doctrine is designated by Mill the Art of Life, which consists of three departments: Morality, Prudence or Policy, and Aesthetics (Mill, *CW, VIII*: 949).

The vertical relationships between different arts and those between different sciences, as well as the corresponding relationships between sciences and arts, make the structure of Mill's knowledge an intricate system: each art is either subordinate to other arts or commands other arts; also, each art presupposes its corresponding sciences; meanwhile, these corresponding sciences are also interrelated with each other. It is a hierarchical and complex structure.

The ends of different arts are different, and each art contains more than one end. As a result, there might be conflict between different ends. Therefore, Mill considers it necessary to have only *one* ultimate standard to be the final objective umpire in cases where principles conflict with each other. For if there were several ultimate principles of conduct, the same conduct might be approved by one of those principles and condemned by another; and some more general principle as umpire between them would be needed. It is well recognized that for Mill the ultimate principle of morality is the promotion of happiness of mankind, or rather, of all sentient beings. In contrast, it is often neglected that the same principle also has the same role in the provinces of prudence and aesthetics in Mill's Art of Life, even though this point has gradually been accepted as a standard view by Mill scholars in the last decade.

Given that morality is only one department of the Art of Life, the principle of utility is a principle of not only the right, but also of the expedient, the beautiful, and the noble in all human conduct and works. It follows that the violation of the principle of utility could be a case which involves moral wrongness, yet it could also be a case which is inexpedient, distasteful or abominable, but irrelevant with regard to moral wrongness.

In addition to the traditional view, there is another possible way to view Mill's Art of Life. Sometimes Mill seems to treat the three departments of the Art of Life as three aspects of an action, rather than three different types of affairs. In his essay 'Bentham', Mill sees Bentham's error as a moralist as lying in his neglecting the aspects of actions and characters other than the moral one, by emphasizing that

> Every human action has three aspects: its *moral* aspect, or that of its *right* and *wrong*; its *aesthetic* aspect, or that of its *beauty*; its *sympathetic* aspect, or that of its *loveableness*.
>
> (Mill, *CW, X*: 112, emphasis original)

This passage leaves a space for us to treat the three departments of Mill's Art of Life as guidance concerning the three aspects of *one* action, in addition to the traditional interpretation, which considers the three departments of the Art of Life as rules for three different types of issues. This route was taken by Alan Ryan to demonstrate how to appraise an act such as repaying a debt with different considerations for the three different dimensions (Ryan, 1991, p. 165). It is not easy to judge which version of two interpretations of Mill's Art of Life is the representative one. Yet there is no doubt that it is Mill's view that a comprehensive value judgement of an action requires considering these three aspects. This view constitutes an important element of his utilitarianism as the Art of Life, which should be distinguished from his utilitarianism merely as the theory of morality.

With this structure in mind, we can easily mark the difference between moral philosophy and morality. The term moral philosophy is used in our discussion to indicate an idea similar to Mill's moral arts as a whole, including the art of life and the various subordinate arts. It follows that moral philosophy is a set of knowledge that covers fields broader than morality. It is worth noting that Mill's concept of morality does not include virtue, yet virtue is indeed part of his moral philosophy. The differentiation between the two terms is not specified by Mill himself, but proposed by this author for the purpose of clarity. Nevertheless, such distinction is consistent with his own usage of the related terms.

To identify the respective realm of moral philosophy and morality as well as their relationship in Mill's system is crucial. This helps us make sense of the manner in which he uses the term utilitarianism and the principle of utility. The principle of utility is sometimes used by Mill to mean the principle guiding all practical reasoning and activities while the same term is sometimes used to refer solely to the principle of morality. Utilitarianism is also used in a parallel way. It is important to note that the principle of utility and utilitarianism are not used interchangeably in Mill's writings. Unlike the principle of utility referring to the first principle solely, utilitarianism is used to refer to a system as a whole, including the rules of moral reasoning and the secondary moral principles. There is vagueness in his usage of these two terms at times, but there is no obvious inconsistency. To grasp an accurate reading of Mill, it is necessary to read these two terms in context.

Morality and virtues

In Mill's writings, 'moral' has more than one meaning. For instance, Mill clearly specifies that 'moral' science in his usage means the science related to the 'mental', rather than science of morality (Mill, *CW, VIII*: 943). Unfortunately, the meaning of 'moral' in moral arts in Mill's writings is not always clear, and the vagueness is one of the key reasons accounting for the confusion about his moral theory.

In the usual philosophical discourse, the word 'moral' sometimes involves the ideas of punishment and obligation, but sometimes it does not. In the latter case, the meaning of moral is often close to the meaning of 'virtuous', which is praiseworthy but not necessarily obligatory. 'Moral judgement' is a typical example in which 'moral' can have two different meanings. Sometimes moral judgement is used to mean judgements which specifically concern moral obligations, but sometimes it is also used to mean judgements concerning moral values in general. For instance, when we make a moral judgement like 'stealing is wrong', it contains an obligatory element, implying that people should be punished for the violation of a presupposed rule that we should not steal. Yet when we make a moral judgement such as 'courage is admirable', we usually do not imply that cowardice should be punished.[6] Similar situations of dual meanings also occur when we use moral to describe the traits of a person or the properties of an action.

The vagueness in the meaning of moral is not a problem unique to Mill's writings. In fact, it is common in the classical literature on moral theory. For instance, David Hume's *An Enquiry concerning the Principles of Morals* is a study of 'morality' in a broad sense, which covers the sphere of virtues (Hume, 1975). Similarly, Adam Smith's *Theory of Moral Sentiments* mainly deals with the issue of virtue, meaning that he uses 'moral' in a broad sense (Smith, 2002). Although they both distinguish the cases in which 'moral' has the connotation of 'obligation' from those concerning common morals, neither Hume nor Smith explicitly spells out how to draw the line. Moreover, 'moral' is commonly used to indicate 'virtuous' in daily usage. The disparity between Mill's usage of the word moral and the traditional usage in literature and daily life is one of the important sources which caused confusion about Mill's utilitarianism as a moral principle.

Traditionally, moral philosophy was an enquiry which covered a greater range of actions and affairs than Mill attempted to confine it to. From the ancient Greek philosophers, including Aristotle and Plato, to the Scottish Enlightenment thinkers, including Hume and Smith, virtues had always been included in the discourse of morals. In contrast, Mill intentionally draws a line between morality and virtues. As Donner notices (2009, p. 43; 2010, p. 90), Mill is explicit about the distinct territory of morality and that of virtue in 'Thornton on Labour and Its Claims' where he wrote:

> Utilitarian morality fully recognises the distinction between the province of positive duty and that of virtue [...] From the utilitarian point of view, the distinction between them is the following: – there are many acts, and a still greater number of forbearances, the perpetual practice of which by all is so necessary to the general well-being, that people must be held to it compulsorily, either by law, or by social pressure. These acts and forbearances constitute duty. Outside these bounds there is the innumerable variety of modes in which the acts of human beings are either a cause, or a hindrance, of good to their fellow-creatures, but in regard to which it is, on the whole, for the general interest that they should be left free; being merely encouraged, by praise and honour, to the performance of such beneficial actions [...] This larger sphere is that of Merit or Virtue.
>
> (Mill, *CW, V*: 650–651)

It needs to be underlined that Mill's exclusion of virtues from the realm of morality does not imply that he downplays the value of virtues in his philosophy. Quite the opposite, Mill highly values virtues as something deserving unlimited pursuit; he explicitly claims that unlike the pursuit of money, power or fame, the pursuit of virtues will not do harm to others and is a thing of which the more the better (Mill, *CW, X*: 236–237). Moreover, in his view, the general cultivation of virtuous character is important to keep utilitarian morality as a sustainable moral system (Mill, *CW, X*: 213–214).

Given that virtues are so important to Mill's utilitarianism, it is curious that Mill insists on delineating morality as a branch of his Art of Life distinct from virtue, which belongs to the province of Worthiness or Nobility (Mill, *CW, X*: 246–247; Donner, 2010, p. 90). There are two possible explanations for this separation of moral duty from virtuous behaviour. First, it could be Mill's main purpose to separate morality from the virtues in order to dispute the misuse of the concept rightness and wrongness, which formed a major misunderstanding about utilitarianism as a moral theory in his time:[7]

> It is often affirmed that utilitarianism renders men cold and unsympathizing; that it chills their moral feelings towards individuals; that it makes them regard only the dry and hard consideration of the consequences of actions, not taking into their moral estimate the qualities from which those actions emanate. If the assertion means that they do not allow their judgment respecting the rightness or wrongness of an action to be influenced by their opinion of the qualities of the person who does it, this is a complaint not against utilitarianism, but against having any standard of morality at all; for certainly no known ethical standard decides an action to be good or bad because it is done by a good or a bad man, still less because done by an amiable, a brave, or a benevolent man, or the contrary. These considerations are relevant, not to the estimation of actions, but *of persons*; and there is nothing in the utilitarian theory inconsistent with the fact that there are other things which interest us in persons besides the rightness and wrongness of their actions.
>
> (Mill, *CW, X*: 220–221, emphasis added)

In short, for Mill the ultimate criterion of moral rightness and wrongness is the *consequences of actions*. The *motivations of the doers* have no role at all in determining whether an act is *morally* right or wrong.

Another possible explanation for Mill's separating morality, which is supposed to be obligatory, from virtues is that he intends to avoid undesirable coercion resulting from public opinion which will be allowed by an inappropriately enlarged scope of morality. This proposition can be supported by Mill's complaint that August Comte's ethics, like the theory of Calvinism, attempted to make every act in life a duty and whatever is not a duty is a sin. In *Auguste Comte and Positivism*, Mill writes:

> It is not good that persons should be bound, by other people's opinion, to do everything that they would deserve praise for doing. There is a standard of altruism to which all should be required to come up, and a degree beyond it which is not obligatory, but meritorious.
>
> (Mill, *CW, X*: 337)

Mill seems to believe that between the region of non-moral actions and that of obligatory actions there should be 'an intermediate space' left for a category of actions which is supererogatory, that is, praiseworthy if performed, but not morally obligatory. Therefore it is reasonable to maintain, as Berger suggests, that in the design of Art of Life Mill intends to leave a space for acts to be meritorious, but not compulsory, by excluding these acts from the domain of moral duty, where 'all moral judgments concern acts the not-doing of which are blameworthy' (Berger, 1984, pp. 26–27).

Both of the above explanations illustrate an attempt to make the judgement of rightness and wrongness based on *impersonal rationality*, without adulterating irrelevant information, such as the character or the motivation of the doer. If these suggested explanations are correct, Mill's attempt should be deemed an advance of moral theory, particularly in the sphere of legislation and public policy, rather than a cause of the neglect of personal virtues, as some scholars have recently charged.[8]

Expediency, morality and justice

Expediency is a term that appears frequently in Mill's *Utilitarianism*; it also repeatedly causes objections to utilitarianism as an ethical criterion. Most of the objections to utilitarianism confuse the notions of expediency and utility, and take the notion of expediency, rather than utility, as the standard of morality. Such confusion is not surprising, since there is an intimate relation between these two ideas. Even though Mill had already tried to clear up the confusion, his treatment is not entirely successful. The unsatisfactory outcome of his attempt is understandable because it is not easy to distinguish expediency and utility by simply defining the two respectively and then drawing a clear line between them. However, it is beyond doubt that for Mill they are two different ideas and in certain occasions definitely not interchangeable. Given that equating these two ideas causes one of the most serious obstacles for utilitarianism to be accepted as an ethical standard, we need to distinguish carefully the idea of expediency from that of utility as a moral standard.

Expedient, literally, means useful, helpful or advisable for a particular purpose. To judge whether something is useful or not, the agent has to weigh up the interests and disadvantages caused by certain means. For a particular purpose expedient always means useful, which means the interests produced by the means outweigh the disadvantages produced. However, this immediate usefulness for a particular purpose might be harmful to the agent in the long term or harmful to other ends and other people. In that case, then expediency is not equivalent to utility. Mill is clear on this point:

> the Expedient [...] generally means that which is expedient for the particular interest of the agent himself; as when a minister sacrifices the interest of his country to keep himself in place. When it means anything better than this, it means that which is expedient for some immediate object, some temporary purpose, but which violates a rule whose observance is expedient in a much higher degree. The Expedient, in this sense, instead of being the same thing with the useful, is a branch of the hurtful.
>
> (Mill, *CW, X*: 223)

According to Mill, the Expedient in these cases 'is opposed to the Right' (Mill, *CW, X*: 223). Since the word 'expedient' can mean useful both to a common good and to a private good, simply equating the Expedient with the Right is definitely a misunderstanding of Mill's moral rules. The expedient or the inexpedient in Mill's utilitarianism as a moral theory is to be interpreted in a social sense, not in an individual sense, for the expediency of individuals may be inexpedient to the society.

Accordingly, when the expediency is breached, it is not necessarily a case of moral wrong. Only the violation of a common good should be considered as a moral issue. In other words, morality is special sector of expediency distinguished from mere expediency (Harrison, 1975, p. 96; Lyons, 1994, p. 49; Gray, 1996, p. 25; Hart, 1982, p. 87).

Similarly, in Mill's system of moral philosophy justice is a part of morality, but not the whole of it (Harrison, 1975, p. 96; Gray, 1996, p. 25). If an action or a policy is called right when it observes the rules of morality and wrong when it violates the rules of morality (we shall sidestep the content of the rules at this point), then being just must be morally right; unjust must be morally wrong. The reverse is not true: being morally right does not necessarily imply justice, being morally wrong does not necessarily imply injustice.[9]

Moreover, if justice is a sector of morality and morality is a sector of expediency, justice must be a sector of expediency, but not the whole. This claim of relationship can be supported by Mill's own words that 'It has always been evident that all cases of justice are also cases of expediency' (Mill, *CW, X*: 259). Yet the reverse does not hold, because some matters of expediency have nothing to do with justice.

This understanding of the structural relationship between expediency, morality and justice is crucial to understanding the role of the principle of utility in Mill's moral philosophy. It also helps us identify the limitations of the act-utilitarian and rule-utilitarian interpretations of Mill's moral system.

Act-utilitarianism or rule-utilitarianism?

In regard to what version of utilitarianism Mill holds as his theory of morality, two separate but related threads of discussion played a significant role in directing the development of Mill scholarship in the twentieth century.

The first thread was generated by J. O. Urmson's 1953 article 'The Interpretation of the Moral Philosophy of J. S. Mill', which is generally regarded as the origin of the rule-utilitarian interpretation of Mill. In fact, it is open to question whether Urmson indeed considered Mill as a rule-utilitarian as commonly believed: he did not use this terminology and more importantly there are some crucial differences in Urmson's construction and the so-called rule-utilitarianism with the strict definition later developed by other scholars. Nevertheless, there is little doubt that Urmson's work inspired many scholars to treat Mill as a rule-utilitarian and fostered the debate between the act- and rule-interpretations of Mill in the literature.

If Harrod is the person who saved utilitarianism in general from the stigma of being a theory that contradicts our moral feeling by allowing people to break customary moral rules whenever doing so will bring in net benefits on balance, then Urmson can be seen as the one who saved Mill's utilitarianism from the same stigma. Despite shedding new light to Mill's moral theory, Urmson's work was unable to provide a definite interpretation of Mill's utilitarianism. Rather than terminating the act-utilitarian interpretation of Mill, Urmson's emphasis on the role of moral rules in Mill's moral system eventually led the traditional version of act-utilitarianism to evolve into one that recognizes the necessity of secondary rules to Mill's moral system while insisting that those rules are merely rules of thumb. On the other hand, Urmson's interpretation was considered unsatisfactory in several aspects. In particular, Urmson was not very clear regarding the status of rules in Mill's moral system and gave the impression that moral rules must be observed without exceptions. This clearly contradicts Mill's texts. In order to reconcile this with Mill's own words, proponents of rule-utilitarianism further revised Urmson's interpretation. A more advanced rule-utilitarian interpretation accepts the exceptions to rules while insisting that the exceptions have to be made on a rule basis, rather than on a case-by-case basis. Eventually, both act- and rule-utilitarian interpretations of Mill accept the indispensable role of moral rules and the unavoidability of exceptions to these secondary rules. The dividing line separating the two virtually resides in the status of these secondary moral rules: act-utilitarianism takes these rules as simplified guides to calculation whereas rule-utilitarianism holds that the secondary rules have much stronger authority because they are associated with compulsory obligations.

The other thread regarding the form of Mill's utilitarianism was initiated by Alan Ryan, who was the first scholar using Mill's discussion of the Art of Life in the *System of Logic* to clarify the scope of morality which Mill tried to delimit (1991 [1965], 1987 [1970]). Ryan's illuminative work led to a new wave of study of Mill's utilitarianism by placing it in the context of the theory of the Art of Life. The interpretation of Mill following this thread is usually known as a revisionary view, which treats his principle of utility as a theory of good, in contrast to the received view, which treats it as a theory of right.

Based on Ryan's analysis, Brown (1973) further argues that Mill's principle of utility is not concerned with the rightness and wrongness of actions, but with the only thing desirable as an end. Note the difference between Ryan and Brown: the former says that the principle of utility is not only the first principle of morality but also the first principle of the other branches of the Art of Life, whereas the latter says the principle of utility is that happiness is the only thing desirable as an end. The two views are compatible but not identical. The former does not deny the role of the principle of utility as a principle of moral right, but the latter does.

Influenced by Brown but diverging from him, Lyons (1976) continued on the path laid by Ryan to reconstruct an analytical framework of Mill's moral system. By identifying the concept of punishment as a crucial difference between the notion of morality and that of expediency, Lyons successfully demonstrated that morality is only a sector of expediency and refuted the received view that Mill's utilitarian moral theory requires one always to maximize total utility, regarding any other way of acting as wrong.

A key argument of the revisionary view is that Mill's utilitarianism does not impose agent obligations to take every action to maximize total utilities or to maximize total utilities whenever taking an action. The structure of Mill's moral system, stated in the previous sections of this chapter, is in line with this revisionary view, except that we treat Mill's principle of utility as a principle of both good and right. It is worth noting that scholars who follow this strain of reading Mill are not necessarily supporters of the rule-utilitarian interpretation. Brown, for one, firmly believes that Mill is an act-utilitarian (Brown, 1974) and one of his recent articles shows that he has not changed his standpoint (Brown, 2010).

These two lines of development significantly improve our understanding of Mill. They clearly save him from the absurd interpretation of being a simple act-utilitarian who would justify people's violating moral rules whenever their calculation of felicity suggests them doing so. Yet there is still no clear evidence to decide whether Mill is an act-utilitarian or rule-utilitarian. Even for those who believe Mill to be a rule-utilitarian, agreement is difficult to reach because some believe that his utilitarianism is an ideal moral code system while others believe it to be an actual or conventional moral code system. Each of the interpretations has support from distinguished Mill scholars.

Here we will focus on three more recent interpretations of the form of Mill's utilitarianism and examine the arguments held by the representative of each interpretation: first, multilevel act-utilitarianism held by Crisp; second, ideal moral code rule-utilitarianism by Fuchs; third, actual or conventional moral code rule-utilitarianism by Donner. We must not forget that the discussion here is constrained to Mill's theory of right or theory of morality, which is only one part of his moral philosophy. These three authors' interpretations are explicitly aimed at answering how Mill defined the rightness and wrongness of actions.

All of these scholars recognize the important role of rules in Mill's moral system. All of them recognize the place of the principle of utility in relation to the art of life, although Crisp, unlike the other two, seems to reject the revisionary view of seeing the principle of utility as merely the theory of good, but not the theory of right (Crisp, 1997, p. 128). All of them appeal to Mill's own words for their arguments, but none has unequivocal support in Mill's texts. Each of them seems to represent some truths of Mill's thought, while all of them encounter difficulties in reconciling Mill's own words. We will introduce and assess these three authors' views respectively.

Crisp's multilevel act-utilitarianism

According to Crisp, Mill is an act-utilitarian, but his utilitarianism is a multilevel version, rather than a single-level one (1997, p. 109). Crisp differentiates utilitarianism as a moral theory providing the criterion of right action from a decision-making process and interprets Mill's theory from both perspectives.

In terms of the criterion, Crisp believes that it is the consequences of an act, rather than whether the act conforms to or transgresses a moral rule, which determines the rightness or wrongness of an act. On the other hand, the multilevel view reads Mill's utilitarianism from the perspective of decision-making procedures. Influenced by Hare's arguments of two levels of moral thinking (Hare, 1981), Crisp suggests that Mill's utilitarianism consists of three levels of moral thinking: the first is a non-act utilitarian level of customary morality; the second an act-utilitarian level of customary morality and the third a philosophical act-utilitarian level. According to this three-level structure of moral reasoning, in daily life agents make their decisions of actions by following customary moral rules. They do not usually adopt the act-utilitarian moral thinking to decide what they ought to do. Only in cases where conflict arises between two or more non-utilitarian customary principles should people directly consult the utilitarian principle. The highest level is independent of the everyday moral practice at the first two levels; it is the philosophical reflection on the customary morality.

By attributing this multilevel view to Mill, Crisp is able to reconcile the important role of rules assigned by Mill with the act-utilitarian criterion of right and wrong, which is strongly supported by the statement laid down by Mill in the beginning of the second chapter of *Utilitarianism*, that is, 'The creed which accepts as the foundation of morals, Utility, or the Great Happiness Principle, holds that actions are right in proportion as they tend to promote happiness, wrong as they tend to produce the reverse of happiness' (Mill, *CW, X*: 210). However, this interpretation faces one critical challenge common to various versions of act-utilitarianism.

Crisp's interpretation, despite recognizing the importance of rules, does not require the secondary moral rules to be authoritative. As a consequence, it is not very clear how his interpretation would support the crucial role of rights granted by Mill to his utilitarianism. Crisp's disagreement with the rule-utilitarian interpretation mainly resulted from his rejection of the *intrinsic* weight given to rules by the latter. He seems to believe that if right and wrong is 'defined' by moral rules, then what 'makes' an action right is its conforming to that set of rules and that rules should always be abided by. Even though it is arguable that the version of rule-utilitarianism in Crisp's mind is not the most reasonable one, Crisp makes his point in saying that what *ultimately* justifies an action is its consequence and that Mill noticeably allows exceptions to moral rules. However, these two points are insufficient to suggest that customary moral rules are merely rules of thumb without any binding force, a claim that seems to be indicated by Crisp's interpretation. It remains unclear how Crisp's three-level act-utilitarianism would integrate with Mill's idea of justice and rights discussed in the fifth chapter of *Utilitarianism*. This is in fact a challenge encountered by all variants of act-utilitarianism that treat moral rules as mere rules of thumb.

Fuchs's ideal moral code rule-utilitarianism

According to Fuchs, Mill's moral theory should be understood as an ideal moral code rule-utilitarianism.[10] It is one form of rule-utilitarianism that evaluates rules by treating rules as component parts of a complex moral code, rather than evaluating each rule in comparative isolation as done by utilitarian generalization, another form of rule-utilitarianism. An ideal moral code is 'a set of rules that together *would* maximize utility if it was adopted and followed by the overwhelming majority of the members of a society' (Fuchs, 2006, p. 145, emphasis in original). Accordingly, morally correct actions are those required by the rules of such a code.

In comparison with act-utilitarianism, Fuchs's version of utilitarianism has a clear strength in interpreting Mill: it assigns an authority to the status of rules, that is, it is not allowed to violate rules *simply* because doing so will marginally increase utility. It recognizes the unavoidability of exceptions to rules, but the authoritative status of rules allows moral rules to protect vital interests required by Mill's idea of justice.

Nevertheless, the ideal moral code rule-utilitarian interpretation is not free from difficulties. One of the major problems is that it would require people to follow the more progressive morality before it is regarded as morally required. Mill expects there to be continuing progress in the rules of morality and continuing widening of the domain of morality in an improving society (Mill, *CW, X*: 338). An ideal moral code would require much more self-sacrifice than the current morality. For instance, it would require people to give much more to charity while it is arguable that Mill would see such sacrifice as supererogatory, part of virtue, not a matter of duty. Imposing moral obligations in accord with the *ideal* moral code would unduly expand the current domain of morality by including those which should belong to the sphere of virtue.

Donner's actual moral code rule-utilitarianism

In deciding that the ideal moral code would unduly expand the domain of morality, Donner considers the actual or conventional moral code rule-utilitarianism to be the interpretation that has the best fit with Mill's conception of morality (Donner, 2009, p. 54). The actual moral code rule-utilitarian interpretation enjoys the merits owned by Fuchs's version, namely, it is compatible with Mill's account of justice. Donner, however, is clearly aware that the actual moral code interpretation also suffers from an obvious difficulty, that is, the actual moral codes of any society are noticeably imperfect and flawed (Donner, 2009, p. 54). In order to answer this problem, Donner proposes a specific concept of the progress of moral reform to help address the difficulty: the reform is made to bring to awareness that the accepted rights were either not being reasonably applied or could be extended (Donner, 2009, p. 54). Donner's solution may lessen the problem to some extent, but it is questionable how widely such a concept of reform can be used to explain real reforms in general.

Having reviewed three of the most prominent interpretations of Mill's moral theory, we can say that despite capturing part of its important features none of these interpretations offers an entirely satisfactory explanation of Mill's theory without stretching or even contradicting his own words. At this point, one cannot but ponder the question raised by Donner: whether the upshot of the above discussion is to reveal weakness in Mill's theory, or rather, limitations in the way that these theories have been classified, conceived or configured in recent dialogues (Donner, 2009, p. 34)? Before answering this question, we will consider another similar but not identical question: if Mill's moral theory could not be interpreted as either act or rule-utilitarianism, what kind of theory is it? Is there any other way to describe it?

Beyond act- and rule-utilitarianism

In addition to the act- and rule-utilitarian interpretations, there is another option: it has been argued by Gray (1996 [1983]), Berger (1984) and West (2004) that Mill's moral theory is neither act- nor rule-utilitarianism. These authors have different reasons for supporting this view and the alternative interpretations they provided to substitute the traditional act- and rule-utilitarian interpretations are also different.

In recognizing the limitations of both act- and rule-utilitarian readings of Mill, Gray proposes the concept of 'indirect utilitarianism' to interpret Mill's utilitarianism.[11] Gray's notion of 'indirect utilitarianism' needs to be carefully differentiated from that used by some theorists to indicate 'rule-utilitarianism', in contrast to 'act-utilitarianism' as 'direct utilitarianism'.[12] Indirect utilitarianism in the sense of rule-utilitarianism is very different from what Gray means since Gray explicitly rejects rule-utilitarian interpretation of Mill (Gray, 1996, p. 15). According to Gray, the indirect version of utilitarianism does not allow the principle of utility to be directly applied to either individual acts or social rules. The key difference between rule-utilitarianism and Gray's version of indirect utilitarianism resides in how to use the principle of utility: the former allows the principle of utility to be used directly as umpire to settle the conflicts between different moral obligations, whereas the latter insists that Mill's principle of utility is merely 'axiological and not practical in force' in any case (Gray, 1995, p. 51). Moreover, rejecting the definitions of moral rightness provided by act- and rule-utilitarianism, Gray considers that the necessary and sufficient condition for an act to be wrong is that 'punishing it has best consequences' (Gray, 1995, p. 31). This notion of right actions is therefore defined by the consequences of punishment, rather than the consequences of actions.

Gray's arguments reveal the incompetence of both act- and rule-utilitarian interpretations in capturing Mill's utilitarianism. However, Gray's treatment is not satisfactory either. As many commentators point out, the textual evidence that Mill considers it necessary to appeal directly to the principle of utility on some occasions is fairly clear (Mill, *CW, X*: 226; Berger, 1984, p. 114). This evidently vitiated Gray's treatment of Mill's principle of utility as axiological only. Also, the punishability criterion is controversial (we will discuss this more carefully in Chapter 3). When referring to punishment as an essential part of the notion of morally wrong, Mill is *analysing*, rather than *defining*, the notion. The latter is to provide a definition with contents while the former is closer to, although not exactly the same as, the meta-ethical reflection as Crisp suggests (Crisp, 1997, p. 128).

Similar to Gray, Berger also considers it problematic to classify Mill as either an act-utilitarian or a rule-utilitarian because those terms are strictly defined, which according to Berger requires that *every* act is either right or wrong (Berger, 1984, pp. 65–66). Berger supported his view by showing that the textual evidences used respectively to support act- and rule-utilitarian interpretations are in fact not mutually exclusive. As an alternative, Berger proposes a 'strategy conception of rules' to explain the role played by moral rules and the consequences of acts in determining rightness and wrongness in Mill's moral system. According to Berger's strategy explanation of rules, Mill is believed to maintain that

> in practical moral reasoning, the determination of what should be done should be made by relatively strict adherence to moral rules, except in exceptional cases, where the right action must be determined by appeal to the consequences of the act (including any rule-related tendencies *it* may have).
>
> (Berger, 1984, p. 115, emphasis in original)

It is interesting to note that unlike Gray, whose version of Mill cannot sit comfortably with either act- or rule-utilitarianism, Berger's position is actually compatible with both the act-consequence and rule-consequence conception of right action, as Berger himself pointed out (Berger, 1984, p. 115).

The compatibility of Berger's interpretation with both the act-consequence and rule-consequence conception of right action is not entirely surprising. The proponents of act- and rule-utilitarian interpretations of Mill, at least Crisp, Fuchs and Donner, all capture some truths regarding Mill's moral theory in certain ways. The differences between the accounts offered by Crisp, Fuchs, and Donner become smaller and reconcilable through the lens of the strategy conception of moral rules offered by Berger. On the one hand, Crisp is right to say that the ultimate criterion to judge the rightness of an action is the consequences of the act. On the other hand, Fuchs and Donner are correct in defining the rightness of an action in accord with the conformity of a moral rule. The former focuses on the *philosophical* level concerning the *ultimate test* of rightness and wrongness, whereas the latter focuses on the *practice* level concerning *immediate working definitions* of rightness and wrongness.

Strictly speaking, Berger's discussion did not provide a definition of rightness. The strategic view of rules concerns mainly how the first principle of utility and secondary moral rules enter into a procedure of determining the criterion of right and wrong. Berger's extensive study of the act-utilitarianism/rule-utilitarianism controversy has another conclusion concerning the substantive part of the concept of right however. For this, Berger argued that Mill's texts suggest two different criteria of rightness and wrongness: proportionality criterion and punishability criterion. Berger considered that Mill did not provide a satisfactory solution to reconcile these two criteria (Berger, 1994, p. 116).

Like Berger, West also gives an extended account of Mill's utilitarianism as moral theory, but unlike him, West rejects the 'strategy conceptions of rule' and proposes a fresh interpretation of Mill:

> he is neither [an act- or rule-utilitarian], if these are interpreted as *exclusive and complete utilitarian moral theories*. On the other hand, if these are interpreted as *forms of utilitarian moral reasoning* he is both and much more.
>
> (West, 2004, p. 77, emphasis added)

West separates moral reasoning from a complete moral theory. This distinction is crucial in reading Mill's ethical writings in that it enables us to read them with an enhanced awareness of the context of Mill's arguments.

West concludes that:

> [Mill] has a place for rights, which are correlative to especially stringent obligations to 'assignable' people; he has a place for praise and condemnation of people's characters as well as their actions (elements of 'virtue ethics'); and he has a place for supererogation. The structure of Mill's moral theory is truly complex, not the simple model of either act-utilitarianism or rule-utilitarianism, or a mixture of the moral reasoning of both.
>
> (West, 2004, p. 95)

From this author's point of view, West's interpretation seems to capture Mill's moral theory most comprehensively. However, Fuchs's comments on West's treatment cannot be ignored. 'Were Mill consistently to embrace this extremely wide concept of 'morality' (that is, to identify morality with all of practical reason)', Fuchs claims, he would agree with West's interpretation (Fuchs, 2006, p. 155). The problem is, Fuchs argues, that Mill did not consistently use the term 'moral' in the broadest sense. Fuchs challenges West on the grounds that his interpretation unduly pushes the boundary of morality to cover all types of practical reasoning while the scope of Mill's morality is much more restricted.

Fuchs's comments are fair on the point that West's analysis goes beyond the scope of morality Mill intentionally delimits. He is also correct in saying that Mill's use of the term 'moral' suffers from the problem of vagueness. However, the scope of Mill's morality is not as unclear as Fuchs suggests. Mill explicitly marks morality off from virtues and supererogation. If we adopt the distinction of moral philosophy and morality made earlier, there is little difficulty in replying to Fuchs's complaints. The scope of moral system which West is dealing with is close to Mill's moral philosophy, which includes virtue ethics and other norms. It is a legitimate realm of study even from Mill's point of view. However, it is not self-evident that the scope which West's analysis intends to cover is broader than the scope of morality usually assigned. This is where the confusion arises. If we read in this light, the confusion can be removed: West's analysis is indeed informative and improves our understanding of the complexity of Mill's moral philosophy.

Notwithstanding, the question 'How does Mill define morally right actions?' remains unanswered in West's treatment. This is the question Fuchs attempted to answer and is the major question which the whole literature on whether Mill is an act- or rule-utilitarian has attempted to answer.

Before we continue to seek for an answer to the question, let's return to Donner's question mentioned earlier: whether the upshot of the above discussion is to reveal weakness in Mill's theory, or rather limitations in the way that these theories have been classified, conceived or configured in recent dialogues (Donner, 2009, p. 34)? The richness of Mill's moral philosophy demonstrated by West highlights the second possibility pointed out by Donner in her question.

The vast literature on the forms of Mill's utilitarianism has been set to search evidence from *Utilitarianism* to provide a definition of right and wrong actions. This might be an attempt doomed to fail, because it may be the wrong place to search for the answer. *Utilitarianism* was written to refute ethical intuitionism and transcendentalism by showing that the principle of utility is the first principle of morality. It was not meant to discuss definitions of right and wrong.

It is fair to say that the main reason why Mill is not a cooperative player in this game is not because his arguments are so unclear that they are unable to give a definite answer regarding the form of Mill's utilitarianism as a moral theory. The deeper truth seems to be close to what is suggested by Sumner: 'Mill's theory undermines the adequacy of the standard distinction between forms of utilitarianism' (Sumner, 1979, p. 111).

An often neglected reality is that any sensible ethical theory can hardly be presented in a fair way by simply defining what morally right and wrong actions are. Any attempt to define a moral theory solely by giving a definition of right and wrong actions is dangerous because it inclines to improperly squeeze other information into an oversimplified formula. A comprehensive discussion of Mill's theory of morality, like a comprehensive discussion of any other ethical theory, should not be limited to the definition of right and wrong. It should also consider such issues as the scope of morality, that is, what kinds of affairs should and should not be the subject matter of the study, the solutions to competing moral duties, principles of sanctions, and so on.

The distinction of act- and rule-utilitarianism tends to constrain the perspectives of reading and interpreting Mill's moral theory. We unconsciously incline to read Mill from the perspectives created by the modern distinction, rather than from his own perspective. In order to square Mill's utilitarianism with these modern classifiers, Mill's texts are often extracted fragmentally and his messages have been read in isolation from the original context to serve the interpreters' own purposes. In view of this problem, the rest of this book will free itself from the framework of thinking created by the act-/rule-utilitarianism distinction and aims to show what we can achieve in understanding Mill's utilitarianism with this liberation. It will provide a utilitarian theory of justice based on a careful reading of Mill in the hope that the result of this study will equip us with enhanced abilities to reflect on the most controversial issues in the field of applied ethics in our own time. It must be emphasized that Mill himself never attempted a full account of justice. Our attempt is a reconstruction of theory, rather than textual elucidation. This is an 'instrumental reading' of Mill, but it requires an 'accurate reading' of Mill as a precondition, borrowing Peter Boettke's distinction of the two ways of reading great texts (Boettke, 2001, pp. 118–122). The remainder of this chapter will be devoted to reconstructing a framework of Mill's moral reasoning as the first step to reconstructing his theory of justice.

Reconstructing the framework of Mill's moral reasoning

The operation of utilitarianism as a moral system, like all other moral systems, requires various secondary principles. The importance of secondary principles in Mill's utilitarianism is beyond doubt. He believes that once people accept the principle of utility as the first principle, we should be

> bending the whole force of our intellects to the establishment of such secondary and intermediate maxims, as may be guides to the *bonâ fide* inquirer in the application of the principle, and salutary checks to the sophist and the dishonest casuist.
>
> (Mill, *CW, X*: 52)

Given Mill's own emphasis on the necessity of secondary principles, it may appear odd that most of his energy and attention in his philosophical writings was devoted to the question regarding the principle of utility as the first principle. However, it is not strange at all because the contents of secondary principles are highly circumstance-sensitive. It is impossible to derive a secondary principle from the first principle without considering the empirical evidence. What moral principles should be adopted by a society is subject to concrete conditions. Therefore, it is unlikely that one would write about secondary principles as if they are universal principles. If the concrete materials are taken away from the discussion, there is not much left to write. The fact that Mill did not demonstrate how to obtain secondary principles does not suggest that it is impossible to reach them in a logical manner. Mill's moral reasoning can be observed from his evaluation of practical rules. Studying Mill's writings which deal with practical issues will allow us to reconstruct a general framework of his moral reasoning.

The necessity of secondary ends

The necessity of secondary principles in Mill's moral system has been widely recognized. In comparison, the importance of secondary ends or goals has not been fully appreciated. Recall Mill's discussion of the respective functions of arts and sciences and the interrelations between arts and sciences. The precepts or rules of arts are not independent from ends in Mill's system – precepts are meant to help us achieve ends. It follows that various secondary principles must presuppose various secondary ends.

Despite his firm belief that happiness is the end of life, Mill shares with non-hedonists the view that when we consciously take happiness as our immediate end, we somehow miss it. This view emerged in Mill's mind as a result of discovering the inadequate view of human nature held by Bentham and by his father James Mill. After his psychological crisis, Mill, as Berger notices, came to see that 'pursuing secondary ends, rather than directly seeking happiness itself, is often the best way of achieving happiness' (Berger, 1984, p. 82). In his *Autobiography*, Mill describes thoroughly the change of his mentality:

> I never, indeed, wavered in the conviction that happiness is the test of all rules of conduct, and the end of life. But I now thought that this end was only to be attained by not making it the direct end. Those only are happy (I thought) who have their minds fixed on some object other than their own happiness; on the happiness of others, on the improvement of mankind, even on some art or pursuit, followed not as a means, but as itself an ideal end. Aiming thus at something else, they find happiness by the way. The enjoyments of life (such was now my theory) are sufficient to make it a pleasant thing, when they are taken *en passant*, without being made a principal object. Once make them so, and they are immediately felt to be insufficient. They will not bear a scrutinizing examination. Ask yourself whether you are happy, and you cease to be so. The only chance is to treat, not happiness, but some end external to it, as the purpose of life. Let your self-consciousness, your scrutiny, your self-interrogation, exhaust themselves on that; and if otherwise fortunately circumstanced you will inhale happiness with the air you breathe, without dwelling on it or thinking about it, without either forestalling it in imagination, or putting it to flight by fatal questioning. This theory now became the basis of my philosophy of life. And I still hold to it as the best theory for all those who have but a moderate degree of sensibility and of capacity for enjoyment, that is, for the great majority of mankind.
>
> (Mill, *CW, I*: 145–147)

If it is true that human conduct has to aim at ends other than happiness in order to achieve the ultimate end, then we need principles other than the greatest happiness principle for achieving different ends. These secondary ends are not the agent's own happiness, and they do not need to be others' happiness either. They can be goals such as pursuing material prosperity, cultivating aesthetic taste, established habits conducive to hygiene, etc. They are not required to contribute to happiness directly, but they should be able to contribute to it indirectly. We demonstrated in Chapter 1 that for Mill the pursuit of things other than happiness, no matter whether a conscious act or not, is a result of association. This also explains why Mill does not see any contradiction between happiness and secondary ends in his utilitarian moral system. Various secondary moral principles are not only compatible with the first principle of utility, but also necessary to a utilitarian moral system.

Mill's utilitarianism as a three-level structure of moral system

Mill's utilitarian morality could be understood as a system of three-level structure. At the highest level, there is only *one* first principle, that is, the principle of utility. This principle only informs us that the final aim of morality is the greatest happiness for all; it does not and cannot specify *how* to reach this aim. It is mainly due to the fact that utility or happiness is not a fixed idea. Although Mill stipulates that happiness means the pleasure and the absence of pain, the content of happiness still needs to be fleshed out.[13] As Hare points out, for utilitarians, 'what happiness is' is an empirical question: it can only be answered in relation to concrete situations, and with an understanding of human attitudes and reactions (Hare, 1981, pp. 5, 159). Therefore, the principle of utility is only a *formal* formula.

Under this single first principle, there are various types of secondary principles which govern different types of affairs. Take the principles of justice as an example. Those principles with which we are familiar, such as 'the principle of distribution according to needs' or 'equal pay for equal effort' and so on belong to this level. As to which principle will be the just one, there is no absolute answer. It will depend on the issue and social background under investigation. Moreover, these secondary principles may conflict with each other on some occasions. When it happens, the first principle will be invoked to be the final judge.

At the lowest level, there are moral and legal rules which govern our behaviour in daily life. They are practical rules in force. Rules like 'not breaking promises', 'the rich should pay more income taxes than the poor' and so on belong to this level. The acceptance of these rules may not be a conscious selection by a particular person or group, it may be the result of custom. However, a certain amount of deliberation can usually be identified in the formation or evolution of such conventional rules.

For an empiricist like Mill, the speculation at both the second and the third levels requires concrete materials. It means that to judge whether a principle is just or not, we need an issue in hand first. Also, we have to consider the real circumstances in which the issue occurs. As situations vary from time to time, from place to place, the principles of justice in the second and the third levels are not universal. On the contrary, they are changeable. Moreover, their binding force is not absolute: they are overridable by other more imperative rules.

It is important to note that the idea of justice shows up not only at the second and the third levels, but also at the first level. To Mill, justice is 'the chief part, and incomparably the most sacred and binding part, of all morality' (Mill, *CW*, *X*: 255). The highest abstract standard of social justice in Mill's utilitarianism is embraced as part of the principle of utility itself:[14]

> this great moral duty rests upon a still deeper foundation, being a direct emanation from the first principle of morals, and not a mere logical corollary from secondary or derivative doctrines. It is involved in the very

> meaning of Utility, or the Greatest-Happiness Principle. That principle is a mere form of words without rational signification, unless one person's happiness, supposed equal in degree (with the proper allowance made for kind), is counted for exactly as much as another's.
>
> (Mill, *CW, X*: 257)

This three-level structure is illustrated in Figure 2.1.

Within this reconstructed framework of Mill's utilitarianism, the author suggests that the derivation of moral principles in force can be summarized into three steps of moral reasoning. First of all, we have to ask: what is the immediate goal of the issue under investigation? The word 'immediate' is used in contrast to 'final' or 'ultimate'. When we are looking for the secondary principles, it will be necessary to consider what the immediate goals are. Otherwise, we will throw away the three-level structure and go back to applying the principle of utility directly, since the final end of every action and institution is always the pursuit of happiness in Mill's view.

It is undeniable that many social institutions were not set up with any particular goals in place; they emerged from diverse reasons. The institution of private property is a typical example. However, once an existing institution is insufficient to meet the current needs of a society, for the purpose of reform it is necessary to think of the *function* of the institution, if we prefer not calling it a 'goal'.

In the second stage we have to ask: among these principles, which one can best serve the immediate end? The answer is neither obvious nor absolute. 'Discussion' and 'evidence' should play a key role in the procedure of making the decision. Once we choose the main principle, we still have to ask: is this principle sufficient to achieve the end? If not, then we have to find other principles to complete the major principle.

It has to be stressed again that this three-level structure is a reconstruction of a theory, rather than textual elucidation. The reconstruction may contain some

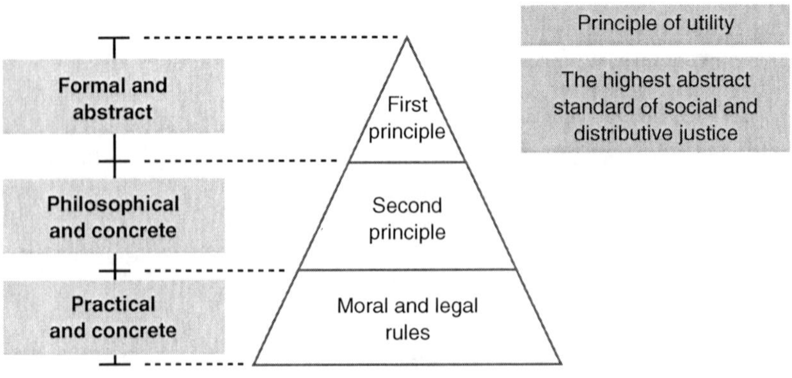

Figure 2.1 The framework of Mill's moral reasoning.

arguments which are not evidently held by Mill, but it is consistent with Mill's texts and his overall standpoint. Most importantly, this structure has the capacity to reconcile some of Mill's views which used to be believed contradictory to each other. Chapters 4 and 5 will use Mill's discussion on economic issues to demonstrate how these three steps can be a promising guide for us to fill the gap between Mill's first principle of utility and the principles of justice in practice, which are what he calls 'the secondary principles' in his *Utilitarianism*. Before that, Chapter 3 will have a closer look at Mill's utilitarianism as a theory of morality.

3 Mill's utilitarianism as a theory of morality

In Chapter 2 we examined Mill's system of moral philosophy with a focus on the *formal* structure and the *formal* relationships between different branches of the system. We examined utilitarianism not merely as a theory of morality, but as a broader moral philosophy governing all sorts of practical reasoning. We also examined whether Mill's theory of morality can be classified as either act- or rule-utilitarianism. The outcome of the discussion showed that the definition of moral right provided by either an act- or rule-utilitarian interpretation of Mill can hardly go beyond *formal* definitions. These definitions bear little substantive content. The attempt to reconstruct Mill's moral reasoning in the last part of Chapter 2 was also carried out at a rather *formal* level without providing substantive contents specific to utilitarianism. In this chapter, we attempt to look for the substantive content of Mill's moral theory. By the substantive contents, we mean how the idea of utility can act as a guide for a moral system. Therefore the scope of this chapter is narrowed down to utilitarianism as a theory of morality, in contrast to utilitarianism as a moral philosophy, as discussed in Chapter 2. Before we can turn to how utility acts as the test of moral standard, we need to resolve a common puzzle regarding Mill's criterion of moral right.

Reading Mill's utilitarianism in context

Nowadays, 'maximization of utility' has become a standard definition of the rightness of utilitarianism, not only for critics of utilitarianism but also its defenders. However, it is highly questionable to interpret Mill's criterion of the right in this way. As illustrated in Chapter 2, since the greatest happiness principle is the ultimate principle for both morality and other departments of Mill's Art of Life, it is inappropriate to suggest that Mill's principle of utility *defines* the right as the maximization of total utility.

This does not exhaust the discussion however. If Mill does not define morally right as maximizing total utility, how does he define it? What is morally right to him? This is a controversial issue and no unanimous conclusion has been reached in literature so far. According to Berger, the 'proportionality' and the 'punishability' criteria are the two most widely acknowledged interpretations of Mill's criterion of rightness and wrongness (Berger, 1984, pp. 105–120; Donner, 1998, p. 283).

The major textual evidence of the proportionality criterion interpretation is the same as the maximization criterion, that is, 'actions are right in proportion as they tend to promote happiness, wrong as they tend to produce the reverse of happiness' (Mill, *CW, X*: 210). This interpretation suffers some difficulties. The title of 'proportionality' criterion is confusing because it is questionable whether the concept of rightness can be susceptible of the idea of proportionality. In a loose daily life usage, we may say something is more or less right, but when setting up the criterion of the right, it would be strange to claim one thing is 'more' right than the other because it produces more pleasures. To avoid this problem, a reasonable interpretation will be that among alternative options, we should choose the one which brings more utility. However, if this is what the proportionality criterion means, then there is virtually no real difference between the proportionality criterion and the criterion of maximization of utility. The proportionality criterion appears to be simply another form of the maximization criterion, hence it should be excluded from the candidates for Mill's definition of rightness and wrongness. This leaves us with the punishability criterion as the most promising interpretation.

The punishability interpretation can be traced back at least to D. P. Dryer, who identifies condemnation as a necessary condition of wrong actions (Dryer, 1969, p. cv). Later a number of scholars, including Brown (1973), Lyons (1976), Copp (1979) and Gray (1995) respectively develop their interpretation concerning Mill's moral theory by connecting the concept of wrongdoing with the appropriateness of punishment. This thread of discussion eventually forms a distinct interpretation of Mill's criterion of right and wrong, and this line of argument remains relevant today. For instance, Dale Miller attributes to Lyons the sentimentalist interpretation of Mill's moral theory in his recent work and overtly endorses Lyons's interpretation (Miller 2010a, 2010b). Similar to the act- and rule-utilitarian interpretations, the punishability interpretation is not a uniform opinion: the interpretations given by Dryer, Lyons, Copp and Brown differ from one other. Here our discussion will focus on Lyons' and Brown's views. The former is deemed by Sumner (1979) as the most plausible among variant punishability interpretations of Mill and the latter is reaffirmed by Brown in one of his recent articles (2010).

Punishment and Mill's notion of moral wrong

The passage below was initially used by Lyons to analyse Mill's distinction of morality and simple expediency and it eventually became the most important textual evidence supporting the punishability interpretation:

> We do not call anything wrong, unless we mean to imply that a person ought to be punished in some way or other for doing it; if not by law, by the opinion of his fellow creatures; if not by opinion, by the reproaches of his own conscience. This seems the real turning point of the distinction between morality and simple expediency. It is a part of the notion of Duty in every

> one of its forms, that a person may rightfully be compelled to fulfil it. Duty is a thing which may be *exacted* from a person, as one exacts a debt. Unless we think that it may be exacted from him, we do not call it his duty. Reasons of prudence, or the interest of other people, may militate against actually exacting it; but the person himself, it is clearly understood, would not be entitled to complain. There are other things, on the contrary, which we wish that people should do, which we like or admire them for doing, perhaps dislike or despise them for not doing, but yet admit that they are not bound to do; it is not a case of moral obligation; we don't blame them, that is, we do not think that they are proper objects of punishment. How we come by these ideas of deserving and not deserving punishment, will appear, perhaps, in the sequel; but I think there is no doubt that this distinction lies at the bottom of the notions of right and wrong; that we call any conduct wrong, or employ, instead, some other term of dislike or disparagement, according as we think that the person ought, or ought not, to be punished for it; and we say, it would be right to do so and so, or merely that it would be desirable or laudable, according as we would wish to see the person whom it concerns, compelled, or only persuaded and exhorted, to act in that manner.
>
> (Mill, *CW, X*: 246)

This paragraph is usually denoted by Mill scholars as V.14 because it appears in the fourteenth paragraph of Chapter V according to the edition of *Utilitarianism* in the *Collected Works of John Stuart Mill*, edited by J. M. Robson. For simplicity of reference, here we will follow suit and call it V.14.

In his 1976 article 'Mill's Theory of Morality', which was reprinted in his 1994 book, Lyons rejects a common interpretation of Mill that every act which fails to maximize utility is wrong. He argues that for Mill wrongness must involve the violation of moral obligations, which are determined by moral principles (Lyons, 1994). To demonstrate this, Lyons analyses Mill's concept of morality and argues that punishment is an indispensable element of Mill's notion of moral wrong. A distinctive feature of Lyons's strategy of analysis is that he distinguishes the formal and material elements of Mill's moral theory. Lyons first explores the division of Mill's morality by discussing the formal relationships between different sectors of his moral theory. The formal structure identified by Lyons is that morality is a sector of expediency and justice is a sector of morality. Based on V.14, Lyons argues that the formal conceptual distinction made by Mill between morality and expediency is drawn by referring to punishment, which has no implication of commitment to utilitarianism. Once this formal structure of Mill's moral theory is established, Lyons continues to argue that the contents of moral rules should be decided by the principle of utility. According to Lyons' reconstruction, whether an act is right or wrong is dependent on whether it confirms or violates a moral rule. The contents of the rule are determined by the principle of utility. Moreover, whether it is worth establishing and enforcing a coercive social rule is determined by the balance of costs and benefits of doing so. Basically, the reconstruction itself does not say much about the substantive material of the moral rules which are supposed to judge the rightness and wrongness of an act.

Lyons's work on Mill in the 1970s was largely motivated in response to Rawls's right-based moral theory which prevailed at the time (Lyons, 1994, p. 12). Lyons's viewpoint of utilitarianism was influenced by Brown's work and in part was developed in response to him (Berger, 1984, pp. 105–113; Miller, 2010b, p. 48). Similar to Lyons, Brown also sees punishment as the essential part of Mill's concept of morality. Unlike Lyons who sees that the appropriateness of *internal* sanctions marks Mill's concept of moral wrong; Brown believes that only if *external* sanctions are justifiable will Mill call an action wrong. The controversy between these two revisionary readings of Mill has been ongoing since 1970s and is still not settled. In one of his recent articles, Brown still considers that it is external, rather than internal, sanctions that mark Mill's notion of morality. This again arouses objections. Standing by Lyons' side, Miller (2010b) argues that Brown is wrong. Riley (2010b) also rejects Brown's interpretation on the grounds that it will allow a wrongdoing to escape external punishment if it is too costly or inexpedient to implement the sanction.

While the internal sanction interpretation is favoured over Brown's external sanction view among scholars, it would be too early to announce the success of the internal sanction interpretation. The internal sanction interpretation in fact suffers from the problem of question-begging, which was noticed and well explained by W. E. Schaller (1991) more than 20 years ago.[1] According to Schaller, if conscience is the desire to do one's duty and if people's conscience makes them feel guilty when they act contrary to their understanding of duty, then 'they must know whether a given action was wrong *before* they can know whether their conscience should approve or condemn their action' (Schaller, 1991, p. 121, emphasis added). In other words, the feeling of guilt is a consequence of a known moral rule and hence cannot be the criterion of morality at the same time. Schaller analyses the problem mainly from the logic point of view. A careful reading of Mill from the context confirms Schaller's analysis.

Scholars who argue along the line of punishability have been searching V.14 for the criterion of right and wrong, or the necessary and sufficient conditions of moral wrong. For instance, following Lyons, Miller maintains that 'Mill regards it as both necessary and sufficient for an action's being wrong that it is appropriate for the agent to experience guilt for it and, indeed, that Mill analyzes wrongness in terms of the appropriateness of guilt' (Miller, 2010b, p. 52). It might be fair to say that this line of reading actually takes V.14 out of context and does not fully recognize the purpose of Mill's argument there.

To appreciate this point, we need to differentiate three closely connected yet distinct types of concepts and related issues: first, the ultimate test of morality, or what makes morally wrong actions wrong; second, immediate criteria in force for making moral judgement, or the sufficient conditions of wrongness, that is, when the conditions are satisfied, then we say it is a wrong act; third, the origin of moral sentiments. It is not exaggerating to say that most misunderstandings of Mill's moral theory are due to the conflation of these three types of concepts and questions.

The aim of Chapter V is to show the origin of the sentiments of justice and its connection to utility. In other words, the motivation and focus of Chapter V is the third type of issue stated in the previous paragraph as well as its connection to the first type. Hence V.14 must be read in this context. Lyons and his followers as well as the critics have been searching answers to the second type of question, and for this reason their effort is doomed to be futile. To correctly understand Mill's argument in Chapter V of *Utilitarianism*, we need to appreciate the motivation and purpose of Mill's writing.

The backdrop of Chapter V and the strategy of argumentation

Mill opens Chapter V with the claim that 'In all ages of speculation, one of the strongest obstacles to the reception of the doctrine that Utility or Happiness is the criterion of right and wrong, has been drawn from the idea of Justice' (Mill, *CW, X*: 240). Today justice remains one of the biggest obstacles for utilitarianism to be perceived as a doctrine of morality. This seeming similarity in the challenges faced by utilitarianism at different times makes it particularly important to notice that the difficulty Mill tried to answer in Chapter V is very different from the difficulty in most modern commentators' mind, even though eventually Mill also comes to answer the question concerned by modern commentators, that is, the utilitarian concept of distributive justice. The importance of understanding the dimension in which Mill proceeds with his discussion of justice cannot be overemphasized.

In Chapter 1, we noticed that Mill was not satisfied with his father's explanation of moral sentiments. It appeared to Mill to be too instrumental and did not allow human beings to genuinely hold these feelings without deliberately calculating the benefits of their every single action. Another serious defect of his father's explanation is that it can only explain moral feeling in a very broad sense, but not the feeling of duty and obligations.

This limitation in the explanation of moral feelings mirrors the limitation of James Mill's utilitarianism as a moral theory: it is unable to mark the difference between morality and general expediency. As a consequence, it cannot leave room for supererogation and tend to force people to act for the general good all the time under pressure from others.

As mentioned in Chapter 1, James Mill's concept of moral feelings is not limited to morality narrowly defined. It is a concept of moral feelings in a broad sense related to all types of common good. His theory is not able to explain the feeling of duty, nor can it explain the feeling of justice. The common view in the nineteenth century regarding ethics is that moral sentiments are innate. James Mill managed to dispute this view by showing that moral feelings are the result of association, but he failed to explain the sentiments of moral obligations, including the sentiments of justice. It follows that he still cannot dispute the view that sentiments of justice are not innate. Sentiments of justice are far stronger feelings that people believe they must be given by God.

This is what Mill sees as one of the strongest objections to the doctrine of utility being the criterion of right and wrong at his time. Chapter V of *Utilitarianism* can be seen as Mill's attempt to close the gap left by his father's theory. At an early stage in that chapter, Mill makes the aim of the study clear:

> Our present object is to determine whether the reality, to which the feeling of justice corresponds, is one which needs any such special revelation; whether the justice or injustice of an action is a thing intrinsically peculiar, and distinct from all its other qualities, or only a combination of certain of those qualities, presented under a peculiar aspect.
>
> (Mill, *CW, X*: 240)

It is evident that Mill is here again confronting ethical intuitionists, who hold the belief that the sentiment of justice is so strong that it must be innate or given by God. Note that it is not Mill's main aim here to discuss how utilitarianism can reconcile with distributive justice, one of the issues of greatest concern in political and moral philosophy in the twentieth century. The major objection Mill is concerned with stems from the psychological fact that the sentiment attached to the idea of justice is so powerful that people believe that the sentiment of justice must be something generically distinct from other sentiments (Mill, *CW, X*: 240).

The strong and distinctly subjective mental feeling of justice leads many people to believe that the moral obligation of justice is predominant and absolute for its own sake, that the source of the moral obligation of justice comes from the dictates of nature and is irrelevant to utility. It follows that in order to remove the obstacle caused by this belief, the major task for Mill is to investigate whether there is some common feature constantly existing in those cases where the feeling of justice occurs; and whether the feelings of justice and injustice are inexplicable or are generated from the general laws of our emotional constitution like other feelings. Mill supposes that if the feeling can be explained by the general laws of our emotional constitution (even it is a sentiment of peculiar character and intensity), the idea of justice should not be an obstacle to the doctrine of utility. On the contrary, if the sentiment is inexplicable, and requires to be regarded as a special provision of nature, this might be a real difficulty for the doctrine of utility and he will have to seek for some other mode of investigation (Mill, *CW, X*: 240–241). The fifth chapter of *Utilitarianism* is devoted to answering this question, and Mill shows little intention of providing the criterion of justice throughout the chapter.

The intent of Chapter V is to refute intuitionism, and Mill's strategy is to provide an analytical investigation of the 'idea' of justice and the 'origin' of the sentiment of justice. It is not his purpose to provide the 'definition' or 'criterion' of morality or justice. In the essay 'Whewell on Moral Philosophy', Mill remarks that 'How these feelings of natural complacency and natural dread and aversion directed towards actions, come to assume the peculiar character of what we term moral feelings, is not a question of ethics but of metaphysics' (Mill, *CW, X*: 184–185). Accordingly, it is fair to say that the analysis in Chapter V is more about metaphysics, and less about ethics.

This setting of Chapter V is explicitly affirmed by Mill himself in his notes to James Mill's *Analysis of the Phenomena of the Human Mind*:

> This feeling of duty or obligation, it is contended, is a very different state of mind from mere liking for the action and good will to the agent. The association theory may account for the two last, but not for the former. I have examined this question in the concluding chapter of a short treatise entitled *Utilitarianism*. The subject of the chapter is "the connexion between Justice and Utility". I have there endeavoured to shew what the association is, which exists in the case of what we regard as a duty, but does not exist in the case of what we merely regard as useful, and which gives to the feeling in the former case the strength, the gravity, and pungency, which in the other case it has not.
>
> (Mill, *CW, XXXI*: 241)

Brown also noticed this passage. However, failing to appreciate the intellectual context and the true intention of Mill's writing, Brown is incorrect in claiming that Mill 'then proceeds to outline the structure of moral requirement' (Brown, 2010, p. 16). In fact Mill only intends to give a conceptual analysis of moral concepts by explaining the origin of these sentiments without specifying the structure of moral requirement.

Mill's letter to Ward, written in 1859, is a further important source for understanding Mill's notion of moral feeling, and should be read in the same light. Mill specifically identifies that the account of moral feelings he gave in the letter has been written in 'a little manuscript treatise', by which he meant *Utilitarianism*.[2] Although considering it imperfect, Mill believes that the short statement made in the letter can convey some notion of his opinions regarding moral feelings. Again, it is not his purpose in the letter to provide a working criterion for making moral judgement, nor to define the scope of morality.

Reading in this light, we can see that punishment is not meant by Mill to be a criterion of moral right in these three places which are usually used as evidence of the punishiability criterion interpretation. Thus the ambiguities and puzzles in Mill's writings suggested by those who hold the punishability interpretation do not in fact exist.

The approach Mill takes in Chapter V of *Utilitarianism* is to first investigate the common concepts of justice and injustice. After reviewing several diverse applications of the terms justice and injustice, Mill found it difficult to 'seize the *mental link*' to hold these cases of justice together. Then, he carried on the discussion with the examination of the etymology of the word 'justice'. By examining the origin and progressive growth of the idea of justice, Mill found that the idea of law, and consequently also the idea of penal sanction, are predominant in the notion of justice.

However, this is only enough to distinguish expediency from morality in general, not to distinguish simple expediency from justice, because 'the idea of penal sanction enters not only into the conception of injustice, but into that of any kind of wrong' (Mill, *CW, X*: 246). Therefore, in order to distinguish justice from simple expediency, Mill has to distinguish justice from general morals as well.

It seems to him that the specific difference between justice and other general morals is 'the idea of a personal right' or 'a right in some person, correlative to the moral obligation' (Mill, *CW, X*: 247). Note again that this claim is not specific to Mill's utilitarian account of justice; rather it is a general observation: in those cases where people think of justice or injustice, the idea of a personal right is always involved. This is fairly clear from the context:

> *In our survey of the various popular acceptations of justice*, the term appeared generally to involve the idea of a personal right – a claim on the part of one or more individuals, like that which the law gives when it confers a proprietary or other legal right. Whether the injustice consists in depriving a person of possession, or in breaking faith with him, or in treating him worse than he deserves, or worse than other people who have no greater claims, in each case the supposition implies two things – a wrong done, and some assignable person who is wronged.
>
> (Mill, *CW, X*: 247, emphasis added)

By this stage, Mill has confirmed that 'Justice implies something which it is not only right to do, and wrong not to do, but which some individual person can claim from us as his moral right' (Mill, *CW, X*: 247). But why can a person claim a right from others? Mill does not raise this question immediately after pointing out that right is the essential element of the idea of justice. Instead, he continues his discussion by analysing the sentiment of justice. Only when the conceptual analysis of the idea of justice and its connection to the sentiment of justice is completed does Mill give his utilitarian account.

Even though it is not Mill's intention in Chapter V to construct a moral theory by using a two-stage approach, Lyons is quite right in pointing out that Mill's analysis up to this point is not a specific utilitarian account of morality or justice. Rather, Mill would hold the view that morality unavoidably concerns such matters as rights and obligations and thus that any theory ignoring these matters is 'conceptually defective' (Lyons, 1994, p. 51). However, it is mistaken for Lyons to move on to use V.14 to suggest punishment as Mill's notion of wrong. Here Lyons is inconsistent with his own interpretation, since doing so would obviously relegate the universal applicability of Mill's conceptual analysis.

The origin of sentiments of justice

The sentiment of justice is the feeling attached to the idea of justice. Before turning to discuss the sentiment of justice, Mill repeated again that the aim of his investigation is to work out which of the following cases is true:

> whether the feeling, which accompanies the idea, is attached to it by a special dispensation of nature, or whether it could have grown up, by any

> known laws, out of the idea itself; and in particular, whether it can have originated in considerations of general expediency.
>
> (Mill, *CW, X*: 248 [V.16])

According to Mill, there are two essential ingredients in the sentiment of justice: first, 'the desire to punish a person who has done harm'; second, 'the knowledge or belief that there is some definite individual or individuals to whom harm has been done' (Mill, *CW, X*: 248). Moreover, Mill believes that the first ingredient comes from two natural sentiments, which either are or resemble instincts. They are 'the impulse of self-defence' and 'the feeling of sympathy' (Mill, *CW, X*: 248). In Mill's view, the impulse of self-defence is an instinct human beings share with others, whereas the much wider range of human beings' sympathy marks the difference between human beings and other animals (Mill, *CW, X*: 248). The former gives the sentiment of justice the impressive force, but there is nothing moral in the desire for punishment which comes from the natural feeling of retaliation or vengeance. It is the 'exclusive subordination of [the sentiment of resentment] to the social sympathies' that gives the colour of moral to the sentiment (Mill, *CW, X*: 249).

In contrast to the brevity of his explanation of how the impulse of self-defence leads to the desire to punish a person who has done harm, Mill gives a relatively detailed account of how the feeling of sympathy works. Human beings are capable of sympathizing not only with their offspring or those who are kind to them, but with all human, and even with all sentient, beings. Mill believes that this capability of sympathy working together with intelligence enables a human being to recognize 'a community of interest between himself and the human society of which he forms a part' (Mill, *CW, X*: 248). Such a concept of unity will lead the person to realize that any conduct which threatens the security of the society which he belongs to also threatens his own and this will call forth his instinct to self-defence. Similarly, the power of sympathizing working together with intelligence will enable a human being to recognize himself as part of a community. The concept of community here can range from a tribe to a country or even to all mankind. As a consequence, when he sees an act which hurts any member of the community, his instinct of sympathy will be aroused and urge him to resist the harmful act.

Mill's discussion of the origin of the sentiment of justice reaches two propositions that are very important to moral theory in general: first, the sentiment of justice is not innate; second, the sentiment must be out of the concern of a good common to all. Compared with the first point, the second has been largely neglected and hence deserves further explanation. Mill's investigation of the sentiment of justice is not a moral theory and its applicability is not specific to utilitarianism. By showing the origin of moral sentiments, Mill is also demonstrating the very origin of the concept 'morality' and the source of moral obligation. Morality must be concerned with the general good. It follows that the source of moral obligation must be the general good. This is true even for Kant, Mill believes; otherwise Kant's categorical imperative has no real meaning as Mill puts it:

> When Kant [...] propounds as the fundamental principle of morals, 'So act, that thy rule of conduct might be adopted as a law by all rational beings,' he virtually acknowledges that the interest of mankind collectively, or at least of mankind indiscriminately, must be in the mind of the agent when conscientiously deciding on the morality of the act. Otherwise he uses words without a meaning: for, that a rule even of utter selfishness could not *possibly* be adopted by all rational beings – that there is any insuperable obstacle in the nature of things to its adoption – cannot be even plausibly maintained. To give any meaning to Kant's principle, the sense put upon it must be, that we ought to shape our conduct by a rule which all rational beings might adopt *with benefit to their collective interest.*
>
> (Mill, *CW, X*: 249, emphasis original)

Note that Mill has not yet identified the common good with general utility here. However, the identification seems to be very natural as the arguments develop.

In Mill's view, to have a right means 'to have something which society ought to defend [one] in the possession of' (Mill, *CW, X*: 250). But why ought? The answer Mill gave to this question is 'general utility' (Mill, *CW, X*: 250). It might be less confusing had he said that it is for the utility of everyone in the society. That said, even if Mill had done so, the difficulty of his answer remains. If right is grounded on utility, then the ideas of justice and injustice must also be grounded on the idea of utility – because the idea of injustice always involves the violation of personal rights. However, if the idea of justice eventually bends to the idea of utility, Mill's discourse comes back to the starting point of his argument – the idea of general utility does not convey the intense feeling which is attached to the idea of justice. To explain this, Mill brings in the notion of qualitative difference between utilities: not every kind of utility will provoke the sentiment of justice; only those 'extraordinarily important and impressive kind[s] of utility' will derive the intensity of the feeling as well as the moral justification of the feeling (Mill, *CW, X*: 250–251).

Therefore, Mill demonstrates that justice must be related to utility. If so, does this mean that the distinction between justice and simple expediency is only an imaginary one? 'By no means', Mill says (Mill, *CW, X*: 255). For him, there is indeed a real difference between justice and usual utility. The nature and origin of the sentiment of justice marks the real distinction between the just and the expedient. The sentiment of justice surrounds the former, but not the latter.

In sum, the cases of justice must be the cases of utility, but not vice versa. Justice is only a name for

> certain social utilities which are vastly more important, and therefore more absolute and imperative, than any others are as a class [...] and which, therefore, ought to be, as well as naturally are, *guarded by a sentiment not only different in degree, but also in kind*; distinguished from the milder feeling which attaches to the mere idea of promoting human pleasure or

> convenience, at once by the more definite nature of its commands, and by the sterner character of its sanctions.
>
> (Mill, *CW, X*: 259, emphasis added)

The principles of justice are 'the classes of moral rules, which concern the essentials of human well-being more nearly, and hence are of more absolute obligation, than any other rules for the guidance of life' (Mill, *CW, X*: 255).

Mill's treatment of the sentiment of justice marks a significant difference between the psychological foundation of his ethics with his father's and other later utilitarians, as noticed by Rawls.

Moral feelings and moral obligations

We must not forget the distinction we made among three types of issues, namely, the ultimate test of moral standard, the immediate criterion of rightness and wrongness, and the origin of moral sentiments. Mill demonstrates that the origin of sentiments of justice is related to general utility, but he does not equate the two. For Mill, the third type of issue is distinct from the first type. It is worth emphasizing this point again, particularly because Mill's utilitarianism is sometimes classified as ethical naturalism. This classification is correct if it means that the moral feeling is originated from our natural feelings. However, it would be a serious misunderstanding of Mill's utilitarianism if ethical naturalism is used to mean a doctrine using subjective pleasant and painful feelings as the criteria of right and wrong.

Mill is clear in differentiating the *standard* or *test* of moral obligation from the *origin* of moral sentiments. This distinction appears as early as 1833 when Mill was criticizing Blakey for confounding the two. The *standard* or *test* of moral obligation is a question regarding 'what rule we *ought* to obey, and why'; the *origin* of moral sentiments is a question regarding 'how our feelings of approbation and disapprobation *actually* originate' (Mill, *CW, X*: 26, emphasis in original). It is important to note that '[t]he former is the fundamental question of practical morals; the latter is a problem in mental philosophy' (Mill, *CW, X*: 240). The two questions are closely connected yet distinct. The same point is reaffirmed by Mill in *Utilitarianism* although in a less straightforward way: there is no necessary connection between the question of the origin of moral sentiments, including the sentiment of justice, and that of their binding force (Mill, *CW, X*: 240).

By moral feeling, Mill means 'a feeling of approving & condemning conscience' (Mill, *CW, XV*: 649). More specifically, a true moral feeling is 'a feeling of pain in the fact of violating a certain rule, quite independently of any expected consequences to themselves' (Mill, *CW, XV*: 649). It deserves the adjective 'true' only when the feeling is independent from the consideration of consequences to the agents. Mill's stress on the independence of moral feelings from the calculation of consequences can be seen as a reaction to the deficiency of James Mill's theory of moral feeling.[3]

Moral feelings are not innate. This claim is held by utilitarianism, but strictly speaking, it is not a utilitarian ethical view. As mentioned earlier, whether moral feelings are innate or implanted is a question of 'mental philosophy', or psychology in today's term. To support the view that moral feelings are not innate does not require accepting utilitarianism as the only legitimate moral doctrine, but rejecting this view necessarily implies the rejection of intuitionism as a plausible moral theory. Remember that Mill's explanation of the formulation of moral feelings is not specific to utilitarianism. This point has significance not only for appreciating Mill's theory, but also for keeping the development of moral psychology in the right direction. We will come back to this point in the concluding chapter.

The right and the good

The above discussion rejects the revisionist view of treating the appropriateness of punishment as Mill's criterion of right and wrong. The likelihood of extracting the criterion of right and wrong from Mill's text in *Utilitarianism* seems to be extremely low. The main reason is not because of the vagueness of Mill's wording, but rather because Mill does not provide, or more accurately intend to provide, an explicit and complete formulation of his criteria for the wrongness of actions, as Brown correctly notices (Brown, 2010, pp. 9–11). For this reason, this section will not continue exploring Mill's criterion of right and wrong. Instead, it will discuss the relationship between the right and the good, which is essential to understanding Mill's practical moral reasoning.

It is clear that Mill's moral theory is a teleological one rather than deontological. For a teleologist, the justification of rules depends on the end, which first has to be ascertained to be good. Accordingly, before deciding what right is, Mill has to answer what good is. This relationship is not constrained to moral good and moral right; it is applicable to the good and the right in general.

'Good' is one of the most frequently used word in daily life and in the discussion of morality, while it is also one of the words of which the meaning is extremely difficult to grasp. Unlike ordinary adjectives which indicate the qualities belonging to things, it is implausible to find some distinctive quality in common existing in things that are good (Dent, 2005, p. 349). If 'good' is not a property which can be found in things themselves, then philosophers have to understand the concept of good by observing the circumstances in which people use the word 'good'. Thomas Hobbes proposed that 'whatsoever is the object of any man's appetite or desire; that is it which he for his part calleth good' (Leviathan, i. 6; cited by Blackburn, 2005, p. 154). Accordingly, good is 'merely the name we gave to those things that in fact we happened to desire or like' (Adler, 1981, pp. 72–73). Mill seems to share this viewpoint since he takes the issue of the good as the issue of the end.

It is not surprising that this view did not become popular among moral philosophers. Such a concept of good will inevitably encounter a difficulty, that people may desire something not really good for them, or desire something that is good for them but bad for others. These two cases need to be considered separately.

In the first case, it is often argued that if what is desired is considered by others to be bad to the agents, there must be some objective criterion of goodness, other than subjective desires, which determines what good is. In other words, there must be some intrinsic good independent from desires. Certainly there is a gap between the real good and the apparent good, but this cannot be used to support an a priori concept of good. The only reason which we can imagine that someone might disagree with the definition of goodness is because the consequence of our initial desires may not be what we really desire if we know the consequence in advance. For example, if someone desires smoking, then smoking is good to him, at least it appears to be good at the time he desires it. If we do not agree that smoking is good for him, what we are thinking must be the belief that the *consequence* of smoking is not good for him. When we say smoking is not good for someone, the only reason we can provide is the belief that smoking is not what he will desire if he knows what the consequence would be. Smoking itself is neither good nor bad. It is the consequence of smoking that makes smoking undesirable and therefore bad to someone.

In regard to the second case, there is also a consideration of consequence. It has to be remembered that for a teleologist like Mill, the concept of the good is prior to the concept of the right and the concept of general good is broader than the concept of moral good. Therefore, it is no contradiction to claim that something is good for someone while it may be morally wrong, since it may be good for that individual, yet harmful to the general good.

As a teleological theory, it is not surprising that utilitarianism encounters a common challenge arising from the worries that undesirable means may be taken: if utility is the standard of morality, whatever means will be sanctified as long as they can reach the end. Yet for Mill this problem, which is a worry not unique to utilitarianism, is only a seeming problem. In reply to a similar challenge raised by Adam Sedgwick, Mill argues that

> In every system of morality, the end, when good, justifies all means which *do not conflict with some more important good.* On Mr. Sedgwick's own scheme, are there not ends which sanctify actions, in other cases deserving the utmost abhorrence – such, for instance, as taking the life of a fellow-creature in cold blood, in the face of the whole people? According to the principle of utility, the end justifies all means necessary to its attainment, *except* those which are more mischievous than the end is useful; an exception amply sufficient.
>
> (Mill, *CW, X*: 72, emphasis added)

In other words, for Mill, the worries of the end justifying bad or immoral means will be superfluous in a *comprehensive* moral system, where means to one end will be denied if they are harmful to other more important ends. Nonetheless, it has to be admitted that it is not an easy job to assess and rank the importance of different ends. It is fair to say that the operation of utilitarian moral theory has been largely limited due to the lack of discussion on this issue. In order to avoid undesirable means, a more urgent and difficult task for utilitarian moral theorists to accomplish is to deliberate what is desirable as ends and how to rank various ends on the scale of desirability. It must be emphasized that such deliberation is not to erect authoritarian morality, for it is 'the greatest happiness for all' that is the ultimate test of the ends. It is time for us to turn to this ultimate test of moral standards, the subject matter of Mill's *Utilitarianism*.

Greatest general happiness as the ultimate standard of morality

Utilitarianism is not a book to depict or summarize a complete view of his morality. Instead, *Utilitarianism* was initially published in three instalments in *Fraser's Magazine* as part of Mill's debate with the prevalent intuitionist view of morality in his time (Robson, 1969, p. cxv). This is commonly known to Mill scholars. However, the significance of this context of writing to understanding Mill is often neglected. When presenting his argument in *Utilitarianism*, Mill has certain opponents in mind. If we keep in mind with whom Mill is debating, most of his arguments will make better sense.

After a few paragraphs explaining of the meaning of individual happiness and pleasures in the second chapter of *Utilitarianism*, Mill shifts his focus to general happiness, including exempting as far as possible from pain. Mill repeats twice the contention that 'the happiness which forms the utilitarian standard of what is right in conduct, is not the agent's own happiness, but that of all concerned' (Mill, *CW, X*: 213, 218). Mill's emphasis on the general happiness is not unfamiliar to modern readers. The aggregative attribute in Mill's utilitarianism even becomes one of the targets most often attacked by modern commentators. Although it is true that Mill's utilitarianism has an aggregative property, it would be biased if we read Mill's arguments without noticing the context of Mill's contention.

In Chapter II, 'What Utilitarianism is', Mill does not address his concerns about the distribution of happiness among individuals, which is later discussed in Chapter V 'On the Connexion between Justice and Utility'. Here Mill's defence of the general happiness principle can be deemed as a response to such objectors as Carlyle and the Stoics, who reject utilitarianism not because of the problem of distribution, but because of the concept of happiness itself. These objectors to utilitarianism renounce the pursuit of happiness as the end of morality or of any rational conduct. They either, like Carlyle, believe that it is an obligation for human beings to learn to do without happiness or, like Stoics, raise virtue above everything. It follows from the denial of happiness as an end that virtues such as sacrifice or other intuitive obligations have an absolute place in ethics for their own sake. Disputing a priori moral duties is the theme of Mill's argument here. In reply, Mill explains that it is possible for individuals to sacrifice their personal happiness, but such behaviour is meaningless and has no moral value if the sacrifice is made without envisaging the possible increase of happiness in the world (Mill, *CW, X*: 217).

Similarly, the tip of bearing in mind the opponents of debate is particularly helpful in understanding Mill's proof of his principle of utility. Berger has an illuminating analysis on this point. According to Mill's plan, in order to prove the principle of utility as the first principle of all human conduct, he has to prove two things respectively: first, happiness is *one* of the ends of conduct; second, happiness is the *only* end of conduct (Mill, *CW, X*: 234). Berger observes that while dealing with these two parts, Mill compresses the first part into one small paragraph while the second part goes on to around ten times that length and at times with excessive detail (Berger, 1984, p. 53).

The most likely reason for this unbalanced discussion, Berger suggests, is that in Mill's mind there are specific opponents who agreed with him on the first point, but would disagree strongly with the second claim for which he tried to argue (Berger, 1984, p. 53). Indeed, the situation described by Berger is acknowledged by Mill somewhere else: the intuitive moralists 'unanimously hold that a large *portion* of morality turns upon the consideration due to the interests of our fellow-creatures' despite believing that there are other intuitive moral obligations and having disagreement with utilitarians over the origin of moral obligations (Mill, *CW, X*: 230, emphasis in original). In other words, to wrestle with intuitionist morality, which was the most influential opinion in Mill's time, Mill has to demonstrate not only that happiness is one of the ends of conduct, but also that it is the *only* end of conduct.

For this, the logic of Mill's proof is straightforward. First, he believes that the ultimate principle for the whole must be the principle for the part as well. Since morality is part of the whole of human affairs, the ultimate principle for all kinds of human affairs is also the ultimate principle for morality. Therefore, the search for the ultimate principle of morality can be approached by looking for the ultimate principle for all kinds of human affairs. Moreover, for a teleologist, the justification of rules depends on the end. Accordingly, in order to find out the ultimate principle for all human conduct, it is necessary to find out the ultimate end of all human conduct. Mill believes that happiness is the ultimate end of all human conduct. If this can be proved to be true, then his proof of the first principle can be considered as successful.

As mentioned above, Mill's proof that happiness is the end of all human conduct is brief and his energies almost exclusively focus on happiness as the 'ultimate' or 'sole' end. Yet this short paragraph of proof is notorious for conflating 'desirable', which is a prescriptive concept, with 'visible' and 'audible', which are descriptive concepts. This criticism is a misunderstanding. What Mill tries to say here is: if happiness is not in reality desired as an end, it cannot be possible for happiness to be desirable. This is as far as Mill can go for the proof of happiness as an end (Mill, *CW, X*: 234). It is important to note that desirability here should not be understood in the moral sense. Mill is demonstrating here that happiness is desired as an end for all sorts of conduct, it is unreasonable to infer that he is arguing for the moral desirability of happiness. The desirability of an end in a moral sense is not justified simply by the fact that people desire it. Thus it is fair to say that Mill does not commit so-called natural fallacy in his proof of the principle of utility.

Happiness, utility and pleasure

According to Mill, even if we accept the principle of utility as the first principle of life, we still have to work out what utility or pleasure is. It is only a starting point for a utilitarian to identify happiness as pleasure and the absence of pain and unhappiness as pain and the privation of pleasure:

> To give a clear view of the moral standard set up by the theory, much more requires to be said; in particular, what things it includes in the ideas of pain and pleasure; and to what extent this is left an open question.
>
> (Mill, *CW, X*: 210)

This passage suggests that Mill leaves the question of happiness open to a certain extent. It is fair to say that Mill would see the concept of happiness as one that continues to change as we better understand the nature of human beings and as the society progresses. What is happiness? is an empirical question. It is impossible for us to exhaust the discussion of the idea of happiness and pleasure here and it is not our purpose here. Instead, we only intend to clarify the fundamental features of these concepts in Mill's theory.

The concept of happiness, pleasure and utility

In order to understand Mill's principle of utility correctly it is necessary to understand his concept of utility, happiness, and pleasure. Moreover, they have to be examined together, for they are three closely linked ideas in Mill's utilitarianism. Unfortunately, as John Gray comments, 'Mill was rarely explicit about the basic notions deployed in his arguments, and it is rare to come across any formal definition of the terms he employs' (Gray, 1996, p. 71). This is also the case in Mill's discussion on happiness and utility. The lack of precise definitions of these three intertwined notions makes it difficult to understand Mill's utilitarianism. Instead of defining these three concepts in accordance with Mill's work, which has been done by abundant literature, the discussion here will only attempt to identify whether there is a difference between them in Mill's utilitarianism.

At a relatively early stage in his discourse of *Utilitarianism*, Mill defined happiness as pleasure and the absence of pain: 'By happiness is intended pleasure, and the absence of pain; by unhappiness, pain, and the privation of pleasure' (Mill, *CW, X*: 210). Nevertheless, it may not be appropriate to interpret this statement as his final definition of happiness. Berger suggests it to be more suitable to see it as the first stage in a strategy for discussion: the definition of happiness is merely 'a preliminary outline of the conception, in need of fleshing out before it could be ultimately accepted' (Berger, 1984, p. 38). We may not be sure whether Mill intended to draw a distinct line between happiness and pleasure when defining happiness at the beginning of the treatise, for he actually never did so. Yet it is a fair comment that happiness and pleasure should not be considered as synonyms in Mill's thought; if we study Mill's words carefully from the context, we will find that these two terms are not always exchangeable.

Although on some occasions Mill uses the word 'happy' in a descriptive sense, namely, being happy means having pleasure, this meaning of happiness cannot represent the comprehensive meaning of happiness in Mill's theory. This can be supported by a subtle feature in Mill's wording. When mentioning the end of life and the doctrine of morality, Mill only uses utility and happiness. For instance, he never identifies pleasure as the end of life or speaks of the principle of pleasure; he always names his first principle, either that of 'utility' or the greatest 'happiness' principle. One possible explanation is that happiness is a concept richer than pleasure. For one thing, happiness means not only pleasure but also the absence of pain. More importantly, happiness consists of various pleasures of diverse qualities. This leaves a space to interpret Mill's concept of happiness as eudemonic rather than hedonic.[4] It seems that Mill subconsciously avoids using pleasure to indicate the end of life, despite the fact that he explicitly declares the identification of happiness and pleasure as well as that of utility and pleasure. Sometimes Mill uses pleasure or utility interchangeably, but this happens mainly when he is describing the causes of the feeling. Only in this sense will there exist a qualitative difference in different kinds of utilities.

Accordingly it is reasonable to infer that for Mill, happiness is not a synonym of pleasure when happiness is used to refer to a moral standard. Similarly, as a moral concept, it is happiness rather than pleasure that is a synonym of utility.

Qualitative and quantitative differences in pleasures

The distinction between quality and quantity in pleasures is one of the most important features of Mill's utilitarianism which marks the divergence of his moral theory from Bentham's. It is also one of the most controversial parts of Mill's utilitarianism.

In his book *An Introduction to Mill's Utilitarian Ethics* (2004), Henry West draws readers' attention to the fact that Mill's position regarding higher and lower pleasures is a combination of three related yet distinct claims. They are first, 'there are qualitative differences between pleasures as pleasures'; second, 'some of these are superior to others on grounds of quality'; third, 'the qualitatively superior are those that involve the distinctively human faculties'. According to West, whether each of these claims is true or not does not necessarily affect the validity of others. By separating Mill's arguments for the distinction of higher and lower pleasures, West's analysis makes a significant progress in Mill scholarship. It helps to recognize that a major difficulty in interpreting and evaluating Mill's distinction largely roots in the entanglement of the different elements in his arguments. This entanglement is key to understanding why it is so difficult for scholars to engage in an effective dialogue on this topic.

Following West's approach, we can further break down Mill's arguments for the proposition that higher pleasures are more valuable than lower ones into five elements: first, there are qualitative differences between pleasures, merely as pleasures; second, the estimation of pleasures, or which pleasure is more valuable, is determined by both the quantity and quality of the pleasures; third, some qualities are superior and therefore more valuable; four, the judgement of the experienced is the only way to determine whether one pleasure has superiority in quality to another; five, the judgement of the experienced will be that those pleasures derived from the distinctively human faculties are qualitatively superior to those from animal appetites. These five elements entangle in Mill's discussion of quality/quantity distinction. This makes the interpretation and assessment of Mill's position particularly difficult. One may agree with the first element, but not the other four. Or one may agree with the first three elements, but not the last two. Therefore, in order to get an accurate understanding of Mill's view on the quality/quantity distinction, it is helpful to examine his discussion by considering the five elements separately. It is worth noting that the first and last elements have a different nature from the other three: they are empirical questions regarding facts while the others are evaluative issues. We will examine these five elements in turn.

For Mill, quality and quantity are two distinct attributes or properties belonging to pleasure. There are not only quantitative differences between pleasures, but also qualitative differences; the former cannot be reduced to the latter. We should note that this statement alone is not an ethical norm, but an opinion regarding facts. It follows that whether it is true or not can and should be tested by empirical evidence.

Mill wrote *Utilitarianism* in the 1850s and 60s when the study of psychology still relied heavily on introspection. It is not surprising that Mill's demonstration of the qualitative differences in pleasures, which is grounded in introspection, is difficult to test as true or false. As West commented, disputes resulting from introspection are notoriously difficult to settle and this is why professional psychologists have turned to overt behaviour (West, 2004, p. 53). West seems to suggest that introspection remains the only procedure available for the subject of qualitative versus quantitative differences in pleasures. If this is really what West meant, he might neglect the possibility of investigating this subject with different methods offered by today's technology and methods of survey. There are at least two possible ways to test whether pleasures differ in quality.

First, the advance of technology has allowed neuroscience to provide evidence which indicates the existence of qualitative differences among pleasures, even though the differences may not be the same as what Mill meant. One may disagree with Mill's approach and the evidence he used to demonstrate the claim that there are qualitative differences between pleasures, but the claim itself is true according to today's scientific evidence. Scientists have proved that pleasure is not merely a sensation. It involves a complicated brain activity which 'actively paints an additional "hedonic gloss" onto a sensation to make a pleasant experience "liked"' (Berridge and Kringelbach, 2011, p. 3). Scientific evidence suggests that the coding of sensory pleasures (such as taste) is processed in an area of brain different from that where pleasures caused by more complex or abstract reinforcers (such as monetary gain and loss) are coded

(Berridge and Kringelbach, 2011, pp. 10–12). It remains unclear how such a fact would change our evaluation of fundamental pleasures and higher pleasures in a moral sense, but it does demonstrate that pleasures differ in quality in the sense that they are related to the brain's networks differently. Admittedly this difference, unlike what Mill intends, is not phenomenological one, since two pleasures might be phenomenologically the same yet correlate with different parts of the brain, or two pleasures might be phenomenologically different yet correlate with the same part of the brain. Nevertheless, the further study of this difference, a promising area suggested by Kringelbach and Berridge (2010) among other scientists, may provide an answer regarding how different types of pleasures contribute to happiness or well-being differently. For instance, they may have different impacts on happiness through different impacts on mind, emotion or body at either a conscious or non-conscious level. Meanwhile, we cannot deny the possibility that someday science may prove that the difference between pleasures in terms of neuroactivities does not lead to any difference in real terms. The other way to test the existence of qualitative differences of pleasures is to conduct general surveys. This approach has been extensively used in the science of happiness or subjective well-being in the last few decades. The qualitative difference of pleasures identified by this type of study is closer to Mill's own intention. We will discuss this approach more in the concluding chapter. For the time being, we point out that this modern approach is actually similar to Mill's own approach, while the former seems to manage to avoid the problem of deciding who the competent judges are.[5]

The second element of Mill's argument, that is, the evaluation of pleasures should take into account both quality and quantity, will become less controversial if we have a better understanding of the nature and properties of pleasures. In other words, whether one accepts the second element will largely depend on whether one sees the first element to be true or not. Whether qualitative differences exist, like whether quantitative differences exist, is a question regarding fact. The question itself is value-neutral. As Wendy Donner suggests, quality is not the synonym of value in Mill's moral theory (Donner, 2006, p. 123; Donner, 2009, p. 21). Nevertheless, once we put pleasures on the scale of value, it is not only reasonable but also necessary to take into account both quality and quantity, that is, both the greater quantity and the superiority in quality are the properties which make a pleasure more valuable. Indeed, if in reality qualitative differences do exist between pleasures and quality, like quantity, is an intrinsic property of pleasures, why should, as Mill questions, the estimation of pleasures be supposed to depend on quantity alone while the estimation of all other things should depend on both quantity and quality (Mill, *CW, X*: 211)? The burden of argument will not fall on Mill alone but also on those who argue qualitative difference should not be taken into account in the evaluation of pleasures.

As to the third element, the claim that some qualities are superior and therefore more valuable, the statement itself is logical. The problem is how we define superiority. The existence of difference in qualities does not automatically imply that one type of pleasures must be more valuable than others. It is possible that some pleasures differ in quality yet are equally valuable in a moral sense. The concept of 'valuable', like the concept of 'good', does not have fixed contents. What is valuable, like what is good, depends on the subject under discussion. What is morally valuable to human beings should ultimately depend on the nature of human beings.

The fourth element is often criticized for its elitism. Donner (1991, 2009) disagrees with this elitist view and argues that for Mill one gains access to appreciating higher qualities of pleasure by cultivation. Moreover, Mill's views on education and self-development suggest that everyone should be given the chance to cultivate the taste for higher pleasures. Hence Mill's approach of assessing the value of pleasures is not an elitist one in nature. It is true that some might not be able to gain access to higher pleasures even after cultivation. Yet it is a secondary question. The key issue here is an epistemological one: how can we know if one pleasure is superior to another? For an empiricist like Mill, there is no way other than having experience of those pleasures under comparison. It is more reasonable to treat Mill's arguments as dealing with general experience of human beings as a whole, rather than suggesting methods of measuring specific pleasures on every occasion.

After breaking down Mill's arguments, we can see that the above four elements should not cause real objections to Mill's distinction of higher and lower pleasures. But the fifth element of Mill's quality/quantity distinction does suffer some difficulties which cannot be easily settled, even if Mill's arguments are read in the most charitable manner. When facing two pleasures how can we decide which is greater in quantity or superior in quality? On both dimensions of quality and quantity, Mill considers, only those who are familiar with both pleasures can answer. Moreover, he believes that between pleasures derived from higher faculties and lower ones, the former will be chosen by those who experienced both on the grounds of quality.

As mentioned earlier, the fifth element is an empirical question in nature. If so, in theory it can be tested by empirical evidence as to whether the experienced will consider pleasures derived from the distinctively human faculties qualitatively superior to those from animal appetites. However, in practice, such evidence is difficult to collect. The following discussion will first classify the reading of Mill's evaluation of pleasures in the literature into two types. It will then argue that the second interpretation is closer to Mill's position, but it also requires the concept of discontinuities in value held by the first interpretation to allow some of Mill's texts in *Utilitarianism* to be reasonably explained. Also, if how people actually evaluate pleasures is the same as the second interpretation of what Mill expects people will do, then it explains why the observable choice or revealed preference of the experienced judge cannot be used to test the validity of the fifth element.

There are two possible readings of Mill's view on the measurement of value. Let's label these two readings as Method 1 and Method 2 respectively and consider the case in which two pleasures are compared:

> [Method 1] If one pleasure is superior to the other in quality, then however great quantity the other pleasure has, the pleasure which has the superior quality will be more valuable.
>
> [Method 2] If one pleasure is superior to the other in quality, it will be granted more value on the ground of quality. However, one pleasure's value in quantity can still outweigh the other pleasure's value in quality.

In other words, for Method 1, the superiority in quality will render the consideration of quantity negligible. For Method 2, the value grounded on the quality is not the dominant determinant of the total value. If one pleasure is far greater in quantity than the other, it is still possible that the pleasure of greater quantity can outrank the other so that the total value of the pleasure superior in quality may be less than that of the pleasure greater in quantity.

Mill never spells out the method of evaluating pleasures in either way. His discussion of the quality/quantity distinction is so ambiguous that both readings of evaluation method appear to be compatible with, or at least not obviously contradictory to his texts. Moreover, neither of them can be fully justified by the texts in *Utilitarianism* alone. Nevertheless, Method 2 seems to be a more plausible theory and will lead to a theory of value which fits better in Mill's theory of life in general.

If we combine these two readings of the evaluation method with the proposition that higher pleasures are always superior in quality to lower ones, then we obtain the following two interpretations of Mill's theory of value. Let's label them as Interpretation 1 and 2, corresponding to Method 1 and 2 above:

> [Interpretation 1] Higher pleasures are always more valuable than lower ones regardless of their respective quantities, and therefore will always be preferred or ought to be chosen by the competent judge.
>
> [Interpretation 2] Higher pleasures are not always more valuable than lower ones even though they are superior in quality. Therefore, they will not necessarily be preferred or always ought to be chosen by the competent judge.

Both views have strong supporters. Commentators who are in line with Interpretation 1 believe that higher pleasures are not only superior in quality but also superior as a whole. Accordingly, they claim that there is a hierarchy of pleasures in Mill's theory or the values of pleasures are lexically ranked. Riley is the leading figure of this view, among others.[6] Commentators who are in line with Interpretation 2 do not think that there is a rigid hierarchical ranking among pleasures in Mill's theory. Donner is the key figure of this view, among others.[7]

Which interpretation better presents Mill's position? The debate over this issue is still carrying on in the literature, and is sometimes rather bitter. In essence, the core of the debate lies in the disagreement over the answer to the question whether 'the slightest distinctively human pleasure is found more gratifying to the feelings than the greatest pleasure from animal appetite' and whether 'the slightest superiority in quality would outweigh any amount of quantity of an alternative *on every occasion*', framed in West's words (2004, p. 64). The answer of Interpretation 1 to both questions would be positive and that of Interpretation 2 would be negative. The debate between the two views is not merely a pure philosophical speculation. Rather, it has significance in practice for utilitarianism to be adopted as a functional doctrine to provide guidance for public policies. What Interpretation 1 argues for is essentially that higher pleasures always do and ought to trump lower pleasures. It follows that, as a matter of public policy, even a small quantity of higher pleasures for some can never be sacrificed for a very large quantity of lower pleasures for many others.

Some commentators, such as West (2004), argue that a theory of value like Interpretation 1 is in effect a very stringent theory and does not seem to be compatible with Mill's theory of life, which suggests that a happy life will consist of many and various pleasures. Hence it is fair to say that Interpretation 2 is closer to Mill's position as a whole, provided the interpretation is supplemented with a crucial condition which is indispensable to Mill's theory. This condition can be better understood by explaining the notion of discontinuity in value, one of the key arguments of Interpretation 1.

For Interpretation 1 to hold there must be discontinuities in value between pleasures (a notion proposed by Griffin, 1986, p. 85), such that no amount of pleasures that are inferior in quality can ever be that more valuable than some finite amount of pleasures that are superior in quality. It is worth noting that not all scholars who hold the discontinuity view agree on the interpretation of Mill's superiority. For instance, Riley insists that Mill's qualitative superiorities must be interpreted as infinite superiorities, while Rabinowicz and Arrhenius argue that Millian superiority does not need to be infinite (Rabinowicz 2003; Arrhenius and Rabinowicz 2005).

Does Mill's utilitarianism endorse the notion of discontinuity in value? This author argues that the notion of discontinuity in value exists in some cases but not all and this can be supported by Mill's discussion of justice, in particular, security. For Mill, justice is 'only a particular kind or branch of general utility' (Mill, *CW, X*: 241). However, not every utility is eligible to be a utility of this kind. Justice is a 'name for certain social utilities which are *vastly more important, and therefore more absolute and imperative*, than any others are as a class' (Mill, *CW, X*: 259, emphasis added). Security is beyond doubt one of the utilities of this kind, since all other earthly benefits are needed by one person, not needed by another, but no human being can possibly live without security (Mill, *CW, X*: 251). As a consequence,

> Our notion [...] of the claim we have on our fellow-creatures to join in making safe for us the very groundwork of our existence, gathers feelings around it so much more intense than those concerned in any of the more common cases of utility, that the difference in degree (as is often the case in

> psychology) becomes a real difference in kind. The claim assumes that character of absoluteness, that apparent infinity, and incommensurability with all other considerations, which constitute the distinction between the feeling of right and wrong and that of ordinary expediency and inexpediency.
>
> (Mill, *CW, X*: 251)

For Mill, the character of absoluteness, infinity, and incommensurability with all other considerations residing in the feelings gathered around the notion of security provide a foundation for granting those utilities deserving the name of justice a value which cannot ever be outstripped by the value of ordinary utilities. The author argues that this is the key to understanding how Mill weighs up the values of different utilities when facing the conflicts of utilities *among different people*.

Interpretation 1 on the notion of discontinuity in value is a reasonable understanding of Mill's concept of utility to a certain extent, but it is questionable to extend this notion so far as to suggest lexical priorities among different kinds of pleasures, especially if the lexical ranking is meant to be fixed and complete or presented in a sequence form.

It is worth mentioning that the following passage should not be considered to be able to indicate the discontinuity in value or infinite superiority:

> If one of the two [pleasures] is, by those who are competently acquainted with both, placed so far above the other that they prefer it, even though knowing it to be attended with a greater amount of discontent, and would not resign it for any quantity of the other pleasure which their nature is capable of, we are justified in ascribing to the preferred enjoyment a superiority in quality, so far outweighing quantity as to render it, in comparison, of small account.
>
> (Mill, *CW, X*: 211)

Riley and Schmidt-Petri once had an acrimonious debate over the interpretation of this passage. The author has no intention of entering their debate here since their arguments are complicated and it is not a suitable place to divert our discussion. Schmidt-Petri's view is not well-known yet worth noting. According to Schmidt-Petri, the above passage should not be read as 'if some pleasure is of higher quality, then it will be or ought to be chosen over the pleasure of lower quality regardless of their respective quantities' (Schmidt-Petri, 2003, p. 103). If we read this passage carefully from the context, we will notice that Mill is not giving a definition or stipulating the necessary or sufficient condition of qualitative superiority. Instead, the purpose of this passage is to propose a way to demonstrate the existence of qualitative difference. All he says in this passage is that if one of the pleasures is preferred in the way as he describes, then we are justified in ascribing to a qualitative superiority to the preferred pleasure. In other words, qualitative superiority can be inferred, but not defined, if competent people would not sacrifice one pleasure for any quantity of the other pleasure which their nature is capable of. If so, the logic of Mill's argument in this passage is that one pleasure will be preferred because of its qualitative superiority, not vice versa, namely one pleasure is qualitatively superior because it is preferred. If this analysis is correct, then the above quotation does suggest the possibility for one pleasure to enjoy superiority in quality which is so great that it causes discontinuity in value. However, it is insufficient to infer from the passage that qualitative superiorities will always cause discontinuities in value because in the quotation Mill gives us only one extreme case of qualitative superiority.

4 Reconstructing Mill's theory of justice

Despite considering justice as 'the chief part, and incomparably the most sacred and binding part, of all morality', Mill never attempted to construct a systematic theory of justice. The most extensive discussion on justice he gave in the last chapter of *Utilitarianism* is not meant to be a comprehensive theory. In this chapter we attempt to reconstruct Mill's theory of justice with a focus on economic justice by gathering the scattered discussion of justice in Mill's writings. One might challenge the legitimacy of such an attempt: isn't it meaningless to construct a separate theory of justice given that Mill grounds his standard of justice on utility? Mill indeed believes that the moral requirements of justice must be dependent on social utility. However, the relationship between justice and utility in Mill's philosophy is usually oversimplified by commentators, and the oversimplification has caused a significant amount of confusion regarding Mill's utilitarian account of justice. For this reason, a sensible reconstruction of his theory of justice is needed in order to remove misunderstandings and to appreciate the strengths of Mill's utilitarian theory of justice. Given that Mill's theory of justice is part of his utilitarianism, the reconstruction in this chapter will adopt the reconstructed framework of Mill's utilitarian philosophy in general introduced in Chapter 2.[1] We will explore Mill's principles of justice at three different levels in accordance with the reconstructed framework of utilitarianism, that is, justice at the highest level as the first principle, justice at the secondary level as philosophical principles, and justice at the third level as practical principles. Moreover, the principles of justice will be examined and explained by connecting them to the idea of equality at each level.

Justice and equality

The idea of equality has a close connection with the idea of justice, and is often treated as the basis for discussions of justice. Indeed, no discussion of justice which does not investigate the idea of equality can ever be considered comprehensive. For his part, Mill certainly does undertake such an investigation, and the idea of equality often appears in his writings. However, whether Mill has an overriding commitment to equality and whether an egalitarian position can be consistent with his utilitarian theory are not questions with straightforward answers. Not surprisingly, there is no agreed view on these issues in the enormous literature on Mill.[2] The difficulty of interpretation arises not only from the fact that Mill rarely if ever provides a clear definition of equality, but also that the idea of equality has several dimensions. The latter, combined with the vague everyday meaning of equality, is a major reason causing complications to the philosophical debates on equality.

According to the *Oxford English Dictionary*, 'equal' means 'the same in size, amount, values, number, degree, status, etc'. In other words, 'equal' means the 'same' in 'something'. Since 'something' can be anything, 'equality' and 'equal' are 'incomplete predicates' (Rae, 1981, p. 132). It follows that it is necessary to ask in what respect equality is under consideration in order to have a sensible discussion; otherwise, the discussion of equality tends to cause rather than solve problems. In this chapter we will introduce Mill's notion of equality in connection with his theory of justice in relation to three aspects in turn, namely equality as the practice of justice, equality as the formal element in the conception of justice, and equality as the substantive element in the conception of justice. The first two will be discussed in this section and the last in the last section on Mill's theory of economic justice.

Today, there is near-universal agreement that equality is an indispensable principle for the practice of justice. 'Equality before the law' is the manifestation of equality in this sense. Clearly, Mill recognizes the importance of equality in the practice of justice. While observing the relationship between justice and equality, Mill points out that the idea of equality 'often enters as a component part *both* into the *conception* of justice and into the *practice* of it' (Mill, *CW, X*: 243, emphasis added). Nevertheless, his discussion of equal treatment or impartiality is more often couched in terms of its being a formal element of the conception of justice. This will also be the focus of our following discussion.

Since Aristotle almost every theory of justice, including Mill's, comprises both formal and substantive elements. Thus the classification between formal justice and substantive justice made by Chaïm Perelman, one of the most important theorists on argumentation in the twentieth century, provides a useful framework for analysing Mill's theory. By examining the six most widely accepted conceptions of justice – 'to each the same thing', 'to each according to his merits', 'to each according to his works', 'to each according to his needs', 'to each according to his rank', and 'to each according to his legal entitlement', Perelman identifies a common feature among these different and even contradictory conceptions of justice. He labels this common element as 'formal justice' or 'abstract justice', in contrast to 'substantive justice' or 'concrete justice', which represents the distinctive part of each conception of justice (Perelman, 1980, Chapter 1). Perelman concluded that despite their differences, all the various conceptions of justice would agree that to be just is to give the same treatment to those who are equal from some particular point of view. Accordingly, Perelman defines formal justice as 'a principle of action in accord with which beings of one and the same essential category must be treated in the same way' (Perelman, 1980, p. 11). In other words, equality is the essence of formal justice: every kind of conception of justice requires impartial treatment according to a certain criterion which has been chosen by that conception of justice.

Perelman's distinction between 'formal' and 'substantive' justice illustrates that the crux of the debates on justice is over the idea of substantive justice, rather than formal justice. That is to say, the key issue in the debate among different theories of justice is not 'equality or not' but 'equality of what'.[3] Equal treatment as a formal justice in a *conceptual* sense should not be conflated with equal treatment as a formal justice in an *administrative or practice* sense mentioned above. The latter is a dictate of treating the subjects of the law or rule impartially without discrimination, whatever the law or rule stipulates. By contrast, equal treatment in a conceptual sense concerns what the content of the law or rule ought to be. One example of equal treatment in a practice sense might be: if the rule is 'No parking on the yellow line' meaning 'No parking on the yellow line for anyone', then no one, including the prime minister, an elderly person, or a disabled person, can park on the yellow line. On the other hand, if the rule is 'No parking on the yellow line except the disabled', then the equal treatment required by the practice of the justice means that any disabled person is allowed to park on the yellow line and those who are not disabled are forbidden to park on the yellow line. In contrast, equal treatment in a conceptual sense plays a role in formulating rules by reflecting whether and why disabled and non-disabled should be treated differently or in the same way regarding the issue of parking.

Formal justice, equality and the greatest happiness principle

Like nearly all other theories of justice, Mill's utilitarian conception of justice also has equality as its formal element. In principle, one notion of justice implies one opinion of equality of something. Mill's theory of justice consists of various principles of justice, each of which corresponds to the requirement of equal treatment in one specific dimension. We start with the requirement of equal treatment contained in his principle of utility in this section. In the last part of this chapter, we will investigate the different notions of equality in his principles of economic justice in relation to three different economic issues, namely remuneration, tax and exchange.

Mill's utilitarianism requires equal treatment as the fundamental standard of social and distributive justice:

> we should treat all equally well [...] who have deserved equally well of *us*, and that society should treat all equally well who have deserved equally well of *it*, that is, who have deserved equally well absolutely.
>
> (Mill, *CW, X*: 257, emphasis original)

This quote is explicitly stipulated by Mill to be 'the highest abstract standard of social and distributive justice'. Mill's highest abstract standard of social and distributive justice in this context only requires that 'society should treat all equally well who have deserve equally well of it'. It implies treating equals equally and therefore also treating the dissimilar dissimilarly. Note that it does not specify the basis of 'desert', that is, 'desert' in this context has no specific content. Therefore, this is only a formal element of Mill's conception of justice.

According to Mill, this great duty of equal treatment is not a corollary from secondary doctrines, but 'a direct emanation from the first principle of morals': 'It is involved in the very meaning of Utility, or the Greatest Happiness Principle' (Mill, *CW, X*: 257). Mill stresses that equality is the integral part of the Greatest Happiness Principle, the first principle of utilitarianism:

> That principle is a mere form of words without rational signification, unless one person's happiness, supposed equal in degree (with the proper allowance made for kind), is counted for exactly as much as another's. Those conditions being supplied, Bentham's dictum, 'everybody to count for one, nobody for more than one', might be written under the principle of utility as an explanatory commentary.
>
> (Mill, *CW, X*: 257)

It is clear from the text that the first principle of Mill's utilitarianism contains *two distinct* elements: the first, the greatest happiness and the second, equal treatment of everyone's happiness.

The first element is universally recognized. The second element is also familiar to modern commentators. However, interpretation of the second element is controversial. H. L. A. Hart's interpretation of Mill quoted below represents a standard view held by a great many of philosophers and economists:

> As many contemporary philosophers, hostile to utilitarianism, have been concerned to show, it in principle licenses the imposition of sacrifices on innocent individuals when this can be shown to advance net aggregate welfare. Such sacrifices may be licensed because the egalitarianism embodied in the maxim 'everybody to count for one and nobody for more than one' is only a weighting principle, to be used in calculating what will maximize aggregate happiness; it treats persons as equals by securing that in the determination of what measures are required by the general welfare equal weight must be given to the equal happiness of all persons. But *it is not a principle requiring the equal treatment of different persons* and it may yield grossly inegalitarian results.
>
> (Hart, 1982, p. 98, emphasis added)

In Hart's reading, the requirement of treating different persons' happiness equally in Mill's utilitarianism is 'only a weighting principle' used for calculating aggregate happiness. The requirement of equal treatment is only a measure to carry out the aggregation procedure. It follows that the principle of utility is purely aggregative in nature, having no distributive attribute; all it cares is that the sum of happiness needs to be maximized irrespective of how the total amount of happiness is distributed.

Hart's interpretation is a misreading of Mill. It is a serious, but understandable misunderstanding. On the one hand, the brevity of Mill's discussion adds difficulty of interpretation to the already obscure subject. More importantly, the intellectual context in which Mill made his argument is very different from the context from which Hart interpreted Mill's writing. Even those most careful and sympathetic commentators of Mill, like Alan Ryan, found it difficult to make sense of Mill's argument.

While recognizing Mill's effort in integrating distributive elements into utilitarianism, Ryan believed that 'Mill fails to show, and *must fail to show*, how a distributive ideal can be subsumed under an aggregative one' (Ryan, 1987, p. 228, emphasis added). When attempting to reinforce his point that equal treatment between different persons is the very principle of utility itself, Mill says that the principle that everybody has an equal right to happiness 'may be more correctly described as supposing that equal amounts of happiness are equally desirable whether felt by the same or different persons' (Mill, *CW, X*: 257–258). Clearly, Ryan was not impressed by Mill's explanation. In fact, it is described by Ryan as 'the exactly wrong answer' (Ryan, 1987, p. 229). In Ryan's view, Mill's explanation of the principle of equality not only failed to refute, but also reinforced the objections to simple aggregative utilitarianism as a moral principle. Like many others, Ryan has presupposed the impossibility of accommodating the distributive side of ethics under the aggregative concept of utilitarianism.

It might be true, as Ryan suggests, that Mill's attempt to reconcile the aggregative requirement of utilitarianism with the distributive element is doomed to fail. But it is certainly true that for a long time Mill's message has been read from a perspective alien to Mill. Hart's interpretation, despite being a misreading of Mill, represents an accurate characterization of most versions of utilitarianism in contemporary moral philosophy and welfare economics. This suggests that neglecting the changes to the content of utilitarianism as a moral theory is one of the main reasons contributing to the popularity of the misinterpretation of Mill. It is fair to say that modern readers are ready to accept the standard interpretation of Mill not merely because of the ambiguity in Mill's own discussion of equal treatment; a more fundamental reason is that they are inclined to understand Mill's argument by interpreting it in the light of the forms of utilitarianism with which they are familiar.

By the mid-twentieth century, utilitarianism had become a doctrine which aims solely at maximizing total utility, whatever utility might mean. In line with this single aim, everyone's utility is given an equal weight in the aggregating calculation. A classic application of such a calculation can easily justify the case in which one innocent is framed or tortured in order to save more lives (see for instance, McCloskey, 1957, 1965; Williams, 1973). Utilitarianism is considered as a simple maximizing arithmetic principle which lacks any concern for distribution. It is treated in this way not only by the critics, but also by the defenders. For instance, J. J. C. Smart used H. J. McCloskey's famous sheriff example in defence of utilitarianism (Smart, 1973, pp. 69–73). In so doing, as Rosen comments, Smart caused a mutation in modern utilitarianism, which justifies cases of the sort envisaged by McCloskey, such as framing innocent people (Rosen, 1997, p. 36). This mutation has led to further confusions in discussions of utilitarianism. Indeed, the affirmation from the defenders of utilitarianism reinforces the belief that utilitarianism gives no respect to individuals at all, and cares only that total utility be maximized, no matter how happiness is distributed among different individuals. Following Rosen, this author terms this view the post-utilitarian paradigm, since it cannot be found in classical utilitarianism such as Bentham's or Mill's (Rosen, 1997).

To many contemporary philosophers and economists, it is the post-utilitarian paradigm, rather than Bentham's or Mill's utilitarianism, that is the version of utilitarianism they first or ever encountered. It is therefore natural for them to use this paradigm as the reference point to understand classical utilitarianism. Studying new theories per se is not a problem, but it would be a problem if a philosopher or economist only studies the latest theory and knows little about the history of the theory. It is evident in the case of utilitarianism that there is detrimental conflation between the post-utilitarian paradigm and the classical utilitarianism articulated by Bentham and Mill. In order to make sense of Mill's claim that a duty of equal treatment is involved in the very meaning of the greatest happiness principle, the importance of contextualizing his arguments cannot be overemphasized. For this purpose, a brief review of the historical background of utilitarianism as a legal and moral philosophy in eighteenth- and nineteenth-century England is necessary. This will be introduced presently with a focus on Bentham, followed by a re-examination of whether the notion of equality is compatible with the first principle of Mill's utilitarianism.

Bentham's utilitarianism as a guiding principle to legal reform

It is often alleged that utilitarianism does not respect the distinction between persons and hence allows the oppression of the minority by the majority. This charge clearly neglects the fact that for Bentham the problem was rather the reverse: it was the ruling minority that tended to oppress the governed majority, and this is the historical background that makes Bentham's greatest happiness principle remarkable (Schofield, 2009, p. 61). In opposition to the accusation made by contemporary critics, the greatest happiness principle was a principle initially appealed to by Bentham to emphasize the significance of the happiness of the neglected majority in society and to enhance and secure their happiness.

It is fair to say that a failure to recognize this setting of Bentham's writings is one of the main reasons for the unsympathetic interpretation of Bentham's utilitarianism. A correct understanding of the historical context of Bentham's principle of utility may not indeed resolve all the challenges it faces, but it helps us avoid biases resulting from the common stereotype of utilitarianism.

By the end of the eighteenth century, the shortcomings of the English legal system had become noticeable. After evolution over centuries, the 'bit-by-bit' development of English law had resulted in a legal system marked by obsolete rules, uncertainty as to its contents, complication of litigation, which notably made the administration 'so expensive that justice was in effect denied to the poor man' (Holdsworth, 1940, p. 580). The need for a thorough reform of English law was obvious. Advocating the codification of law, Bentham was one of the leading figures of the legal reform in eighteenth- and nineteenth-century England. The principle of utility was adopted by Bentham as the foundation of his critical analysis of the then existing law and institutions, and as the lodestone for legislators. This is the context in which his greatest happiness principle should be read.

With this historical context in mind, it becomes easier to understand Bentham's greatest happiness principle. In several places Bentham presents the 'each for one' idea codified by Mill's words. For instance, in Plan of Parliamentary Reform, Bentham wrote:

> The happiness and unhappiness of any one member of the community – high or low, rich or poor – what greater or less part is it of the universal happiness and unhappiness, than that of any other?
>
> (Bentham, 1843d, p. 459)

In Constitutional Code, Bentham also phrased the same idea in a different way:

> The happiness of the most helpless pauper constitutes as large a portion of the universal happiness, as does that of the most powerful, the most opulent member of the community. Therefore the happiness of the most helpless and indigent has as much title to regard at the hands of the legislator, as that of the most powerful and opulent.
>
> (Bentham, 1843e, p. 107)

> If the possession of a share in the supreme constitutive power is a means of, or security for, happiness, there is as much reason why a share in that means of security should be in the hands of the most helpless and the most indigent, as why it should be in the hands of the most powerful and the most opulent.
>
> (Bentham, 1843e, pp. 107–108)

It is important to note that in neither passage was Bentham talking about an abstract philosophical theory. Rather, the context of the above passages is the justification of universal suffrage, which, according to Bentham, is an application of his greatest happiness principle.

As Schofield points out, ill-informed commentators incorrectly describe Bentham as 'against rights', whereas what he is truly against is the idea of 'natural' rights (Schofield, 2009, p. 63). His commitment to an equal right of voting is not impaired but supported by his greatest happiness principle. Writing as a law reformer, Bentham argues that the constitutive power should be spread as widely as possible among the people, and that its extension is an essential means to achieve the greatest happiness. This implies that how the voting rights are distributed among people does matter in Bentham's felicity calculation, since it has impact on the sum of total happiness. In other words, Bentham's logic of calculation implies that excluding the helpless pauper from the right of voting (a right which is itself seen by Bentham as a means of security) does not meet the equal treatment condition required by his greatest happiness principle, because the exclusion itself means that the happiness of the pauper is likely to be simply ignored in the account of the happiness of the community.

Bentham believes that a representative democracy is the form of government that will have the greatest happiness of the greatest number for its effect. Throughout his writing of Constitutional Code, the greatest happiness of the greatest number is largely used in explicit contrast to the happiness of the corrupt few (namely the monarch and the subordinate holders of power who owe their privileged position to his goodwill) who wield power in the unreformed monarchy. If political reform is necessary, if monarchy or aristocracy should be replaced with representative democracy, isn't it evidence that the greatest happiness principle tends to justify the sacrifice of the few for the gain of the majority? To some extent, it is. It is a reality that no reform programme would ever get off the ground without some form of sacrifice of vested interests, as Schofield candidly puts it (Schofield, 2009, p. 63). However, it should not be forgotten that this is also why Bentham takes seriously the greatest happiness *of all concerned*. Bentham's balanced position on reform is well summarized by Paul Kelly: 'the reform-minded legislator must pay as much attention to the disappointment of those who are deprived of superfluous benefits by a reform measure, as those whose happiness depends on the reform of existing institutions' (Kelly, 1990, p. 179). This disappointment prevention principle is a substantive principle of Bentham's theory of justice.[4] If there is anything unsatisfactory in Bentham's arguments for universal suffrage, it is that he places the burden of justification on those who are against it, without justifying directly the desirability of equality:

> If a man who calls for the right of suffrage to be given to any one human being, calls for its being refused to any other human being, it lies upon him to give a particular reason for such refusal.
>
> (Bentham, 1843e, p. 107)[5]

It is a received view that utilitarians have to rely on the assumption of diminishing marginal utility to reconcile the goal of maximizing total happiness with the pursuit of equality.[6] However, this view seems to unduly downplay the importance of equality in Bentham's philosophy. Over the last two decades, Bentham scholars, including F. Rosen (1983, 1998), Paul Kelly (1990), Gerry J. Postema (1998, 2006), and Michael Quinn (2008), have argued that distributional equality plays a fundamental role in Bentham's utilitarianism. The revisionist view first recognizes that Bentham is very clear in identifying security, subsistence, abundance and equality as four subordinate ends of legislation. It then argues that Bentham's position of maximizing utility demands maximizing the production of security, subsistence and abundance, and distributing them among individuals with as much equality as is practicable. This interpretation can be supported by Bentham's own text as Michael Quinn notices: 'it is in the interest of all that *by each of them* the matter of subsistence, the matter of abundance, security in all its shapes or branches, be possessed and enjoyed in the highest degree possible' (Bentham, 1989, p. 153, emphasis added; Quinn, 2008, p. 321). In other words, spreading security, subsistence and abundance is a crucial way of maximizing the sum of happiness for Bentham.[7] According to the revisionist view of Bentham, the key to understanding why his utilitarianism is sensitive to equality relies on an understanding of 'individualist conception of happiness', in contrast to the traditional 'abstract conception of happiness'. The latter implies that happiness is 'abstracted from those who experience it', whereas the former believes that 'happiness is the happiness *of someone* is of fundamental moral importance' (Postema, 1998, pp. 149–150, emphasis in original). It is beyond the scope of this book to give a thorough examination of the debate between the traditional and revisionist views of Bentham. For the purpose of this study, it is sufficient for us to notice that it is Bentham's intention, successful or not, to promote total happiness by endorsing distributional equality in security and subsistence.

The respect to each as a human being who is the real bearer of happiness has been lost in the post-utilitarian paradigm in the twentieth century. The historical background of the greatest happiness principle emerging as a guiding principle of legal and social reforms in the eighteenth- and nineteenth-century England has been largely forgotten. These two factors acting together increase the difficulty of interpreting Bentham's theory.

The exegesis of Mill's utilitarianism suffers from a similar problem. Mill's principle is often read in isolation from the historical and intellectual context. To a large extent, Mill's greatest happiness principle is a continuation and extension of Bentham's principle with modifications. It is beyond doubt that Mill is familiar with Bentham's legal writings and the philosophy behind his proposals for legal and political reform. The dictum 'Every individual in the country tells for one; no individual for more than one' appears in Bentham's *Rationale of Judicial Evidence, specially applied to English practice*, which was edited by Mill with great care before age 20 (Schofield, 2009, p. 63; Mill, *CW, I*: 117–118). Mill knows well the true meaning of Bentham's dictum each for one, and adopted this particular legacy from Bentham without reservation.

Whoever understands how Bentham and Mill grounded their arguments for legal and social reform on the principle of utility would find it odd that this once radical philosophy, which aimed at promoting everyone's happiness, is now understood as an absurd doctrine which justifies framing and torturing. It has become a doctrine warranting the tyranny of the majority.

Understanding the origin of the principle of utility as a radical and progressive philosophy can help us appreciate the motivation for Mill's integrating equality into the first principle, but it does not imply that Mill's arguments are necessarily free from logical flaws. We shall now consider whether it is logically possible to combine equality and the greatest happiness principle as Mill intended. We will first explore why Mill considers equal treatment and utility as two indispensable elements of the first principle. We then analyse the logic behind Mill's arithmetic.

Mill on distributive justice and the first principle of utilitarianism

Before starting the discussion, it is important to bear in mind that in this section we examine the idea of distributive contained in the principle of utility as the *first* principle of a system of philosophy. The standard of justice or the notion of equality we discuss here is also related to this highest level. We are not concerned with the practical principles or rules of justice in daily life or those which are invoked directly to instruct institutions, which will be the topic of the last part of this chapter.

Let's start with recalling the relationship between the duty of equal treatment and the greatest happiness principle in Mill's utilitarian moral theory by reading again the key passages cited before:

> If it is a duty to do to each according to his deserts, returning good for good as well as repressing evil by evil, it necessarily follows that we should treat all equally well (when no higher duty forbids) who have deserved equally well of *us*, and that society should treat all equally well who have deserved equally well of *it*, that is, who have deserved equally well absolutely. This is the highest abstract standard of social and distributive justice; towards which all institutions, and the efforts of all virtuous citizens, should be made in the utmost possible degree to converge. But this great moral duty rests upon a still deeper foundation, being a direct emanation from the first principle of morals, and not a mere logical corollary from secondary or derivative doctrines. It is involved in the very meaning of Utility, or the Greatest Happiness Principle. That principle is a mere form of words without rational signification, unless one person's happiness, supposed equal in degree (with the proper allowance made for kind), is counted for exactly as much as another's.
>
> (Mill, *CW, X*: 257, emphasis original)

We can infer from the above passage three important propositions: first, equal treatment and the greatest happiness principle co-exist as the first principle of Mill's utilitarian philosophy; second, the greatest happiness principle and the requirement that 'one person's happiness is counted for exactly as much as another's' are the two sides of the same coin; third, different individuals' happiness has to be given equal weight if happiness is equal in degree and it follows that different weights should be given to happiness which is different in kind.

To a great many commentators, the requirement that 'one person's happiness is counted for exactly as much as another's' has no real distributive effect. If the requirement does have real implications for distribution, then equal treatment and the greatest happiness are irreconcilable rather than two sides of the same coin. To what extent can Mill's claim be sustained? Let's take McCloskey's well-known sheriff example to illustrate how Mill's utilitarianism would differ from modern versions of utilitarianism in calculating total happiness. Below is the scenario constructed by McCloskey in his 1957 essay 'An Examination of Restricted Utilitarianism'. The language he used might be insensitive and politically incorrect from today's viewpoint. However, to avoid distorting McCloskey's story, we cite the original text in full rather than rephrasing it:

> Suppose that a sheriff were faced with the choice either of framing a Negro for a rape that had aroused hostility to the Negroes (a particular Negro generally being believed to be guilty but whom the sheriff knows not to be guilty) – and thus preventing serious anti-Negro riots which would probably lead to some loss of life and increased hatred of each other by whites and Negroes – or of hunting for the guilty person and thereby allowing the anti-Negro riots to occur, while doing the best he can to combat them.
>
> (McCloskey, 1957, p. 468)

How would a utilitarian sheriff decide what to do? According to the post-utilitarian paradigm, the utilitarian formula of happiness calculation can be expressed as the function below:

$$\text{TU (Total Utility)} = 1{*}U_1 + 1{*}U_2 + \ldots + 1{*}U_n \qquad (1)$$

The idea that everyone's happiness should be given equal weight is presented by the same coefficient of everyone's happiness (let's say one). Now assume person 1 is the innocent Negro. Let's use TU′ to denote the consequence of not framing person 1 and TU″ the consequence of framing person 1. According to McCloskey, for an extreme utilitarian, or act-utilitarian, as long as TU″ > TU′, framing the innocent would be justified by utilitarianism.

In contrast, such a calculation is inconsistent with Mill's utilitarianism. Mill's answer to the imaginary scenario would be that to frame an innocent is to deny that person's claim to happiness. For Mill, it is the highest abstract standard of social and distributive justice of his utilitarianism that 'society should treat all equally well who have deserved equally well of it'. Accordingly, an innocent person should be treated equally like all other innocent people in regardless their ethnic background. The utility of protecting an innocent person's life and liberty is universally essential to everyone's happiness in a civilized society. It is such an important utility that Mill's utilitarianism would argue that every innocent person's life and liberty should be protected from framing. It is an issue about justice: every innocent person should be entitled a claim to protection from framing, and the claim should be recognized as a right to be protected by the society with the law grounded on the principles of justice. The justification of the claim to protection as a right is for the happiness of all – the true meaning of social utility. Only by protecting everyone's happiness can the total happiness of the society be truly maximized. Therefore, according to Mill's greatest happiness principle, framing the innocent Negro is unjust. It is arguable whether Mill's thought can be captured by a simplified equation, but if we really want to use the equation to express Mill's idea, there are two possible ways to present it. First, for Mill, framing the innocent person 1 would imply that the coefficient of U_1 is less than the coefficient of U_2 to U_n. In other words, the requirement of equal coefficient in the above equation (1) is not satisfied. TU′ is a result derived from TU, in which everyone's happiness is given an equal weight, but TU″ is not. Hence, comparing TU″ with TU′ makes little sense since they are outcomes of two different functions. This view is to connect Mill's principle of utility to the equation from the perspective of whether all concerned are taken into account. We can also examine the happiness calculation from the perspective of whether different kinds of utilities are given different values in the calculation. For Mill, when framing an innocent person, the total utility would be

$$TU_M'' = 1^* (-\infty) + 1^*(+) + \ldots + 1^*(+) = -\infty$$

This is because if person 1 is innocent, then the loss of his happiness should be considered as infinite. Therefore, there is no chance for TU_M'' to be greater than TU′ and thus it is impossible to justify TU_M'' in the name of maximizing total utilities. It has to be underlined that the loss of every kind of utility will not be deemed as an infinite loss. Only the 'extraordinarily important and impressive kind of utility', needed by nearly everyone, is qualified. The second interpretation can be seen as an explanatory note to the proviso of equal treatment of everyone's happiness 'when no higher duty forbids' and 'with the proper allowance made for kind', both of which appear in the above quotation of Mill.

To sum up, the requirement by Mill's utilitarianism to treat different individuals' happiness equally is not equivalent to a formal weighting principle which gives equal weight to each unit of happiness. The former is an integral part of the principle of the greatest happiness of the greatest number, while the latter is only a principle subordinate to the aggregating formula. A key difference between the two is that Mill's equal treatment is distribution-sensitive, while the equal weighting principle is not.

One might tend to argue, as Kymlicka (1988) did, that equal consideration is a condition prior to maximizing total happiness in utilitarianism. However, the textual evidence suggests that Mill would not agree with this. In reply to Herbert Spencer, Mill explicitly refutes the view that perfect impartiality between persons is the anterior principle of the principle of utility. When commenting on Spencer's arguments, Mill does not seem to be comfortable with the term 'right', and thus rephrases Spencer's 'everybody has an equal right to happiness' into that 'equal amounts of happiness are equally desirable, whether felt by the same or by different persons'. Then he rejects its interpretation as 'a premise needful to support the principle of utility' by arguing that it is '*the very principle itself*; for what is the principle of utility, if it be not that "happiness" and "desirable" are synonymous terms?' (Mill, *CW, X*: 257–258, emphasis added). Mill leaves a big puzzle here. His reply does not seem to give much attention to the notion 'equal'. Instead, it appears to focus only on happiness. This might disappoint those who wish to see Mill as an egalitarian in an absolute sense: his position is clearly a teleological one. The notion of equality alone has no significant meaning unless it is associated with happiness as a desirable end. It is the recognition of happiness as desirable to everyone, and as the ultimate aim of all human conduct, that justifies the equal claim of everybody to happiness. In other words, for Mill 'good' must be prior to 'right', 'just' and 'rights'. The adjective 'prior' here is used in an epistemological sense, not in a normative sense. It does not imply that equality and distributive justice are not important. The point here is that it is impossible for the notions of equality and distributive justice to exist independently from the notion of good in Mill's teleological moral theory. Equality makes sense here only because it has been attached to happiness. Equality alone is not a prima facie duty. For Mill, 'a right to equal concern and respect' per se has no significance unless it is aimed to benefit one's happiness.

So far, we have shown that equal treatment as a formal element of the conception of justice is an integral part of Mill's first principle. It is a requirement of treating people equally well if they deserve to be treated equally well. Formal justice in this sense is a rather vacuous form, for it tells us nothing about how to formulate the judgement of people's 'desert'. Moreover, merely emphasizing the significance of equality cannot guarantee the prevention of extremely unjust social states. As Mill points out, it is ironic that even in slave countries the rights of the slave were believed to be as sacred as those of the master, and it was deemed an injustice if a tribunal failed to enforce the slave's rights with equal strictness (Mill, *CW, X*: 243–244). Therefore, despite playing a central role in Mill's theory of justice, equal treatment is only a necessary, rather than a sufficient, condition of justice. In order to gather a full account of Mill's theory of justice, we still have to examine the substantive part of his conception of justice.

Differential treatment as the essence of substantive justice

Since the French Revolution in 1789, the slogan 'liberty, equality, and fraternity' has become deeply rooted in people's minds. But are people really born equal? The truth is the very opposite. Human beings are born very different. This fact is recognized by Mill and becomes one of the crucial foundations on which his view of social and distributive justice is based.

In many cases, Mill thinks that the requirement of simple equality without considering personal circumstances will lead to an unjust result. For instance, when commenting on the principle of giving equal payment to each who shares the work equally, a principle often favoured by communists, Mill considers it to be 'a very imperfect standard of justice', in that people have unequal mental and bodily capacities for work, so that to demand the same amount of work from everyone is to allocate a bigger burden to those whose capacities are weaker (Mill, *CW, V*: 743–744). In other words, because of the fact that human beings are in general different in certain aspects, substantive justice will require treating people differently. Because of the diversities among human beings, equal treatment might actually require differential treatment in reality.

But what should be the criterion for differential treatment? Mill indicates that 'social utility' to be the guide. However, Mill does not provide a plain demonstration of how to apply this abstract guide to address the problems in the real world. 'Social utility' is such a vague idea that Mill left a huge gap between the instruction and its implementation. Despite the difficulties, the last part of this chapter will try to analyse Mill's opinions regarding the rules for remuneration, income taxation and exchange of commodities, and suggest how Mill derives moral principles in practice from the principle of utility in the abstract. Before turning to Mill's theory of economic justice, we shall first clarify our terminologies.

Social justice, economic justice, and distributive justice

To avoid unnecessary confusion it is essential to clarify the use of the terms 'social justice', 'distributive justice' and 'economic justice' in our discussion in that these terms are often used to indicate different ideas by different scholars. The intention here is not to specify the substantive content of these three terms, but to explain the relationships between them in our discussion.

In *The New Palgrave: A Dictionary of Economics*, under the entry 'distributive justice', Edmund S. Phelps writes

> [s]ocial justice is justice in all of the relationships occurring in society: the treatment of criminals, children and the elderly, domestic animals, rival countries, and so forth. Distributive justice is a narrower concept for which another name is economic justice. It is justice in the economic relationships within society: collaboration in production, trade in consumer goods, and the provision of collective goods.
>
> (Phelps, 1987, pp. 886–887)

This approach treats economic justice as a synonym of distributive justice and the sphere of economic or distributive justice is smaller than that of social justice.

Another way to relate these three ideas is to equate social justice and distributive justice and then treat economic justice as part of distributive justice. John Rawls for one adopts this approach. According to Rawls's treatment, the scope of social justice in his discourse does not include the attitudes and dispositions of persons, or the rules and practices of private associations. Commutative justice is excluded from his study of social justice. In his mind, the concept of social justice is to provide an initial standard for the basic structure of society in regard to its 'distributive' aspects (Rawls, 1999, pp. 7–8).

Mill rarely if ever used the term 'economic justice'. Nevertheless, it is apparent from his discourse that the idea of justice has an important role in his opinions regarding economic issues. Hence, economic justice is used in our discussion to give some indication of Mill's idea of justice related to economic affairs, and we will not be concerned at this point to spell out in detail the content of his economic justice. Moreover, we follow Phelps in using 'social justice' to mean 'justice in all of the relationships occurring in society' (Phelps, 1987, p. 886). Again, this meaning refers only to the realm of social justice, but not the content. Consequently, economic justice is a branch of social justice in our discussion.

Furthermore, we can divide social affairs into two types according to their nature: one is individual-to-individual affairs and the other individual-to-community affairs. If we use Aristotle's examples, the former includes sale, purchase, loan for consumption, and pledging, and the latter includes distributions of honour or money. In our discussion, commutative justice is used to govern the rules of individual-to-individual affairs and distributive justice is used to govern the rules of individual-to-community affairs. Again, no specific content is implied in relation to what the rules of commutative or distributive justice ought to be. We must admit that it is not always clear-cut whether one particular affair is commutative or distributive in nature, and hence it is not always clear whether one affair should be regulated by the idea of commutative justice or by that of distributive justice. For instance, some economists believe that taxation is a sale–purchase relation between the government and the people. Those who hold this view will naturally take benefit-principle rather than the ability-to-pay principle as the just principle of taxation. Therefore, investigating and identifying the nature of an affair should be included as an indispensable part of a comprehensive theory of justice.

According to the realms assigned above, in our use social justice contains elements of both commutative and distributive justice, and similarly economic justice too contains elements of both kinds of justice. However, we cannot say that distributive justice is a concept narrower than economic justice, since some issues regarding distributive justice may not be economic in nature. The realm of distributive justice and that of economic justice overlap because the limits of each are determined by different criteria.

The relationship between social justice, economic justice and distributive justice characterized above is consistent with the way Mill uses these terms. For instance, Mill claims that the abstract ideal of social justice is involved in the very meaning of the Greatest-Happiness Principle, the first principle of his moral philosophy which is the ultimate criterion of all human conduct and affairs (Mill, *CW, X*: 257). Moreover, both the notion of distributive justice and commutative justice appear in Mill's political economic writings. On the one hand, Mill refers to the idea of distributive justice when discussing taxation and property institutions; on the other hand, it is also obvious that the concept of commutative justice exists in Mill's discussion about the exchange of commodities, although he does not use the term 'commutative justice' explicitly. It is important to remember that the term economic justice in our use does not have a concrete or fixed meaning; nor does it hold a certain standard or principle as *the* just one. Moreover, depending on the context, the principles of economic justice in our discussion may refer to the principles of justice at the philosophical level (the second level) or at the practice level (the third level).

Based on the connection between social justice, economic justice and distributive justice articulated above, the relationship between different principles of justice in Mill's system can be described as follows: under the single ultimate principle – the principle of utility, there are plural principles of justice. The abstract ideal of social justice itself is embraced in the very meaning of the greatest happiness principle and those various principles of justice can be seen as what Mill calls secondary principles of utilitarianism. These secondary principles of justice govern different areas, including the economic field in which there are miscellaneous affairs requiring different principles of justice. When these secondary principles conflict with each other, the principle of utility has to be appealed to as the final arbiter. Now we are going to explore Mill's theory of economic justice. We will start with identifying the features which characterize Mill's theory of economic justice in general, followed by the investigation of the specific principles of economic justice in three different areas.

Mill's theory of economic justice

Mill's theory of economic justice has two significant features. First, no principle of economic justice characterized by substantive and concrete content can be universal. Despite claiming that the distribution of wealth is solely a matter of human institution, Mill does not suggest that the adoption of institutions is a free choice without any constraints. On the contrary, Mill is all too aware that for an institution to be feasible and successful, certain conditions, such as the social character and moral mentality of the people, are required (Mill, *CW, II*: 199–200).

From this viewpoint, Mill's utilitarian account of justice has the characteristic of relative validity. It is relativistic not in an extreme sense of being ethically relativist,[8] but in a sense that people's judgement about the facts of a situation which are the basis of moral thought is actually a fact about the dispositions of people in the society in question.[9] To borrow Hare's words, the characteristic of relative validity in Mill's moral theory reflects only the truth that 'moral judgements about concrete situations have to be made in the light of facts about those situations, of which facts about attitudes and reactions are one very important kind' (Hare, 1981, p. 159).

The objective realities of mental and material conditions restrict the subjective conceptions of utility in certain times and societies. The principles of justice grounded in utility are hence also constrained by objective circumstances and human nature. In other words, the problem of choosing which principles of justice to be the ruling principles is a matter related to the real circumstances in a certain society at a certain time.[10] Therefore, it is impossible for principles of justices to be universally applicable. They can only be 'relatively' valid, namely, valid for a certain society during a certain period. As civilization and human nature evolve, the ideas of utility and therefore the conceptions and the principles of justice will also change accordingly. It follows that as soon as we try to make Mill's highest abstract standard of social justice – a universal but rather empty form of justice – contain any substantive materials, the secondary principles derived from this absolute form immediately become only relatively valid. In Aristotle's words, if the principles are universal, they will not be substances; for everything that is common indicates not a 'this' but a 'such', and substance is a 'this' (Aristotle, 1940, Book 3, 6 (12)).

In addition to the relative validity of principles of economic justice, pluralism is another feature of Mill's theory of economic justice. For Mill, there is no such *a* principle as the principle of economic or distributive justice grounded on which a just institution can be constructed and a just society can be achieved. It has been noted in Chapter 2 that in addition to the first principle of utility, the operation of a society needs various secondary principles, including moral and non-moral principles. The institutions of a society are constituted of these various secondary principles.[11] Of these principles, some are based on different conceptions of justice so that they can be named as principles of justice. For instance, while reviewing the popular opinions regarding the matters of taxation and remuneration in *Utilitarianism*, Mill points out that each of these popular opinions can be considered just from each of its own views. As to which one should be chosen as *the* principle, Mill does not give a determinate answer. He leaves it to different societies and different generations to search for their own answers. It is important to bear in mind that these secondary principles of justice are not the principle of justice as the highest abstract standard of social justice, despite the former being derived from the latter.

Now we are going to explore Mill's principles of economic justice by examining his discussion of the just principles for remuneration, income taxation and the exchange of commodities in a capitalist society. It is important to note here that we are not concerned with the ideal of socialism. Instead, we investigate how Mill worked out operational just rules for the system of private property from his ideas and philosophical principles of justice. This is a type of moral reasoning corresponding to the second and third steps of analysis introduced in the last section of Chapter 2. Moreover, we will adopt Perelman's framework of formal and substantive justice to analyse the requirement of equality in each of the three cases.

Principles of remuneration

In *Utilitarianism*, Mill presents two popular yet conflicting views regarding whether the principle 'to each according to merits' is a just principle for remuneration (Mill, *CW, X*: 253–254). One view holds that the talented or skilled should be given a title to superior remuneration because society owes the more efficient labourers a larger return for the more useful services they provide to it. The other argues that those with superior abilities already have more than enough advantages, and that society should make compensation to the less favoured for the unmerited inequality of inborn advantages, rather than aggravate it. How do we decide which of these two conflicting principles to adopt as the principle of justice for our society? Mill considers that making a choice between them in the name of justice must be arbitrary, because each of them can be deemed as a just principle from the perspective of different conceptions of justice respectively. One adopts the perspective of what the individual should receive, and the other the perspective of what the community should give. The idea of justice alone is unable to decide which one to choose; Mill believes that only social utility can answer the question. But how?

Principles of remuneration such as 'to each according to their merits' or 'to each according to their exertion' are the secondary principles in the reconstructed three-level framework of Mill's utilitarianism. None of these secondary principles can be universally applicable to any society at any time and any place. The answer to which is the best one depends on the society under consideration. In addition, social utility or greatest happiness is the ultimate standard of human action and affairs, including policies and institutions. In most cases, the selection of the secondary principles cannot be answered by directly invoking social utility. Rather, the identification of secondary ends is needed. How can we identify the end of the system of remuneration?

The principle of remuneration is part of a bigger question regarding how to distribute the products of a society, an issue occupying a central place in the debate between the supporters of socialism and those of private property. Despite his inclination towards socialism later in his life, Mill never suggests 'to each according to their needs' as the just principle of distribution. Mill considers that people in his time were still too ignorant about private property in its best form and socialism in its best form to judge which of the two should be the ultimate form of human society, even thought he seems to believe a 'qualified socialism' to be 'the ultimate prospects of humanity' (Mill, *CW, I:* 199; *II*: xciii, 208). Based on his observation of the social character of English people, Mill judged that it was not time yet to implement socialism in nineteenth-century England, since socialism is an institution requiring a much higher moral condition of people which was lacking in his time. Instead, it was highly expedient to carry on the institution of individual property since it fitted well with the 'selfish type of character formed by the present standard of morality and fostered by the existing social institutions', and Mill expected these institutions to be 'more likely to prove immediately successful, than an attempt at a higher ideal' (Mill, *CW, II*: 210). Mill's argument here is not to justify people's selfishness; he actually considers it important to improve English people's moral state through education. Rather, the key point here is that the choice of social institution of remuneration is not a choice free from constraints.

If Mill's assessment is correct, what would be the just principle of remuneration for a society implementing private property according to Mill? We shall start from Mill's view on the main purpose or function of private property as a social institution. It needs to be stressed that in Mill's view private property, when established, did not owe its origin to any of the considerations of utility which are used to plead for the maintenance of it (Mill, *CW, II*: 201). Indeed, private property may not be established for any specific aim or function which we now attribute to it. Nevertheless, to plead for maintaining it we need to consider its function as an institution for our society.

It is Mill's view that the foundation of the private property is 'the right of producers to what they themselves have produced', that is, 'a right to the exclusive disposal of what he or she have produced by their own exertions, or received either by gift or by fair agreement, without force or fraud, from those who produced it' (Mill, *CW, II*: 215). What Mill intends to emphasize here is not the right per se, but the *content* of the right. The institution of private property is supposed to mean the guarantee or protection to individuals of the fruits of their own labour and abstinence; it is 'upheld and commended principally as being the means by which labour and frugality are insured their reward' (Mill, *CW, II*: 208, *CW, V*: 712). It follows that the principle of remuneration according to merit or exertion is a principle of justice consistent with the ideal of private property institution.

Accordingly, the idea 'desert' in Mill's highest standard of social and distributive justice can be interpreted as 'to each according to their merit or exertion' within the context of remuneration in a society holding the private property institution. If we use Perelman's framework, the requirement of equality as the formal element of Mill's conception of justice in this case chooses 'merit/exertion' to be the criterion of equal treatment. Therefore, the substantive justice of remuneration requires that those who display the same merits/exertions should be rewarded with the same amount of income, and those who display different merits/exertions be rewarded with different amounts of income. As to how to treat different merits/exertions differently, Mill considers that the very idea of distributive justice requires *proportionality* between success and merit or between success and exertion (Mill, *CW, V*: 714). That is to say, proportionality between success and merit/exertion is an outcome of two requirements of justice: one is the requirement of formal equality, and the other is the requirement of the substantive principle of justice which identifies 'merit/exertion' as the just, that is morally relevant, basis for differentiation in treatment.

Certainly, the notion of rewards in accordance with exertion is not the same as the notion of rewards in accordance with performance or contribution. Unfortunately, Mill did not discuss further which one would be the better principle of justice to govern remuneration. Nevertheless, it is fairly clear that exertion plays an important role in Mill's assessment of the distribution of income in his time:

> the produce of labour [...] apportioned as we now see it almost in an inverse ratio to the labour – the largest portions to those who have never worked at all, the next largest to those whose work is almost nominal, and so in a descending scale, the remuneration dwindling as the work grows harder and more disagreeable, until the most fatiguing and exhausting bodily labour cannot count with certainty on being able to earn even the necessaries of life.
>
> (Mill, *CW, II*: 207)

The principle of remuneration in accordance with labour is a principle of justice at the secondary level in the reconstructed framework. The ideal pursued by the requirement of equal treatment at this philosophical level may be prevented by some disturbing causes at the practice level and thus equal treatment in accordance with the criterion selected at the philosophical level will become an unfair treatment. There are various factors in the real world which prevent the ideal of justice aimed at by the philosophical principle 'to each according to his exertion/merit' from being achieved.

For instance, it is Mill's view that the unequal opportunity will hinder the implementation of the principle of proportioning remuneration to labour from achieving the ideal of justice pursued by this principle. Mill recognizes the unfairness of inequality in opportunities resulting from the social arrangement in his time and argues that a just and wise legislation would endeavour to ensure all of the competitors a fair start. It is important to note that Mill does not advocate the pursuit of absolute equality of income or wealth. On the contrary, he considers that once the government has done all it can do, by instruction and by legislation, to diminish the inequality of opportunities, the inequalities of property which arise from unequal industry, frugality, perseverance, talents, and to a certain extent even opportunities, are inevitable and should be tolerated (Mill, *CW, II:* 225, *III*: 811). In other words, Mill's advocacy of equal opportunities is similar to what Robert Sugden calls 'starting-line equality', which is 'a principle of *ex ante* compensation' for disadvantages (Sugden, 2004, p. 217). Equality of opportunities in this sense does not require that *ex post* rewards have to be determined only by effort, and therefore does not guarantee that individuals will not suffer *ex post* disadvantages which result from circumstances beyond their control.

In addition, the fact that people were born unequal in their physical and mental capabilities will also render the principle of equal pay for equal merit an unfair principle. Mill considers the proportioning of remuneration to work done to be really just '*only in so far as the more or less of the work is a matter of choice*' (Mill, *CW, II*: 210, emphasis added). Recognizing the difference in people's strength and capacity, Mill accepts the principle of reward in accordance with work done as a just principle with a crucial proviso. It is Mill's view that 'the true idea of distributive justice consists not in imitating but in redressing the inequalities and wrongs of nature' (Mill, *CW, III*: 808). Note that Mill does not advocate using the principle in accordance with needs as the principle of distribution to level the inequality in human beings determined by nature. As mentioned earlier, he believes that the principle in accordance with exertion or performance is a more practical principle in regard to the social character in his time. Therefore, his compensation rule works only as a precondition to ensure that the operation of the principle of reward in accordance with exertion will lead to a result which is closer to the ideal that principle pursues.

Because of the unequal conditions in the real world, the just principle of remuneration at the second level should be qualified in practice. The formal requirement of equal treatment to equal exertion needs to be supplemented by the rule of equal opportunities and the rule of compensation. Otherwise, the principle of equal pay for equal exertion/performance cannot be considered to be a just principle.

Principles of income taxation

Similar to the case of remuneration, Mill also identifies in *Utilitarianism* four popular views which are often considered as just principles of taxation: taxation should be in numerical proportion to pecuniary means; those who have more to spare should be taxed at a higher percentage; everyone should pay the same absolute amount of tax; all should pay an equal capitation tax for the protection of their persons (since life is of equal value to all) and pay an unequal tax for the protection of their property, which is unequal (Mill, *CW, X*: 254–255). Again, in Mill's view, invoking the idea of justice is not helpful in choosing from these conflicting principles of justice; only social utility can decide which one is the best and hence just for a particular society.

In the *Principle of Political Economy*, Mill starts his discussion on the fundamental rules of taxation by quoting Smith's four maxims: equality, certainty of taxation, convenience of payment, and economy in collection (Mill, *CW, III*: 805–806; Smith, 1976, vol. 2, pp. 350–352). Mill considers these four maxims classical, and states that, except for equality, they require little further explanation or illustration than Smith has already given them (Mill, *CW, III*: 806). Mill's evaluation seems to be fair, in that what Smith means by equality is unclear since he equates ability with the benefits from the government's protection:

> The subjects of every state ought to contribute towards the support of the government, as nearly as possible, in proportion to their respective abilities; that is, in proportion to the revenue which they respectively enjoy under the protection for the state.
>
> (Smith, 1976, vol. 2, p. 350)

However, the sentence immediately following the quotation clearly indicates that by equality Smith means the benefit-principle rather than the ability-to-pay principle:

> The expence of government to the individuals of a great nation, is like the expence of management to the joint tenants of a great estate, who are all obliged to contribute in proportion to their respective interests in the estate.
>
> (Smith, 1976, vol. 2, p. 350)

This view is the main point which Mill considers unsatisfactory.

In contrast to Smith's treating taxation as something similar to the price paid in exchange for public service, Mill takes taxation mainly as a common burden which has to be shared among the members of the society (Mill, *CW, III*: Book 5 Chapter 2). Mill explicitly rejects adopting 'the principles of bargain and sale' as the principles of taxation (Mill, *CW, III*: 807). He argues that since the purposes and functions of government are comprehensive and its existence is a concern of all, it is improper and impossible to charge people according to how much they benefit from the government (Mill, *CW, III*: 807). Mill considers the application of the benefit principle on taxation as the reverse of the idea of distributive justice, because it requires those who are weakest in mind or body and hence least capable of helping or defending themselves to pay the greatest share of the price. In Mill's view, this is against the true idea of distributive justice which aims at redressing the inborn inequalities between individuals (Mill, *CW, III*: 808). Therefore, Mill believes that 'all are thought to have done their part fairly when each has contributed according to his means, that is, has made an *equal sacrifice*' for a purpose in which all are interested (Mill, *CW, III*: 808, emphasis added). In short, for Mill it is the ability-to-pay principle, rather than the benefit-principle, that should be the equality principle of taxation, and equal sacrifice is the embodiment of the principle. Both the ability-to-pay principle and the equal sacrifice principle are equivalent to the philosophical principles at the second level in the three-level structure of Mill's utilitarianism constructed in Chapter 2.

In a formal sense, the ability-to-pay principle requires people with equal capacity to pay the same amount of tax and people with greater ability to pay more. If we use Perelman's framework, the requirement of equality as the formal element of Mill's conception of justice in this case is joined to 'ability to pay' as the criterion of equal treatment which informs the substantive part of taxation justice, while ability can be assessed by the sacrifice individuals suffer due to the taxes. In order to apply this principle to establish taxation institutions in the real world, we still have to deal with the questions regarding how to measure ability to pay, and how different abilities should be treated. The specific rules constituting the institutions are the rules belonging to the third level.

In regard to income tax, a typical approach to dealing with the ability-to-pay principle in the literature is to investigate the capability to pay by looking into tax base and tax rate structure separately. The former is considered as an indication of horizontal equity and the latter of vertical equity.[12] According to this classification, Mill's concept of equality of sacrifice is often classified as a principle only for tax rate structure. It follows that Mill's ability-to-pay principle is interpreted as: people with the same amount of income should pay the same amount of income tax; people with different amounts of income should pay different amounts of income tax. The interpretation, despite capturing some features in one dimension, fails to give a full account of Mill's notion of equal sacrifice, which is relevant not only to tax rates but also the tax base and allowances.

To Mill, there are three conditions necessary for making income tax consistent with the requirements of distributive justice, and the requirement relating to tax rate is only one of them. These three conditions are:

> first, that incomes below a certain amount should be altogether untaxed [...] The second condition is, that incomes above the limit should be taxed only

> in proportion to the surplus by which they exceed the limit. Thirdly, that all sums saved from income and invested, should be exempt from the tax.
>
> (Mill, *CW, III*: 830–831)

In today's terminologies, the first condition is concerned with tax allowances; the second, with tax rate structure; the third, with exemptions. How does Mill integrate these three conditions into one tax system?

First of all, Mill rejects grounding his theory of taxation on the assumption that the marginal utility of money is diminishing because he thinks it is 'not true to a sufficient extent, to be made the foundation of any rule of taxation [...] on which a legislator or a financier ought to act' (Mill, *CW, III*: 810). Considering the theoretical basis not solid enough, Mill does not advocate a progressive income tax. Instead, he believes proportional taxation to be closer to the idea of equal sacrifice: 'I can see no fairer standard of real equality than to take from all persons [...] the same arithmetical proportion of their superfluities' (Mill, *CW, III*: 810).[13] It is important to note that this statement concerns not just tax rate structure, but also allowances. A key word here is 'superfluities'.

Mill's proportional income taxation is conditioned: it is the most crucial part of Mill's proposal for income taxation that 'incomes below a certain amount should be altogether untaxed' (Mill, *CW, III*: 830). 'To tax all incomes in an equal ratio', Mill remarks, 'would be unjust to those, the greater part of whose income is required for necessaries' (Mill, *CW, III*: 810). But why unjust? Because for Mill *the sacrifice resulted from taxing the income for the support of existence is 'entirely incommensurable' with the sacrifice resulted from taxing the income for the comfort of existence* (Mill, *CW, III*: 809). This is the essence of Mill's idea of distributive justice. This is clearly a utilitarian way of weighing sacrifice. Moreover, Mill grounds his arguments in relation to economic institutions on one of the most central claims of his utilitarianism, namely that utilities with different qualities have different moral significance. Utilities which are related to survival and maintenance are given higher value by Mill in comparison with those which are related to comfort or enjoyment only.[14] If income for survival is treated as the same income for enjoyment, according to Mill's utilitarianism this is not the true equal treatment required by the principle of equal sacrifice and is unjust. Differential treatment between income for survival and income for enjoyment is one of the most crucial and distinct parts of Mill's opinion on income tax. It marks the comprehensiveness of his tax theory and the consistency between his philosophy and economic policy.[15]

Accordingly, the principle of imposing equal ratios of tax on income alone can hardly constitute a just income tax system.[16] Given the fact that each human being requires minimum levels of materials for survival, the principle of proportional taxation has to be supplemented by other rules in order to achieve the ideal of justice. After taking into account the unequal conditions between individuals in the real world, the secondary principle of equal sacrifice will in fact require differential treatment between income for subsistence and income for superfluities at the practice level.

Principles of the exchange of commodities

Before examining the principles of justice for the exchange of commodities, we should make it clear that the discussion in this section does not include labour. The principles for the rewards of labour have been discussed under the heading 'Principles of remuneration' above. It is important to notice that Mill's treatment of remuneration and that of exchange of other commodities are based on different ideas of justice. The form is treated as an issue of distributive justice, while the latter is an issue of commutative justice.

Like most other economists, Mill believes that if there is no fraud and force, the agreement of exchange must be fair because people will exchange their own goods only for what they esteem equivalent (Mill, *CW, II*: Book 3 Chapter 1).[17] In other words, the exchange of commodities occurring on a voluntary base can be seen as consistent with the idea of commutative justice. The element of equality in formal justice can also be found here. A just principle for exchange of commodities requires equal treatment of commodities with equal value. In other words, a fair transaction in accordance with the principle of commutative justice requires that the commodities exchanged should be equal in value.

In his *Principles of Political Economy*, without judging whether the market can guarantee people just prices, Mill simply describes how the mechanism of competition in a market system works. Though Mill's theory of value is based on the labour theory of value, he has found that not only costs of production but also subjective utility play crucial roles in determining the exchange value of commodities (Mill, *CW, II*: Book 3 Chapter 1). He believes that in the long run market value will lie in between the cost, which is the lower limit of exchange value, and the utility of use, which is the upper limit of exchange value (Mill, *CW, II*: Book 3 Chapter 1). In addition, Mill seems to believe that utility, a subjective element of exchange value, will enable the market to formulate a mechanism for agents to seek the just price of commodities for exchange.

Indeed, if we examine one economic transaction in isolation from the socio-economic background, voluntary exchange implies fairness. As exchange is an affair between individuals, the idea of commutative justice will be fulfilled by the agreement between individuals if the agents are free and equal. Accordingly, the voluntary transaction principle can serve the purpose of fair exchange between people well. However, when the real social and economic circumstances are taken into account, some factors may prevent the implementation of the just principle of exchange from achieving the ideal. The most important reason for this is that agents are not on an equal footing in the market in the real world. As a result, the principle of respecting voluntary transactions cannot guarantee the fairness of transactions or just outcomes.

For example, in the financial market, generally speaking enterprises will have superior positions to individual investors or creditors. Taking this factor into account, the rule of voluntary exchanges needs to be supplemented by other rules in order to act as a principle of justice. Not until 1855 were joint-stock companies with limited liability allowed by English law. On the issue of legalizing this sort of company, Mill's stand was far more advanced and liberal than his contemporaries. He urges the lifting of the ban on the formation of joint-stock companies with limited liability. Nevertheless, Mill, despite his consistent position of laissez-faire, is cautious in relation to economic injustice which may be caused by asymmetry of information. Therefore, he argues that the laissez-faire principle, the general principle in economic transactions, should be supplemented by regulations regarding the enforcement of information disclosure (Mill, *CW, III*: 898). The major types of transactions in Mill's mind are business loans resulting from the trades between two enterprises. Nevertheless, Mill would agree that the requirement of disclosure of financial information is also applicable to the contemporary business environment. The publicity of information about listed companies is particularly essential to sustain the real equal freedom of transaction of individual shareholders and bond buyers, and hence is a condition of economic justice.

At the beginning of this chapter, we argued that the relationship between utility and justice in Mill's utilitarianism is usually oversimplified. The discussion in this chapter has demonstrated that Mill's theory of justice is far more complicated and comprehensive than it is usually thought to be. Treating Mill's principle of utility as *the* principle of justice is a seriously mistaken interpretation of Mill's theory. The principle of utility is the first principle of Mill's utilitarian philosophy. Under this principle, there are many various principles of justice governing issues belonging to different areas. In Mill's writings, the principles of justice for remuneration, those for income taxation and those for exchanging commodities are all different, while they are all derived from the principle of utility. Around a half century ago Elizabeth Anscombe, a well-known British analytic philosopher of the twentieth century, wrote in her 1958 essay 'Modern Moral Philosophy' that '[Mill's] position was stupid, because it is not all clear how an action *can* fall under just one principle of utility' (Anscombe, 1958 p. 9, emphasis in original). Anscombe seems to suggest that the principle of utility is the one principle for everything. There is little doubt that the complexity of Mill's utilitarianism got lost in plain sight by a philosopher who was considered by many to be one of the most gifted philosophers of the twentieth century. If the principle of utility was an all-in-all principle, and no other principles were needed for stipulating moral good, moral right and justice respectively, not only would Mill's position be stupid but his theory would be simply impracticable in reality. This author hopes that the discussion of this chapter has demonstrated that Mill's position was not as stupid as Anscombe claimed, and as many others have believed it to be.

5 Economic justice, liberty and utilitarianism

John Stuart Mill's firm stand on liberalism is beyond doubt: as an economist, he asserted that the principle of laissez-faire should be the general principle of the government in practice; as a political theorist, he argued that representative government and universal suffrage are indispensable conditions of political liberty; as a philosopher, he believed that liberty is essential to self-development and individuality, which are key elements of happiness and well-being. The influence of Mill's works on liberty on intellectual history and on later political and economic institutions has been far-reaching. However, it is often believed that his granting liberty a privileged place among other values is inconsistent with his utilitarian philosophical position. This allegation is in fact only part of a broader accusation that Mill displayed no coherent doctrine in his writings. Up until at least the mid-twentieth century, most commentators were unsympathetic and some exponents of the traditional account of Mill, as John Gray notices, have even gone so far as to claim to discern 'an intellectual schizophrenia' in Mill's writings (Gray, 1979a). This received view was dominant until the late 1970s when the revisionist wave was rising.

The revisionist position begins with Alan Ryan's (1970) clarification of Mill's principle of utility by connecting it with the Art of Life expounded in his *System of Logic*. Following Ryan, scholars such as Brown (1973) and Lyons (1976) all suggested that the utility principle does not impose a moral obligation to maximize utility or condemn not maximizing utility as a moral wrong. Following a similar stream, Gray (1995, 1996) further argued that Mill's utility principle is an axiological principle and hence his utilitarianism should be understood as neither act- or rule-utilitarianism but rather as indirect utilitarianism. Fred Berger (1984) also put forward a similar view. Both Gray and Berger re-examined Mill's principle of liberty by placing it within a reconstructed utilitarian framework where secondary principles are necessary to supplement the principle of utility. Moreover, Gray and Berger contend that Mill's idea of happiness is characterized by its being hierarchical, pluralistic, and non-hedonistic.[1] This revisionary interpretation of Mill's conception of happiness allows Gray and Berger to embrace individuality, or autonomy, as an essential element of happiness and therefore to justify the protection of liberty, a key condition of individuality. They hence were able to demonstrate that Mill's principle of liberty is coherent in a utilitarian manner.

In addition to the coherence between Mill's theory of liberty and his utilitarianism, the role of justice marks a significant difference between the traditional view and the revisionary interpretations of Gray and Berger. Berger argued that Mill's theory of liberty is an application of justice by connecting Mill's discussion of rights and justice in the last chapter of *Utilitarianism* with 'the doctrine of the rights of individuality' in *On Liberty* (Berger, 1984, pp. 229–230). He suggested that autonomy is such a vital interest for individuals that it should be treated as a right and protected by rules as a matter of justice. Gray (1996) also suggested treating the principle of liberty as a major part of Mill's substantive theory of justice grounded on an argument similar to Berger's. According to both Gray's and Berger's interpretations, Mill's utilitarianism would not allow the trading-off of rights of liberty for other advantages.

Nevertheless, Gray saw the issue concerning equity to be a weakness of Mill's theory of liberty. Unlike Berger (1984, p. 238) – who states that 'freedom and equality imply one another' in Mill's theory – Gray believes that a principle of equity, a principle distinct from and independent of the principle of liberty, is needed for Mill's theory of liberty. This is because he does not think that Mill's principle of liberty has complete action-guiding force or is able to provide determinate guides as to 'how much liberty may be traded away for how much harm-prevention' (Gray, 1996, pp. 66–67). Gray's concerns with equity become more obvious in his book *Liberalism*. There he claims that Mill fails in developing 'a satisfactory account of liberal justice in utilitarian terms' (Gray, 1995, p. 52). It is Gray's view that a principle of equity guaranteeing equity in the distribution of freedom is 'indefensible in utilitarian terms' (Gray, 1995, p. 53).

Despite defending forcefully Mill's theory of liberty in his early work, Gray ultimately agrees with John Rawls's criticisms of utilitarianism as a theory of justice, holding that Rawls's theory of justice as fairness has decisive advantages over Mill's theory because the former prohibits the unjust distributions of unfreedom allowed by the latter (Gray, 1995, p. 54). Although the revisionary interpretations have answered the charge of inconsistency between giving priority to liberty in *On Liberty* and treating utility as the fundamental value in *Utilitarianism*, they have not provided a satisfactory reply to the accusation that utilitarianism is ready to sacrifice the freedom of some in the name of social utility and hence is unable to secure equal distribution of freedom for all. This is a long-standing characterization of utilitarianism, running from at least James Fitzjames Stephen (1993 [1874]), one of the most formidable critics of Mill in the nineteenth century, who saw liberty as instrumental and hence of no inviolable value in utilitarianism, to Rawls, whose influential work *A Theory of Justice* reaffirmed and reinforced the assertion that utilitarianism tends to foster sacrificing the freedom of some in the name of the social utility of the whole.

This chapter aims to demonstrate that this popular assertion is not applicable to Mill's utilitarianism and that his utilitarianism in fact supports real freedom for all. The remainder of this chapter will first re-examine Mill's principle of liberty from two separate aspects: the principle in the self-regarding area and the principle in the other-regarding area. Mill's defence of individual liberty in self-regarding matters has been studied extensively in the literature; therefore our discussion of the principle related to self-regarding matters will be restricted to the necessary extent to serve the purpose of contrasting it with the discussion of other-regarding matters. In contrast, we will give more attention to interpreting the principle in relation to other-regarding matters. Moreover, this author argues that Mill's principle of liberty should be understood not only as a principle of justice protecting autonomy, as suggested by Gray and Berger, but also as a principle of distributive justice endorsing equal freedom. This perspective of examination singles out the element of positive freedom in Mill's principle of liberty and shows that it is justice grounded in utility that protects real freedom for all in the conflict of individual liberties. Following a similar reasoning, we can derive a principle from Mill's utilitarianism concerned with the relationship between economic freedom and distributive justice. This principle suggests that, for Mill, justice grounded in utility requires constraints upon the economic freedoms of some to prevent threats to the subsistence of others.

Individual liberty in self-regarding matters

In respect to self-regarding matters, Mill's commitment to liberty is clear and firm:

> when a person's conduct affects the interests of no persons besides himself, or needs not affect them unless they like (all the persons concerned being of full age, and the ordinary amount of understanding) [...] there should be perfect freedom, legal and social, to do the action and stand the consequences.
>
> (Mill, *CW, XVIII*: 276)

> The only part of the conduct of any one, for which he is amenable to society, is that which concerns others. In the part which merely concerns himself, his independence is, of right, absolute. Over himself, over his own body and mind, the individual is sovereign.
>
> (Mill, *CW, XVIII*: 224)

It has to be noted that the word 'absolute' in the second sentence of the second quotation should be understood from the context: it is not used as a contrast to the superiority of utility, but to the *relativity of liberty in public matters*. Given Mill's undisputed commitment to individual liberty, the focus of the debate in the literature has been how Mill grounded his liberalism on his utilitarianism on the one hand, and whether this attempt is logically consistent on the other.

With regard to the first issue of how Mill reconciles liberalism and utilitarianism, it is *individuality* that Mill used as the pivotal link to harmonize the tension between individual liberty and the greatest general happiness. Two frequently quoted passages in Mill's *On Liberty* are crucial to this connection:

> I forego any advantage which could be derived to my argument from the idea of abstract right, as a thing independent of utility. I regard utility as the ultimate appeal on all ethical questions; but it must be utility in the largest sense, grounded on the permanent interests of man as a progressive being.
>
> (Mill, *CW, XVIII*: 224)

> in things which do not primarily concern others, individuality should assert itself. Where, not the person's own character, but the traditions or customs of other people are the rule of conduct, there is wanting one of the principal ingredients of human happiness, and quite the chief ingredient of individual and social progress.
>
> (Mill, *CW, XVIII*: 261)

Taking these two passages together, Mill's argument becomes clear. First, utility has to be understood 'in the largest sense', i.e. as grounded on the permanent interests of human beings as progressive beings. Moreover, we have to search out the components of utility or happiness by reflecting on human nature and by observing human experience in the real world. For Mill, character or individuality is one of the principal ingredients of happiness; also, they are the chief ingredients of individual and social progress (Mill, *CW, XVIII*: 267). As Jonathan Riley comments, if each individual can develop themselves by cultivating individuality, it will maximize social improvement and lead the whole society to the best state (Riley, 1998, p. 159). If the observation that individuality is the principal ingredient of happiness is an observation close to the truth, we have nearly no difficulty in reconciling individual liberty with utilitarianism. Social improvement, a permanent ingredient of human happiness, will only come about through the cultivation of individuality; and the cultivation of individuality requires the absolute liberty of self-regarding actions (Riley, 1988, pp. 226–234). Liberty, as one of the indispensable conditions of individuality, must be an essential condition for happiness (Gray, 1995, p. 52). Mill's defence of individual liberty is based on general human happiness and therefore his defence of individual liberty is consistent with his utilitarianism.

Nevertheless, despite sharing the view that there is no inconsistency problem in Mill's theory, some insist that Mill's argument for absolute liberty in self-regarding matters is not a utilitarian one. The debate over whether Mill's argument for individual liberty can be considered as utilitarian in fact boils down to whether Mill's utilitarianism, with his distinction of higher and lower pleasure, can still be deemed as utilitarianism. The qualitative difference of pleasures is required in Mill's justification of absolute individual liberty. As Riley puts it,

> a person's liberty in self-regarding matters is infinitely more valuable than any satisfaction the rest of us might take at suppression of his conduct. The utility of self-regarding liberty is of a higher kind than the utility of suppression based on mere dislike in that any amount (however small) of the higher kind outweighs any quantity (however large) of the lower.
>
> (Riley, 1998, p. 159)

If it is accepted that differences in kind between utilities are genuinely integral to utilitarianism as Mill claims, then the justification of absolute individual liberty in self-regarding matters is indeed a utilitarian one.

Principle of liberty and its relation to distributive justice

The discussion above is confined to the self-regarding area, with which justice is not concerned. It is Mill's view that private matters do not involve the concept of justice (Mill, *CW, X*: 249). When matters involve other people's interests, however, the harmonization of individual liberties is not as straightforward as weighing one's own real interests against others' mere likes or dislikes. On the contrary, in other-regarding matters the liberties of different people often conflict. Consequently, it is a matter for debate whether Mill's principle of utility is sufficient to operate as the final just arbiter of different people's conflicting freedoms.

Despite considering Mill's argument successful in defending absolute liberty in the self-regarding area, Gray suspects that his utilitarian defence of liberty is unsustainable in the other-regarding area: 'Whenever there is harm or a risk of harm to others, liberty restriction is in principle justified – and may always be justified on balance if the calculus of utilities shows that such restriction promotes the general welfare' (Gray, 1995, p. 53). Rawls also considers that this is an insoluble problem inherent in all forms of utilitarianism because 'Whenever a society sets out to maximize the sum of intrinsic value or the net balance of the satisfaction of interests, it is liable to find that the denial of liberty for some is justified in the name of this single end' (Rawls, 1999, p. 185). In brief, most critics are convinced of the charge that it is highly probable that utilitarianism will lead to unjust results, because its aim of maximizing total utility cannot guarantee equity in the distribution of liberty.

The crux of the problem here is the idea of justice. In the self-regarding sphere, because the idea of justice is not involved, the relation between liberty and utility is simple. Liberty and social utility can sit together in harmony as long as the matter does not concern other people's real interests; individual liberty can always promote social utility in the largest sense through promoting personal utility. However, this harmony no longer exists as soon as more than one person's interests are involved. Therefore, the concept of justice must step in. Since most affairs in daily life are other-regarding matters and every public policy is clearly other-regarding, it is not surprising that there are so many arguments concerning the conflict between individual liberty and social utility.

Social justice as real liberty for all

One of the main purposes of Mill's writing *On Liberty* was to find 'one very simple principle' to identify 'a limit to the legitimate interference of collective opinion with individual independence' (Mill, *CW, XVIII*: 220, 223). The principle proposed by Mill is that

> The sole end for which mankind are warranted, individually or collectively, in interfering with the liberty of action of any of their number, is self-protection. That the only purpose for which power can be rightfully exercised over any member of a civilised community, against his will, is to prevent harm to others.
>
> (Mill, *CW, XVIII*: 223)

This passage is generally labelled as Mill's principle of liberty. When interpreting this passage, most scholars focus on the concept of negative liberty, meaning that as long as people do not harm others, they are free to do whatever they want. This is also the reason why this principle is also called the harm-prevention principle. This conventional interpretation is indeed what Mill intended to argue in *On Liberty*. But we can also read Mill's principle of liberty from a different perspective.

Emphasizing the notion of negative liberty is to interpret Mill's principle from the position of the stronger members in a community. If we look at the same principle from the perspective of the weaker members of the same community, Mill's principle is actually a protection of their *positive* liberties. In other words, the purpose of limiting some people's liberty is to protect *everyone*'s liberty of life and body. Moreover, concerning the purpose of proposing this principle, we should bear in mind that Mill's principle of liberty is a principle not only concerning liberty, but also justice. This reading, despite not focusing on his original intention, is consistent with Mill's utilitarian philosophy and can be supported by Mill's own texts.

First, as already noted, Mill's concept of happiness or utility should not be understood merely as the feeling of pleasure. We have to realize happiness through resources in the real world. Based on his psychology of association, Mill claims that happiness is composed of a lot of different things, such as virtue, health, fame, power, money, and so on. All of them are part of happiness (Mill, *CW, X*: 234–235). In doing so, Mill includes liberty in his idea of utility and happiness.

These various utilities are not of the same quality. For Mill, the difference between utilities is not just quantitative but also qualitative (Mill, *CW, X*: 211). 'Security' is one of the examples he gives. Unlike most utilities which are generally needed by some people but not by others, security is needed by everyone. Security is so vital that it is different from other common utilities, not only in degree but also in kind. When security is infringed, the desire for revenge will be provoked. That is to say, security is protected by our natural feeling of revenge. Mill believes that the sentiment of justice is merely this natural feeling moralized by our social sentiment. This then is how Mill connects utility and justice; he thinks that justice is just the name for certain social utilities. It is important to notice that not every kind of utility is qualified to be considered as a matter of justice. Only those utilities which are vastly more important and therefore more absolute and imperative than others are matters of justice. Once a utility is so important that it is protected by the sentiment of justice, the society should protect this utility by law. This is why Mill claims that the idea of justice is always attached to the idea of personal rights.

The above argument shows that Mill's principle of liberty is one not merely of negative liberty but also of the condition of real liberty. This assertion is based on the fact that where there is no security there is no real liberty. This also implies that, in Mill's utilitarianism, *justice is for the real liberty of everyone.*

Distributive justice and real economic freedom for all

The liberties with which Mill's principle of liberty deals are those of action, speech and thought. With a similar reasoning, we can derive from Mill's writings a principle concerned with the liberty of economic behaviour, including the liberty of property. This can be deemed the underlying principle of several policies related to distribution advocated by Mill.

Principle of economic liberty: justice as real economic freedom for all

The reasoning of a new principle starts from the assumption that in addition to security, there is another fundamental utility which is universally needed by everyone. The sentiment towards this desire is so intense that the difference between this utility and others is not just one of degree, but of kind. Therefore this utility ought to be, and naturally is, accompanied by the sentiment of justice. Whenever it is violated, the sentiment of justice will be provoked. The utility indicated herein is *subsistence.*

Under this assumption, this author proposes a principle of economic liberty:

> A limit on one's economic liberty is justified to prevent threat to others' subsistence, and for this purpose power can be rightfully exercised over any member of a civilised community.

This principle is named so as to be analogous to Mill's principle of liberty. A comparison will make the analogy clearer: the principle of liberty claims that people's liberty of action should be restricted for others' security; and the principle of economic liberty claims that people's liberties of economic behaviour and property ownership should be restricted for the sake of others' subsistence, which is the most fundamental type of economic security. There is a similar paradoxical logic in the principle of economic liberty and Mill's principle of liberty: in order to protect everyone's real liberty, it is necessary to constrain everyone's liberty. Such restrictions required by both principles are sustained for the sake of *justice* and therefore they are not determined arbitrarily.

The principle of economic liberty can explain some of the exceptions to the laissez-faire principle argued by Mill. In his *Principles of Political Economy*, Mill asserted that laissez-faire 'should be the general practice: every departure from it, unless required by some great good, is a certain evil' (Mill, *CW, III*: 945). Given the proviso that exception is 'required by some great good', the laissez-faire principle is not universal. It is important to remember that not every kind of utility can override the laissez-faire principle; only a utility which is extraordinarily important and imperative to everyone concerned is eligible. Building on this, this author suggests that 'subsistence' is a qualified utility which can override the laissez-faire principle in economic issues for reasons of justice.

It is worth underlining that the proposed principle of economic liberty is grounded in Mill's understanding of human nature. It is Mill's view that the first and strongest want of human nature is liberty, with the precondition that the primary needs of food and clothing are satisfied and secured (Mill, *CW, II*: 208). In other words, for Mill the realization of freedom is not always a problem purely of human will: it requires the fulfilment of some conditions as a prerequisite. This view is captured perfectly by Virginia Held's comment on the relationship between human actions and the means of subsistence: when people live in want and deprivation, the need for self-preservation will form an unavoidable limitation on human actions; we cannot act freely when we have no means to stay alive and act at all (Held, 1989, p. 124). This understanding of human nature constitutes the essence of Mill's concept of distributive justice.

Roger Crisp once commented that Mill's utilitarianism is 'a humane and progressive doctrine, which in practice brought to an end many injustices based on conservative orthodoxy' (Crisp, 1997, p. 17). This is indeed true and we can say it is the recognition of and respect for human nature that makes Mill's theory 'humane and progressive'. For Mill subsistence is one of the most vital utilities, and his opinions on practical economic policies always granted it the greatest priority. Much of his discussion of policy accommodates the requirement of distributive justice by ensuring everyone's dignity of life.

Policy implications for wealth distribution

The principle of economic liberty, based on the observation of human nature, asserts that some people's liberty of economic action should give way to others' subsistence, which is a necessary condition of making choices freely. It follows that the fulfilment of the principle will require the interference of the public authority and the redistribution of wealth to a certain extent, given that in the modern economy some people's subsistence will be threatened by the existence of serious economic inequality, such as inequality of income, wealth and so on. As Held observes, it is an obvious false assumption of a modern society that people not interfered with can adequately acquire what they need to live. Except for a minority, most people in modern society have almost no other ways to make a living other than selling their labour. The myth that anyone selling his or her labour does so voluntarily merely masks the reality for those who prefer not to see it (Held, 1989, pp. 123–124). In other words, the principle of economic liberty requires a restriction on the economic liberty of those who already have economic privileges and property to ensure everyone's substantive liberty, especially those who lack such privileges and property.

In Chapter V of his *Utilitarianism*, where Mill discusses his conception of justice, he stipulates that '[t]he equal claim of everybody to happiness in the estimation of the moralist and of the legislator, involves an equal claim to all the means of happiness' (Mill, *CW, X*: 257–258). If we place Mill's statement within the context of our discussion here, a modern meaning of 'an equal claim to happiness' needs to include 'an equal right to the means of subsistence'. This is the necessary condition of substantive liberty because the equal liberty of people in contemporary society, as Held observes, cannot be interpreted in the traditional negative sense, but must be enlarged to include the freedom to live, to work, and to develop (Held, 1989, p. 130). It is important to note that the protection of everyone's subsistence does not imply equal amounts of the means of subsistence. On the contrary, Mill would argue that the diversity among different persons will require unequal amounts since he believed that 'the true idea of distributive justice [...] consists not in imitating but in redressing the inequalities and wrongs of nature' (Mill, *CW, III*: 808).

On the other hand, economic inequality should not be levelled merely as a result of the prejudice in favour of egalitarianism. The principle of economic liberty is not a requirement for levelling the distribution of wealth. Economic inequality is acceptable and 'the differences of fortune arising from people's won earnings could not justly give umbrage' if the inequality is not from accident alone, and 'if all were done which it would be in the power of a good government to do, by instruction and by legislation, to diminish this inequality of opportunities' (Mill, *CW, III*: 811). Above levels of subsistence, redistribution of wealth may still be desirable. However, society does not have a duty to guarantee everyone can have enough resources to reach their personal goals; the failure to fulfil personal wants is not a violation of free will.

It should be emphasized that Mill never explicitly argued for any specific principle of distribution as an absolute. The principle of economic liberty is a proposition inferred from Mill's work and it seems to do justice to his opinions on various policies related to distribution. Furthermore, it does not represent the only principle of distribution Mill would suggest. Instead, it only suggests Mill's view of distribution in relation to protection of the minimum level of economic liberty. Thus the principle of economic liberty is merely *one* of many secondary principles derived from the principle of utility. It should not be expected to solve every problem of wealth distribution. It deals only with the issue relevant to the guarantee of subsistence. Other secondary principles which are compatible with the first principle are still needed for various problems of distribution.

The following subsection will take Mill's discussions on economic policies as examples to examine how well his suggestions for practical economic problems were consistent with the abstract principle of distributive justice that this chapter suggests.

Application of the principle of economic liberty

We can easily find examples in Mill's writings which are endorsed by the proposed principle of economic liberty. This section will examine Mill's discussion of policy concerning the remedies for low wages. This example suggests that maintaining the minimum subsistence plays a key role in Mill's idea of distributive justice and real freedom and the principle of economic liberty essentially acts as a fundamental principle underlying Mill's economic and social policies.

There are two types of issues concerning freedom in the labour market: one is connected to the wage relation, the other the level of wages. Significant inequalities in market power between employers and employees can prevent the weak from real freedom in the labour market. According to the principle of economic liberty derived from Mill's theory, it is morally justifiable and just to take some pecuniary means away from those who have more than enough to satisfy basic needs for the purpose of assuring every labourer basic means of subsistence, which is the precondition of real freedom.

For most classical economists the operation of labour markets is similar to that of other commodity markets, in that the market price of labour depends mainly on the supply and demand of labour. For example, after describing the mechanism of population adjustment through the price mechanism of markets, Adam Smith concluded that 'the demand for men, like that for any other commodity, necessarily regulates the production of men' (Smith, 1976, vol. 1, p. 89). Moreover, classical economists hold that labour, like all other things which are purchased and sold, has not only a market price but also a natural price. The natural price of labour is that price which is necessary to enable the labourers to subsist and to reproduce, without either increase or diminution.[2] They also recognize that unlike commodities which are dead, waged labourers, who are alive, will confront the problem of the cutting-off of income when the market is over-stocked with labour.

The low wage caused by the over-supply of labour was a serious social problem in eighteenth- and nineteenth-century England. Mill also regarded over-population as the main cause of workmen's poverty, and hence believed that the proper restriction of population was the only solution for the labouring classes to avoid miserable lives (Mill, *CW, II*: 351–354). Yet he did not agree with repressing population via a rising death rate, which was considered by most classical economists, including Smith, as the only way to raise wages back to the proper rates. Holding the postulations that no one is responsible for having been born and that all persons already in existence have the right to live, Mill advanced several remedies for low wages. A legal minimum wage is one among others (Mill, *CW, II*: 357–358).

Either in the nineteenth century or in modern times, when it comes to the problem of low wages, the simplest expediency that can be imagined is to fix the minimum wage by law. Mill for one was willing to be 'the most strenuous supporter for it' (Mill, *CW, II*: 357). However, it is worth noting that while assessing whether a minimum wage is practicable and how it should be implemented, the basis of Mill's analysis was not blind philanthropy, but logical economic theory. This led to his cautious attitude towards interference by authority: Mill insisted that a minimum-wage scheme can be supported only if legal measures for control of population numbers are required as a condition (Mill, *CW, II*: 357).

Even if birth control is required for minimum-wage legislation, the feasibility of minimum-wage laws remains debatable. If the minimum wages fixed by law are higher than the level determined by competitive markets, how could we assure employment for all the people who are able and willing to work? This is an awkward question for the classical economists who upheld the wages-fund theory. According to the wages-fund theory of the classical school, wages depend upon the relative amount of capital and population (Mill, *CW, II*: 357–358).[3] If the law succeeds in fixing wages above the rate which results from competition, some labourers will be kept out of employment. Therefore, a provision of work for all who apply for it has to be part of the scheme; otherwise, it is pointless to fix a minimum wage (Mill, *CW, II*: 356). Accordingly, the minimum-wage legislation has to regulate both the level of wages and employment at the same time. Now, if legislation for a minimum wage fixes the level of wages and employment, it implies that the amount of wages-fund needed is fixed by the legislation as well. Unfortunately, the existing wages-fund was usually insufficient. The wages-fund doctrine presumes that the amount of capital and level of technology is fixed at a given time. Provided this supposition is true, it is impossible to raise the wage rates by increasing capital in the short run. Then, when wages are lower than the level of subsistence resulting from the over-supply of labour, the labouring classes are doomed by the deficiency of food. Hence, the classical economists encountered the most difficult task with which the minimum wages regulation has to cope: how should we finance this fund? Ultimately, the minimum wage is a question of the distribution of wealth. Mill suggested that

> if the moral influence of opinion does not induce the rich to spare from their consumption enough to set all the poor to work at 'reasonable wages', it is supposed to be incumbent on the state to lay on taxes for the purpose, either by local rates or votes of public money.
>
> (Mill, *CW, II*: 356)[4]

As a result, wages will be raised not by allowing some of the existing population to die, but by increasing capital. In other words, if the market wage rates are too low to support the subsistence of the labouring classes, the government's interference in the distribution of wealth will be justified by Mill's idea of distributive justice.

It should be emphasized that Mill had no intention of disturbing the free competition of labour markets by the regulation of minimum wages. In principle, he respected the self-adjustment mechanism of competitive markets. For Mill, the main purpose of minimum wages is the protection of everyone's basic subsistence. Therefore, he never advocated that the level of minimum wages should be set higher than the level which is required to ensure basic necessities. This view is very different from the standard analysis in economic textbooks today, stating that the level of minimum wages has to be set at a level higher than the equilibrium wage determined by the market, otherwise it is ineffective. As a consequence of this reasoning, many modern economists allege that the minimum-wage legislation is a policy that will inevitably disturb free labour markets. This modern view and Mill's view on minimum-wage laws actually reflect two different ideas of free markets: free, because the government plays no role in the markets; or free, because everyone is ensured a minimum level of freedom in the markets.

Part III

Dialogues – justice and liberty in focus

By examining the corpus of Mill's own work, Part II has argued and demonstrated that in Mill's utilitarianism social justice and individual liberty are not two ideas inevitably clashing with each other. In Part III, we will further support this claim by examining the arguments underlying the common criticism that the utilitarian idea of justice is incompatible with individual liberty and explaining why these arguments have not really defeated Mill's theory of justice.

6 Rawls versus Mill

Deontological versus teleological theory of justice

In the preface to *A Theory of Justice*, John Rawls explicitly states that the aim of his book is to offer an alternative systematic account of justice superior to the utilitarian theory which had been dominant for a long time (Rawls, 1999, pp. xvii–xix). Rawls expresses the rationale for his book straightforwardly: the liberties of equal citizenship are insecure if social institutions are founded on utilitarian precepts of justice, which are derived for the sole end of attaining the greatest balance of satisfaction. For Rawls, it is one of the most striking features of the utilitarian view of justice that it does not matter how the greatest sum of satisfactions of a society is distributed among individuals. As the consequence of this feature of maximizing total utility,

> there is no reason in principle why the greater gains of some should not compensate for the lesser losses of others; or more importantly, why the violation of the liberty of a few might not be made right by the greater good shared by many.
>
> (Rawls, 1999, p. 23)

In Rawls's eyes, this causes a fatal flaw in the utilitarian theory of justice.

It is important to note that in Rawls's discussion of utilitarianism Mill is always intentionally separately cited and discussed. When contrasting his theory of justice with that of utilitarianism, Rawls explicitly specifies that the utilitarians in his mind are classical utilitarian philosophers, such as Jeremy Bentham and Henry Sidgwick (1838–1900), as well as utilitarian economists such as F. Y. Edgeworth (1845–1926) and A. C. Pigou (1877–1959) (Rawls, 1999, p. 20). Clearly, Rawls notices the difference between the utilitarianism held by these philosophers and economists and that by Mill. More importantly, Rawls believes that Mill's principle of utility would share several essential conclusions of his theory of justice.

Despite recognizing the tendency of supporting freedom, Rawls argues that Mill's utilitarianism is unable to secure 'an equal liberty for all'. A passage specifically referring to Mill shows that Rawls believes that Mill's utilitarianism, like all other variants of utilitarianism, suffers the intrinsic flaws of the teleological doctrine:

> Whenever a society sets out to maximize the sum of intrinsic value or the net balance of the satisfaction of interests, it is liable to find that the denial of liberty for some is justified in the name of this single end. The liberties of equal citizenship are insecure when founded upon teleological principles.
>
> (Rawls, 1999, p. 185)

Mill's utilitarianism is indeed a teleological moral theory, as specified by Mill himself. Yet it is open to question whether Mill's utilitarianism contains the features which Rawls attributes to the utilitarian teleology and thus suffers the problem of failing to secure individual liberty.

The remainder of this chapter will first demonstrate that Rawls's account of classical utilitarianism cannot be applied to Mill's utilitarianism, and hence that his criticism that classical utilitarianism's acceptance of sacrificing individual liberty for the common good is unjust is inapplicable to Mill's theory. It will then compare Mill's and Rawls's fundamental principles of distributive justice, and show that there are actually significant similarities between their theories. The last part of the chapter will argue that Rawls's theory does not enjoy absolute superiority to Mill's, since it cannot answer the challenge Mill raised to the a priori view of moral theory.

Rawls's reading of Mill

In his slim yet weighty book *Ethics*, William Frankena distinguishes teleological moral theories from deontological ones by identifying how they connect the concept of the good and the right (Frankena, 1963, pp. 13–14). Following Frankena, Rawls also maintains that the structure of an ethical theory is largely determined by how it defines and connects the concepts of good and right. A teleological theory defines the good independently from the right, and then defines the right as that which maximizes the good (Rawls, 1999, pp. 21–22). In other words, a teleological theory holds that the good is prior to the right. In contrast, a deontological theory holds that the right is prior to the good. It does not specify the good independently from the right or define the right as maximizing the good (Rawls, 1999, p. 26). By the priority of the right over the good, Rawls means that those interests which require the violation of rights have no value (Rawls, 1999, p. 28). Rawls considers this priority essential because it does not allow the loss of freedom for some to be compensated by a greater good shared by others (Rawls, 1999, p. 25). In Rawls's view, it is a serious problem of teleological theory that it allows the judgement of goodness to be made without referring to what is right (Rawls, 1999, p. 22).

Rawls's understanding of utilitarian view of distributive justice is grounded on his understanding of utilitarianism as a teleological theory. Rawls sees the just distribution for utilitarianism as distribution of the means of satisfaction which yields the maximum satisfaction. This conception of distributive justice is in fact a logical corollary from the two features which Rawls attributes to the utilitarian teleology, that is, the right is defined as maximizing the good and the good is defined as the satisfaction of desire.

At first glance, Rawls's characterization of utilitarianism as teleology seems to be able to capture Mill's utilitarian moral theory. A closer examination will show that despite being sympathetic, Rawls's reading of Mill is strongly influenced by his understanding of the more modern versions of utilitarianism in the twentieth century. This causes the problem of smuggling modern elements into his interpretation of Mill's utilitarianism, even though Rawls is careful to separate Mill from other utilitarians.

Since parts of Mill's *Utilitarianism* were published in 1861, utilitarianism as a moral theory had gone through significant transitions by the time Rawls published *A Theory of Justice* in 1971. As the specialization of the social sciences was growing in the late nineteenth century, the development of utilitarianism in different disciplines started to diverge. It is not exaggerating to say that the increasing difference between the meaning of utility in economics and in moral philosophy accounts for the major confusions about utilitarianism as a moral doctrine. It is not possible to give a full account of the evolution of the theory during this period here. For the purpose of our discussion, it will be sufficient to identify some key transitions which can potentially cause conflation between Mill's utilitarianism and the modern version.

After the marginal revolution in the late nineteenth century, the concept of utility in economics had already become a notion very different from utility in philosophy. By the time Pigou wrote *The Economics of Welfare* in 1920, the term utility had become to mean 'intensity of desire', a concept used by Pigou as an approximate to satisfaction (Pigou, 1932 [1920], p. 23). Pigou's definition of utility was widespread among economists because Pigou's welfare economics was dominant in Britain up to 1930.

In the 1930s, the meaning of utility underwent another significant transition. In order to eschew the difficulty of measuring and comparing interpersonal utilities, which was deemed unscientific by economists at the time due to the influence of logical positivism, welfare economists took inspiration from the Italian economist Vilfredo Pareto and developed the ordinal concept of utility to replace the cardinal concept in the British tradition of welfare economics (Backhouse and Nishizawa, 2010, p. 3). According to Broome, the new meaning of utility was fully formed by John Hicks and Roy Allen in their 1934 article 'A Reconsideration of the Theory of Value'. The figure attached to utility no longer stands for the level of the satisfaction of economic agents. Instead, their utility function ranks alternatives and assigns a greater utility to the one that is preferred. Hence the term 'utility' acquired the meaning of 'the value of a function that represents a person's *preferences*', and this is has become the official definition of utility in economics (Broome, 1991, p. 3, emphasis added). Harsanyi, for one, equates utility with satisfaction by treating value judgments concerning social welfare as 'a special class of judgments of preference' (Harsanyi, 1953, p. 434, see also 1977, p. 54).

Around the same period when Hicks and Allen developed a new meaning of utility, another important notion of utility was constructed by J. von Neumann and O. Morgenstern. Neumann and Morgenstern's concept of utility is close to the cardinal utility used in the theory of choice involving risk (Harsanyi, 1953, p. 343) and was adopted by Harsanyi for his social welfare analysis, in particular, to establish an 'additive cardinal social welfare function' (Harsanyi, 1955, p. 310).

The term utility has continued to be used by economists despite its meaning having undergone constant change since the term was used by Bentham and Mill. Similarly, the idea of maximizing total utility also persists in economics even after the meaning had changed considerably, especially after experiencing the changes during the 1930s and 40s. It has been developed in two different ways. One is by microeconomists in studying the rational agent's decision-making process; the other is by welfare economists in studying the social welfare function and policy decision-making. Rawls notices the difference, and emphasizes that his principles of justices are concerned with the second one (Rawls, 1999, pp. 49–50). Thus the second meaning is particularly relevant to our discussion.

Corresponding to the replacement of cardinal utility with personal preference ordering, the social welfare function largely abandoned the concept of maximizing total utility as a cardinal notion, and adopted social states ordering as a new method of judging the states of social welfare. This replacement was first proposed by Bergson in his influential 1938 article. Similar to Bergson, Arrow's framework permits neither the measurement of cardinal individual utilities nor interpersonal comparisons of utility differences (Pattanaik, 2008). Yet Arrow went on to derive the social orderings from individual orderings of preference. This led him to formulate a concept of social welfare function different from Bergson's. Arrow's novel approach to social welfare analysis opened up a new direction for welfare economics, which led to a thriving body of literature known as social choice theory.

In the rise of the wave of ordinal utilities generated by Bergson, Harsanyi, writing after Arrow (1951), did not dismiss the possibility of making social welfare judgements by incorporating cardinal and interpersonally comparable individual utilities. Moreover, he incorporated the concept of uncertainty into his work. This changed the notion of maximization of total utility from actual utility maximization to expected utility maximization. It is evident that his work attracted Rawls's attention, both as a utilitarian theory and as a theory of choices involving risk.

Similarly to Harsanyi, Sen disagrees with Arrow's standpoint regarding the interpersonal comparison of utility. Nevertheless, Sen constructed a highly formal and technical theory of social choice and welfare by following this new approach established by Arrow, that is, the rules of collective choice are concerned with the preference-ordering of the society, which is a function of individual *preference orderings* (Sen, 1970, p. 2). His *Collective Choice and Social Welfare*, published in 1970, is the climax of the new approach of social welfare studies. The term utilitarianism is still used by Sen in his book, but in a very different manner from that in which it was used by Mill. Utilitarianism is used by Sen as an expression of 'the approach of maximizing aggregate individual welfares' in a broad sense (Sen, 1970, p. 98). As Sen pointed out, utilitarianism in this broad sense does not necessarily have any connection with Bentham's utilitarianism or his idea of utility. It is worth pointing out that in *Collective Choice and Social Welfare*, Mill was not mentioned once. This shows that there is little, if any, connection between the modern maximization doctrine in social choice theory and the greatest happiness principle in Mill's utilitarianism.

The main purpose of presenting this brief history of welfare economics in the first three-quarters of the twentieth century is to show how the notion of utility and that of maximizing total utility have gone through considerable transitions. Rawls's understanding of classical utilitarianism as a moral theory is in fact strongly influenced by the modern concept of utility maximization in welfare economics and social choice theory. Those who learn classical utilitarianism through Rawls's lens will naturally obtain a distorted perception. This is not to accuse Rawls of being responsible for the conflation of utilitarianism in welfare economics and utilitarianism in moral philosophy. The key point here is to suggest the importance of understanding the history of ideas in avoiding unnecessary confusion caused by the superficial similarity between the concept of utility maximization in modern economics and Mill's greatest happiness principle in the classical sense.

Clearly Rawls studied the latest welfare economic theories at his time (even though Harsanyi criticized Rawls's for relying on the maximin principle, which despite being popular three decades ago, was discredited by the time his *Theory of Justice* was published). Not only did he study the avant-garde economic theories, he also tried to incorporate these theories into his moral theory. The former no doubt led to the admirable breadth of Rawls's theory, but the latter is perhaps an unfortunate move. Broome once commented that it is unwise for philosophers to adopt the notion of utility developed by economists (Broome, 1991, p. 3). This seems to be true in Rawls's case in this author's view.

The modern meaning of utility and the maximization principle in economics has a clear impact on Rawls, arguably largely through the work of Harsanyi and Sen. The influence of utilitarianism as an economic theory on Rawls can be seen from the following features attributed by Rawls to utilitarianism. First, the good is defined as the satisfaction of desire; second, utility maximization is treated as a decision-making rule of rational individuals in both a descriptive and prescriptive sense; third, utilitarian moral theory for the society is understood as an extension of the decision-making principle of individuals; fourth, the principle of average utility can be viewed as the ethics of a single rational individual under uncertainty, a point obviously obtained from Harsanyi; fifth, a set of assumptions are required for utilitarianism to work, including such assumptions as a certain similarity among individuals and the diminishing marginal value of basic rights. In his discussion of Mill, Rawls seems to suggest that these features also exist in Mill's utilitarianism. However, all these five elements are exclusively the characteristics of the utilitarian theory in economics in the twentieth century. Mill's utilitarianism as a moral theory holds none of them.

First of all, for Mill happiness is not the same thing as the satisfaction of desires. Despite the fact that what Mill means by happiness is still controversial in the literature, there is little doubt that he does not define happiness as the satisfaction of desire, either rational or irrational. His well-known example that dissatisfied Socrates is happier than a satisfied fool provides strong evidence that he does not consider 'happiness' and 'satisfaction' as identical (Mill, *CX, X*: 212). Rawls does not give this discrepancy between happiness and satisfaction in Mill's utilitarianism enough attention. He rarely mentions in his *Theory of Justice* the quantitative and qualitative difference of pleasure proposed by Mill. When discussing how utilitarianism calculates the greatest balance of utility, Rawls specifically points out, by referencing Bentham's work, that utilitarianism asks no questions about the source or quality but only about the levels of satisfaction or dissatisfaction of individuals (Rawls, 1999, p. 27). In fact, it is arguable that utilitarianism as simple preference satisfaction would be just as alien to Bentham as it is to Mill.

Moreover, Mill is immune from the criticism that the morally right thing to do is defined by the principle of utility as maximizing total utility irrespective of difference of individuals and hence neglecting distribution. This criticism is mainly targeted at the version of utilitarianism holding the second and third elements listed above. As noted in Chapter 2, for Mill the greatest happiness principle is the ultimate principle of rightness and wrongness, but it does not follow that we are always required to maximize happiness, or that failing to maximize happiness must always be wrong. Rawls does not appear to make the common mistake by claiming that Mill's utilitarianism requires individuals always to maximize total utility on every occasion. However, he seems to believe that ultimately Mill's utilitarianism cannot explain why it is not allowed to sacrifice the liberty of some for others if the good is prior to the right.

It is worth noting that Rawls differentiates Mill from classical utilitarianism by classifying his utilitarian theory as one holding the principle of average utility, which requires society 'to maximize not the total but the average utility (per capita)' (Rawls, 1999, p. 140). The principle of average utility takes into account the impact of the size of population on the utility level. Rawls considers the principle of average utility more reasonable than the classical principle, and as a plausible alternative to his two principles of justice (Rawls, 1999, p. 140). Despite being deemed by Rawls as a more reasonable version of utilitarianism, the principle of average utility does not seem to be able to capture Mill's utilitarianism as Rawls suggests (Rawls, 1999, p. 141). It is true, and well known, that Mill had strong concerns about population growth, and believes that unlimited growth of population will suppress the living conditions of labouring class. However, these facts are not sufficient to suggest that Mill holds the principle of average utility.

Apart from taking into account the impact of population, average utilitarianism is essentially the same as the traditional version in terms of its purely aggregative nature. Average utilitarianism does not take into account the issue of distribution. Average utility only reflects the level of utility which can be enjoyed by everyone if it is distributed equally, but it does not suggest that the utility should be distributed equally. On this point, the relationship between

Rawls's version of classical utilitarianism and average utilitarianism is similar to that between total gross domestic product (GDP) and GDP per capita. GDP per capita of a nation is a better indicator than total GDP in giving an idea of its people's material living standards. However, like total GDP, GDP per capita does not give any information about how the national product is distributed among the people, and therefore is unable to suggest that the increase of GDP will benefit everyone in the economy. Similarly, an increase in average utility does not necessarily entail an increase in the utility of everyone in the society; maximizing average utility might benefit only some, rather than all. The principle of average utility described by Rawls is indifferent to the distribution among individuals because the average utility per capita is just the quotient of the maximized total utility divided by the number of population. Therefore, this version cannot appropriately represent Mill's utilitarianism.

The utilitarianism characterized by Rawls is a post-utilitarian paradigm, in Rosen's terminology. It is a model which prevailed in the twentieth century, and which was alien to Mill. For this reason, Mill's utilitarianism is resistant to Rawls's criticisms of utilitarianism that target its modern version. In fact, not only can Rawls's criticisms of utilitarianism not apply to Mill's version of utilitarianism, but Rawls's theory of justice shares several important aspects with Mill's theory of justice. In order to reveal the similarities between Mill and Rawls, it is necessary to make sure that what is compared is indeed comparable.

The primary principles of distributive justice

In both the first and second editions of *A Theory of Justice*, Rawls states that he confines his study of justice to those perspectives that concern only the fundamental structure which regulates the assignment of basic rights and duties. He excludes commutative issues from his theory of justice. Moreover, the theory is 'not a complete contract theory' (Rawls, 1971, p. 17; 1999, p. 15). By this Rawls means that his book does not set out to deal with all types of virtues; instead, it concerns only the political virtues, particularly justice. In *Justice as Fairness: A Restatement*, Rawls stresses the boundaries of his theory again in a more explicit and organized manner. He systematically spells out the three limits of his inquiry. The first is that his justice as fairness is not a comprehensive moral doctrine, but a political conception only (Rawls, 2001, pp. 12, 14). As a subject of political justice, it is applied only to the basic structure of political and social institutions (Rawls, 2001, pp. 12, 14). The second limit is that justice as fairness is an ideal theory for a 'well-ordered society' (Rawls, 2001, p. 13). The third limit is that justice as fairness does not deal with just relations between people. Nor is it a universal theory (Rawls, 2001, p. 13). In addition to the initial difference in methodology, these three limits of scope further distance Rawls's theory of justice from Mill's.

In contrast to Rawls's justice as fairness, which is limited to the political domain, Mill's utilitarianism is a comprehensive moral theory, which is supposed to deal with all kinds of moral issues. This difference is recognized and emphasized by Rawls (Rawls, 2001, p. 14). Given the limits Rawls puts on his theory of justice, it is clear that it does not have an equivalent status, in terms of moral theories, with Mill's utilitarianism. It follows that *the principle of utility as the first principle of Mill's utilitarianism is not the counterpart to Rawls's two principles of justice as the first principles of his theory of justice*. As a result, any attempt to compare Mill's principle of utility directly with Rawls's two principles of justice will not make much sense. To identify the counterpart of Rawls's principles of justice in Mill's utilitarianism, we first need to recognize the difference between their notions of social and distributive justice.

At a rather early stage of his work, Rawls distinguishes between a conception of justice and the concept of justice, in order to identify the role of his principles of social justice (Rawls, 1999, p. 5). Rawls believes that people will accept a characteristic set of principles for the purpose of distributing the benefits and burdens of social cooperation despite having disagreement about which principles should define the appropriate distribution (Rawls, 1999, p. 5). He defines the concept of justice 'by the role of its principles in assigning rights and duties and in defining the appropriate division of social advantages' and defines a conception of justice as an interpretation of this role (Rawls, 1999, p. 9). In short, the concept of justice is defined by its *formal role* and a conception of justice by its substance, or *contents*. If we follow Rawls's definitions to compare him and Mill, we will see that not only does Mill have a different conception of justice, but also that his concept of justice is not the same as Rawls's. The following analysis is a comparison of their terminologies. It helps to clarify a common confusion caused by the fact that the same phrases are used by Mill and Rawls to denote different concepts.

Rawls defines the principles of social justice as those principles which are 'to govern the assignment of rights and duties' in the basic institutions of society and 'to determine the appropriate *distribution* of the benefits and burdens of social life' (Rawls, 1999, pp. 4, 47, emphasis added). Moreover, his conception of social justice 'is to be regarded as providing in the first instance a standard whereby the *distributive* aspects of the basic structure of society are to be assessed'; therefore, 'they may not elucidate the justice [...] of voluntary cooperative arrangements or procedures for making contractual agreements' (Rawls, 1999, pp. 7–8, emphasis added). Accordingly, the scope of social justice in Rawls's discourse does not include commutative justice. Social justice can be seen as the synonym of distributive justice in Rawls's use.

On the other hand, it is intriguing to notice that Mill seldom uses the term social justice in his writing, in spite of being usually considered as one of its leading defenders. In *Utilitarianism*, he mentions the phrase social justice only once. In contrast to Rawls, who excludes commutative justice from his discussion of social justice, Mill's discussion of the idea of justice in the last chapter of *Utilitarianism* contains both distributive and commutative justice. The latter includes corrective and reciprocal justice. Although Mill does not explicitly use the term commutative justice, it is clear that the concept is present in his discussion of the rules for the exchange of commodities and punishment. Therefore, if Mill intends to deal with both the concept of distributive justice and commutative justice at the same time, without separating them into different categories, it is reasonable to suggest that in Mill's mind both concepts are commanded by the same principle, which is at a higher level. As discussed in Chapter 4, we suggest that the principles of distributive justice and the principles of commutative justice are both governed by the ultimate principle – the principle of utility – and that social justice covers both distributive and commutative justice.[1] Therefore, in order to make the comparison of their principles of distributive justice more effective, we need to find the principles of distributive justice in Mill's utilitarianism, the status of which is parallel to that of Rawls's two principles of distributive justice.

The derivation of the two principles starts from Rawls's design of the original position. The essential feature of the original position is that 'no one knows his place in society, his class position or social status, nor does anyone knows his fortune in the distribution of natural assets and abilities, his intelligence, strength, and the like' (Rawls, 1999, p. 11). The state of the original position constitutes 'a veil of ignorance' behind which the principles of justice will be chosen (Rawls, 1999, p. 11). This veil of ignorance ensures that 'no one is advantaged or disadvantaged in the choice of principles by the outcome of natural chance or the contingency of social circumstances' (Rawls, 1999, p. 11). Since all are similarly situated in the initial position, and no one is able to design principles to favour their particular condition, the principles of justice which are agreed to can be considered as the result of 'a fair agreement or bargain' (Rawls, 1999, p. 11).

Rawls's design of the original position aims to build up a fair procedure which can ensure that any principle agreed by all is just. Rawls believes that 'one conception of justice is more reasonable than another, or justifiable with respect to it, if rational persons in the initial situation would choose its principles over those of the other for the role of justice' (Rawls, 1999, pp. 15–16). Since people in the original position do not know how their decision will affect their particular situations, including their class and social status, nor will they know their potential or capability as well as their psychological features, such as optimism, pessimism and so on, it is reasonable to assume that they are not willing to take irrational and unwise risks. It follows that they will have a strong tendency to follow the maximin rule as the strategy of making choices (Rawls, 1971, pp. 136–137).

The so called maximin rule means that first the objects of choices have to be ranked in accordance with the worst possible results and then we have to choose the one which is best in this respect. If the maximin rule can describe the psychological tendency of those who are in the original position well, then Rawls's prediction about the principles of justice to be agreed will be correct. Rawls suggests that people in the original position will choose the following two principles:

> First: each person is to have an equal right to the most extensive scheme of equal basic liberties compatible with a similar scheme of liberties for others.
> (Rawls, 1999, p. 53)

> [Second:] Social and economic inequalities are to be arranged so that they are both (a) to the greatest expected benefit of the least advantaged and (b) attached to offices and positions open to all under conditions of fair equality of opportunity.
>
> (Rawls, 1999, p. 72)[2]

Rawls places a lexical order between the above two principles, namely, the first principle (the principle of equal liberty) is prior to the second principle (the difference principle). This order implies that the violation of equal freedom, which is required by the first principle, cannot be justified or compensated by greater social economic benefit.

In addition to the original position and the maximin rule, the assumption of primary goods is another important feature in Rawls's theory of justice. Despite the assumption that people in the initial situation do not know their particular aims of life, a certain basic knowledge about the good is required to 'explicate the notion of rationality underlying the choice of principles in the original position' (Rawls, 1999, p. 349). Hence, Rawls has to make some basic assumptions about the notion of the good. However, these assumptions must not jeopardize the prior place of the concept of right; otherwise the whole deontological methodology Rawls adopts will be endangered. Therefore, the theory of the good used for arguing for the principles of justice has to be restricted to 'the bare essentials'. In order to fit this purpose, Rawls proposes a distinction between the 'thin' theory of the good and the 'full' theory. The principles of justice have to be chosen with the concept of good offered by the thin theory, namely, primary goods. Only after the principles of justice are established is one allowed to flesh out the contents of the good by other things in the full theory (Rawls, 1999, p. 348). The thin theory of the good requires only the existence of a certain structure in different people's conceptions of the good, rather than the detailed contents of the good. Rawls believes that this assumption is sufficient to enable people with different conceptions of the good to choose principles on a rational basis (Rawls, 1999, p. 349).

According to Rawls's definition, primary goods are things that every rational man is presumed to want whatever else he wants (Rawls, 1999, pp. 54, 79). The concrete examples of primary goods given by Rawls include rights, liberties, opportunities, income and wealth, as well as the bases of self-respect (Rawls, 1999, pp. 54, 79). Rawls calls these goods 'social' primary goods in contrast to other 'natural' primary goods such as health and vigour, intelligence and imagination, which are not so directly under the control of the basic social structure (Rawls, 1999, p. 54). Hence the natural primary goods are excluded from consideration in the original position.

Mill never attempted to construct a theory of justice in a systematic way as Rawls does. Nevertheless, it is still possible to propose the principles of justice by summarizing his discussion of justice:

1 [S]ociety should treat all equally well who have deserved equally well of it, that is, who have deserved equally well absolutely. (Mill, *CW, X*: 257)

2 The equal claim of everybody to happiness in the estimation of the moralist and of the legislator, involves an equal claim to all the means of happiness. (Mill, *CW, X*: 257–258)

Let's call these first principles of distributive justice the principle of equal happiness. As mentioned in Chapter 4, Mill treats these principles as 'the highest abstract standard of justice'. The contents of just principles can be obtained only by considering the circumstances of the society under discussion and by taking into account the empirical data. Therefore, it is important to bear in mind that these propositions are merely a formal form without substantive contents.

We can also find propositions in Mill's work which correspond to the difference principle in Rawls's two principles of justice, which regulates the institutions and policies concerning the distribution of resources, income, wealth, etc.:

a After the primary necessities of food and raiment, freedom is the first and strongest want of human nature (Mill, *CW, XXI*: 336).
b If all were done which it would be in the power of a good government to do, by instruction and by legislation, to diminish this inequality of opportunities, the differences of fortune arising from people's own earnings could not justly give umbrage (Mill, *CW, III*: 811).

Statements (a) and (b) together (let's call them Mill's difference principle), suggest that inequalities of income and wealth are allowed if and only if the means of subsistence is ensured to everyone, and if differences in contingent social fortune have been reduced to a minimum level. Similar to Rawls's case, there is also a lexical order between Mill's first and second principles. The principle of equal happiness is prior to the difference principle. This means that the unequal treatment of different individuals' happiness cannot be justified in the name of greater social economic benefit.

This analogy between Mill and Rawls suggests that the substance of their theory of distributive justice shares significant similarities. Both Mill and Rawls's first principles of distributive justice require treating each individual with equal consideration. For both of them, the first principles are prior to the second principles, yet the first principle alone is insufficient to lead to a just system. The second principle is indispensable to make the primary principles of distributive justice complete. Before turning to exploring the institutions grounded on these primary principles of distributive justice, we will take a closer look at Rawls's substantive conception of justice.

Justice for equal prospects of life

The idea of equality plays an important role in Rawls's theory of justice. Rawls clearly points out that the equality he pursues is not merely equality before the law, even though it is a crucial part of his concept of justice. He claims that 'law and institutions may be equally executed and yet be unjust' (Rawls 1971, pp. 58–59). Rawls, following Perelman's analysis, distinguishes the idea of formal justice from that of substantive justice (Rawls, 1999, p. 51). He calls the impartial and consistent administration of laws and institutions formal justice: 'formal justice requires that in their administration laws and institutions should apply equally to those belonging to the classes defined by them' (Rawls, 1999, p. 51). In addition to such impartial application, formal justice implies the consistent interpretation of rules according to such precepts as the treatment of similar cases in a similar way (as defined by statutes and precedents) (Rawls, 1999, p. 441). Rawls is clearly aware that 'treating similar cases similarly is not a sufficient guarantee of substantive justice' because basically there is 'no contradiction in supposing that a slave or caste society, or one sanctioning the most arbitrary forms of discrimination, is evenly and consistently administered' (Rawls, 1999, p. 51). Therefore, the focus of his theory of justice is not equality before the law, the formal element of justice in practice, but equality in the conceptual sense.

Can we summarize the substantive part of Rawls's theory of justice as equality of something? Amartya Sen suggests that Rawls's idea of justice is a call for 'equality of primary goods'. Yet Sen does not consider equal distribution of primary goods among individuals to be just. The issue raised by Sen against Rawls is that if the amount of primary goods is the same, then those who have less capability to transfer primary goods into well-being will have fewer opportunities to enjoy the same level of well-being. When considering the ability to transfer primary goods into well-being, Sen seems to focus solely on material goods, such as income or wealth, rather than basic liberties, such as political liberty, liberty of thought, freedom of the person, and so on. If this reading of Sen on Rawls is correct, Sen's interpretation can only include the substance of the first of Rawls's two principles of justice, not the second one. Curiously, Rawls does not seem to recognize this point in his response to Sen's critiques in his *Restatement* (2001). However, Rawls's omission does not imply that his two principles of justice are equivalent to the endorsement of equality of primary goods as Sen narrowly defines. If we include the second principle and examine the two principles together, we find that the two principles as a whole do not argue simply for equal basic liberties, but for 'an equal prospect of life' or 'equal opportunity to carry out the life desired' or 'equal claim to the advantages of social life'. We can infer this proposition from Rawls's description of 'just' institutions: 'institutions are just when no arbitrary distinctions are made between persons in the assigning of basic rights and duties and when the rules determine a proper balance between competing claims to the advantages of social life' (Rawls, 1999, p. 5). Moreover, it is a pre-constitutional idea, that is, this notion of equality is *ex ante*, rather than *ex post*. Hence, it aims at eliminating the inequality caused by natural and social contingencies, but it does not guarantee everyone equal outcome of life achievement.

This proposition can be better supported by examining carefully the second principle, namely, the difference principle. The difference principle contains two parts: the requirement that inequality should be in everyone's interest and that positions should be open to all. Each requirement can have two possible meanings: everyone's interest can mean either. Consequently, two requirements with two possible meanings for each allow a matrix of four possible interpretations for the difference principle. Rawls gives each of these four possible interpretations a name: system of natural liberty, natural aristocracy, liberal equality, and democratic equality (Rawls, 1999, p. 57). Rawls examine each of them and concludes that democratic equality is the best interpretation. It is a combination of 'equally open' interpreted as equality of fair opportunity and 'everyone's advantage' interpreted as a difference principle.

Rawls mentions several times in his book that his principles of justice seek to prevent arbitrary factors from playing significant roles in determining one's prospect of life. The arbitrary factors in Rawls's mind include not only 'the contingencies of social circumstance' but also 'the accidents of natural endowment'. When excluding 'equality as careers open to talents' as a proper interpretation of 'equally open' for the second principle, Rawls clearly intends to mitigate the influence of 'the contingencies of social circumstance' on the distribution of wealth (Rawls, 1999, pp. 62–63). For Rawls, real equality of opportunity has to go beyond a formal sense which ensures everyone 'the same legal rights of access to all advantaged social positions' (Rawls, 1999, p. 62). However, formal equality of opportunity can at most eliminate the influence of social contingencies, 'it still permits the distribution of wealth and income to be determined by the natural distribution of abilities and talents' (Rawls, 1999, p. 63). In order to mitigate the influence of natural contingencies on distributive shares as well, Rawls stands for 'fair' equality of opportunity. Within a market system, this requires a framework of political and legal institutions which regulates the overall trends of economic events, such as preventing excessive accumulation of property and wealth and maintaining equal opportunities of education for all (Rawls, 1999, p. 63).[3]

Therefore, equating Rawls's theory of justice as a theory aiming at the equality of primary goods tends to be misleading: the latter implies that the amount of income and wealth for basic needs and capabilities should be equally distributed while the former does not. In his reply to Sen in *A Restatement*, Rawls defends the index of primary goods as a flexible index by refining the notion of the index of primary goods as 'an index of expectations of these goods over the course of a complete life' (Rawls, 2001, p. 172). Accordingly, 'an equal prospect of life', 'equal opportunity to carry out the life desired' or 'equal claim to the advantages of social life' might be a better summary of Rawls's substantive justice than equal primary goods.

Background institutions for distributive justice

In Rawls's view, the main problem of distributive justice is the choice of a social system (Rawls, 1999, p. 242). We shall presently turn to this key question of distributive justice identified by Rawls: what kinds of institutions are required in accordance with Mill's and Rawls's principles of distributive justice? Before that we will review one common misinterpretation which we should avoid.

Presented as principles for determining the basic structure of political and economic institutions, Rawls's two principles of justice have important implications for the distribution of wealth in its primary signification. Some economists have tried to apply Rawls's theory of justice to economic theories and policies. However, there seems to be a huge gap between Rawls's original intention and economists' applications.

In economics, the most widely accepted interpretation of Rawls's difference principle with regard to the distribution of wealth suggests that the principle gives attention solely to the worst-off individuals or class. It follows from this interpretation that any kind of redistribution which makes the worst class better off, or maximizes the income of the bottom class will be justified. This viewpoint is held by Musgrave and Musgrave (1989), H. R. Varian (1990), P. J. Lambert (1993), and D. C. Mueller (2003, p. 611).[4] It is obvious that this understanding of Rawls ignores the fact that the final form of the difference principle is derived from the primitive form of the second principle: the inequality is allowed only if it is for *everyone*'s advantage.

Focusing on maximizing the income or wealth of the least well-off class alone has the danger of distorting the initial intention of Rawls's theory. We should not forget that the *starting point* of his theory is the intention of avoiding arbitrary invasion of equal liberties of *every* individual, including those members other than the worst-off class. It is necessary to understand the difference principle through examining how Rawls reached the final form of the second principle instead of focusing on the final statement alone, since the final statement of the second principle emphasizes only the benefits of 'the least advantaged'. In the first statement of the difference principle, the key word is not the least advantaged, but 'everyone':

> social and economic inequalities are to be arranged so that they are both (a) reasonably expected to be to *everyone*'s advantage, and (b) attached to positions and offices open to all.
>
> (Rawls, 1999, p. 53, emphasis added)

The transition from everyone to the least advantaged does not imply any change in the nature of the principle. Rather it is because Rawls, when refining the statement of his difference principle, adopted the idea of Pareto improvement, a principle aiming at making everyone better off without harming anyone else (Rawls, 1999, pp. 58–62). More specifically, Rawls's second principle is based on the strict Pareto improvement, for it does not allow total welfare increase occurring by potential or actual compensation, which is allowed by other welfare criteria, such as Hicks–Kaldor criterion. When deriving the principles, Rawls was cautious about the problem of the interpersonal comparison of utility and it seems that he consciously tried to avoid this problem (Rawls, 1999).[5] There is a difference between Pareto improvement and Rawls's difference principle though: the former is a criterion for a specific circumstance while the latter is a constitutional idea.

While translating Rawls's conception of justice into mathematical function, economists often fail to preserve the liberal element required by the first principle. For instance, Varian creates the Rawlsian social welfare function as $W(u_1, \ldots, u_n) = \min\{u_1, \ldots, u_n\}$ (Varian, 1990, p. 529). However, if social welfare is entirely determined by the utility of the worse-off in the society as indicated by Varian's formula, there is no mechanism in principle to prevent the redistribution of wealth being done in a way that violates the basic rights of those who are better-off or in other unfair ways (e.g. the redistribution might completely deny the necessity of allowing principles such as 'to each according to his exertion' to function). It is questionable that the first principle of Rawls's two principles of justice would allow this to happen.

If the dominant interpretation of Rawls's theory of justice in economics literature is incorrect, the policy implications suggested by the interpretation will be wrong as well. If so, what would the policies or institutions look like according to Rawls's principles of distributive justice? In section §43 of his book, Rawls gives a description of the major supporting institutions in a properly organized democratic state that will ensure that the social and economic processes, and hence the resulting distribution, are also just (Rawls, 1999, pp. 242–251). The institutions he specifically indentifies include those which can ensure equal chances of education (such as subsidizing private schools or by establishing a public school system), those which can ensure equality of opportunity in economic activities and in the free choice of occupation, those which can guarantee a social minimum (such as family allowances and special payments for sickness and employment or negative income tax), and those which can prevent concentrations of power (such as inheritance and gift taxes, as well as restrictions on the rights of bequest).

A major aim of those background institutions in Rawls's list is to ensure equality of opportunities. Rawls's notion of equality of opportunities goes beyond the classical notion, which aims to remove unfair discrimination (Sugden, 2004). He wants to remove the inequality of opportunities resulting from factors which one can hardly be responsible for. As Rawls himself puts it, 'the idea of justice as fairness is to use the notion of pure procedural justice to handle the contingencies of particular situations' (Rawls, 1999, p. 243). Fairness is an important aim of the design of original position and the veil of ignorance. It is obvious that Rawls intends to minimize the impact of birth, which is a random factor out of one's control. There is a striking similarity between Mill and Rawls in this respect.

In several places of his various writings, Mill clearly holds the view that no one can be held responsible for his birth and that the injustice resulting purely from the factor of birth should be minimized, if not eliminated.

This view plays a significant role in the second part of the second principle stipulated above, i.e. (b) of Mill's difference principle. His advocacy of compulsory elementary education and inheritance taxation can be deemed as the manifestation of this principle. We will discuss Mill's views on these two institutions in turn. As to the first part of the second principle of Mill's distributive justice (a), we discussed the policy implication of this principle in Chapter 5 and will not explore it further here.

Before we start, it is worth stressing that for Mill these institutions do not serve only as the means of ensuring an equal starting line. Mill's justification for these institutions is far richer than that. Yet for the purposes of making a sensible comparison between Mill and Rawls, our discussion will focus as much as possible on how these institutions in Mill's design are just in the sense that they can ensure a minimum level of freedom, and allow individuals to pursue more freedom.

Universal elementary education

It is beyond doubt that Mill awards education paramount value. He believes that education, when it is really such, necessarily strengthens as well as enlarges the active faculties, and its effect on the mind is favourable to the spirit of independence (Mill, *CW, III*: 949). Accordingly, a fitting education can enable one to provide not only food for the body, but instruction and training for the mind so that one can perform one's part well in life towards others and towards oneself (Mill, *CW, XVIII*: 301–302). Hence, from the view of either the individual's or the whole society's long-term interests, it is essential to equip human beings born into the community with certain primary elements and means of knowledge during childhood (Mill, *CW, III*: 948). In short, Mill thinks that education has two main functions: one is to make individuals capable of leading an independent life (both in the material and spiritual fields); the other is to enable individuals to develop their potential, and then push the society to keep developing progressively.

To exercise these two functions of education, Mill argues, the government has to interfere in education properly. In contrast to common commodities, which serve the daily uses of life, Mill argues that the need of education is least felt where the need is greatest. Moreover, even if people desire it, they would be incapable of finding the way to it by their own lights. Since consumers are incompetent judges of education, the laissez-faire or non-interference principle, deemed as the general rule of government action by Mill, is not applicable in the case of education. Education, therefore, is one of those things which it is admissible in principle that a government should ensure its people receive (Mill, *CW, III*: 948).

Education is discussed by Mill as one of the examples of exceptions to laissez-faire, since the demand for it in the market is by no means a real test of the need (Mill, *CW, III*: 947). As a consequence, many economists centre the problems of education on the failure of the market-price mechanism, and regard education issues as a problem concerning the inefficiency of resource allocation. However, for Mill it is equity of distribution, rather than efficiency of allocation, that justifies government's intervention. Moreover, the key point of Mill's assertion is that the government should interfere in education by the provision of funds rather than interference in the content of education.

As mentioned, obtaining the independent ability to acquire the means of subsistence is one of the fundamental functions of education. Considering government interference in education from this perspective, we can connect education and individual liberty with the security of minimum economic independency. In Mill's view, the degree of education received is in proportion to the choices of employment. Even though the proportion may not hold accurately, it is generally true that education can enlarge a person's choices of occupations. Hence, government's intervention in the funding of elementary education will not be an obstacle to liberty, but will grant real rights of liberty to every individual. In Mill's time, all employment which required even the basic education of reading and writing could be recruited only from a select class and the majority had no opportunity of acquiring those attainments. As a consequence all such employment was immensely overpaid, as measured by the ordinary remuneration of labour. That is to say, the inequality in the opportunity of receiving education causes a natural monopoly in favour of skilled labourers against the unskilled, which makes the difference of reward (Mill, *CW, II*: 386). For those workers who had no access to basic education, when the supply of labour so far exceeded the demand they must take whatever they can get. Consequently, the most revolting occupation always devolved on the most helpless and degraded, either from squalid poverty or from want of skill and education (Mill, *CW, II*: 383). As such, equality of opportunities or equal freedom for occupations would merely be a slogan with no significant meaning. From this point of view, universal elementary education can ensure every labourer's equal freedom in choosing employment.

Furthermore, Mill's discussion of education concerns distribution in another respect. It is Mill's design that once the government uses its binding authority by law to impose on parents the legal obligation of giving elementary instruction to children, the government has to take measures to insure that such instruction shall be always accessible to them, either gratuitously or at a trifling expense (Mill, *CW, III*: 948–949). Otherwise, the imposition of legal obligation on parents cannot fairly be done (Mill, *CW, III*: 949). We should not forget that in the nineteenth century the general rate of wages in England was barely over the level of subsistence and thus not high enough to bear the expenses of education, so the expenses for children's education must be financed by sources other than wages. As a result, Mill considers it the government's duty to give pecuniary support to education, and treats it as a present investment which will reduce the help needed in the future.

Inheritance taxation

In eighteenth-century England, it was a popular view that property right was a sacred natural right, the absoluteness of which should not be challenged or invaded. Bentham's adoption of the greatest happiness principle as the foundation of social and legal reform started a new era of moral and legal philosophy. Bentham dismissed the notion of natural right, and used the utilitarian philosophy as the foundation of his arguments for the reform of the law of escheat and inheritance taxation. In Bentham's time the law of escheat, a law prescribing that property with no assignable heir should revert to the state, applied only to landed property. Accordingly, the collateral relatives of a deceased person were entitled to inherit the full amount of such property if he or she had no children. In his Supply without *Burden*, or Escheat vice Taxation (1843b), Bentham attempted to extend the scope of the law of escheat. According to Bentham's plan, the state would be entitled to half the value of any estate in cases where there were no direct heirs, with the other half to be distributed in accordance with the will of the deceased proprietor. Where a property holder without direct heirs died intestate, the estate would escheat to the state in its entirety. Bentham's arguments for this reform are entirely utilitarian. In his view, the reduction or elimination of claims on the part of potential collateral claimants would not harm them, since people would not usually have cause to expect to inherit property other than from their parents.

Mill's views on inheritance taxation are basically an extension of Bentham's views, but his position is even more radical than Bentham's. While aiming to limit collateral inheritance, Bentham did not intend to limit inheritance in direct lines. Mill went further. He proposed not only to abolish collateral inheritance, but also to impose strict limits on the inheritance of direct heirs. Mill's position on inheritance taxation is often believed to be highly socialist. This is a mistaken impression. Mill's position on the issue regarding the right of bequest and the right of inheritance is in fact rather individualistic. To understand this, we need to know how Mill approaches the issue of inheritance taxation.

Despite the extensive discussion of inheritance systems and inheritance taxation given in his *Principle of Political Economy*, Mill emphasizes that questions regarding inheritance cannot be answered by knowledge of political economy alone (Mill, *CW, II*: 218). Instead of getting straight to such issues as tax rates or tax base, Mill starts his discussion of inheritance with an observation of the evolution of the concept of property. According to Mill's analysis, the idea of property has been closely linked to the mode of production and the corresponding constitution of society in history. In early ages, the children and close relatives were usually in some sense joint owners of the property of a deceased person because normally the acquirement and the preservation of assets were the result of collective effort. However, as the mode of economic activities changed, the unit of modern society was no longer the family or clan, but the individual, or at most a pair of individuals, with their unemancipated children (Mill, *CW, II*: 219). It used to be a reasonable and expedient measure to allow children, collaterals or close family to inherit estates in ancient times, but it is no longer appropriate in modern times.

It is Mill's view that the idea of property in the modern sense includes the following rights, and no more:

> the right of each to his (or her) own faculties, to what he can produce by them, and to whatever he can get for them in a fair market; together with his

> right to give this to any other person if he chooses, and the right of that other to receive and enjoy it.
>
> (Mill, *CW, II*: 218)

It follows that the right of bequest forms part of the idea of private property, but the right of inheritance does not. The distinction between the right of bequest and that of inheritance has important implications for the government's power of taxing. It implies that when imposing inheritance taxation government does not invade the property right of the inheritors. The only person who is entitled to bargain with the government on the ground of property right is the dead one.

Taking a different approach from Bentham, who dismisses the concept of right in his discussion of the taxes on collateral succession, Mill makes his arguments by appealing to the concept of property right to support inheritance taxation. Mill's approach appears to be even more forceful and more difficult for right-based theorists to refute: since it has never been the right of inheritors to claim inheritance, imposing inheritance taxation cannot be seen as the infringement of property right, and the loss of utility resulting from disappointment is not in the same category as the loss of utility resulting from the invasion of right.

For Mill the true spirit of private property is a system aiming at ensuring everyone the fruits of their own labour and abstinence. If the law permits or even encourages people to accumulate huge amounts of wealth by receiving inheritance or gifts rather than by personal exertion, such a law is inconsistent with the ideal of private property. When the incidental consequence of such a law reaches a certain height, it 'does not promote, but conflicts with, the ends which render private property legitimate' (Mill, *CW, II*: 208). It is a natural tendency of capitalism that economic activities and power will be concentrated in the hands of few capitalists. If capital and wealth can be passed on and accumulated without limitations from one generation to another within a family or clan, eventually whether one will be successful or struggle to survive in the system will be determined to a large extent by birth, an accidental factor. For those who were born in poor backgrounds, the so-called freedom of the property right is virtually an empty right. For Mill this clearly violates the ideal of distributive justice.

It should be emphasized that Mill's advocacy of heavy inheritance tax does not imply that he is advocating an absolutely equal distribution of income or wealth, or using it as a tool to pursue equality for its own sake. For the sake of the public interest, what has to be restrained are 'not the fortunes which are earned, but those which are unearned' (Mill, *CW, III*: 811), in particular, the property people can obtain from others' benevolence without employing their own talents (Mill, *CW, II*: 225). Mill never argues that equality in the amount of income or wealth is a distribution pattern desirable for its own sake. On the contrary, it is his belief that

> The inequalities of property which arise from unequal industry, frugality, perseverance, talents, and to a certain extent even opportunities, are inseparable

> from the principle of private property, and if we accept the principle, we must bear with these consequences of it.
>
> (Mill, *CW, II*: 225)

However, it should be a precondition that the government has done its best to diminish this inequality of opportunities (Mill, *CW, III*: 811). In other words, for Mill the law that sets limits on the amount of inheritance is designed to ensure *ex ante* equality, as Ekelund and Walker comment (1996, p. 575). It is not Mill's intention to achieve *ex post* distribution of wealth by using inheritance taxation as a measure to expropriate the fruit of people's labour. Admittedly, it is impossible to make everyone start on perfectly equal terms in a society running the system of private property. Nevertheless,

> if as much pains as has been taken to aggravate the inequality of chances arising from the natural working of the principle [of private property], had been taken to temper that inequality by every means not subversive of the principle itself; if the tendency of legislation had been to favour the diffusion, instead of the concentration of wealth

such a system of private property would not result in the injustices often attacked by the proponents of socialism (Mill, *CW, II*: 207–208).

Mill's argument that the right of inheritance is not an intrinsic or indispensable part of the notion of private property has not exhausted the discussion of bequest. Despite dismissing the right of inheritance, Mill recognizes the right of bequest as people's property right. Is there any case in which interference in it from the government should be justified? If so, what is the rationale of the interference and where is the boundary of regulations?

Mill is very cautious with the power of bequest, since he believes that the abuse of it will lead to 'conflict with the permanent interest of the human race' in a greater degree than most other proprietary rights (Mill, *CW, II*: 226). Given that property is only a means, not an end, the right of bequest is not absolute, and the exercise of the power of bequest should be limited by law. Despite agreeing that each person should have power to dispose by will of their whole property, Mill insists that it would be wrong 'to lavish it in enriching some one individual, beyond a certain maximum, which should be fixed sufficiently high to afford the means of comfortable independence' (Mill, *CW, II*: 225). As to the methods of imposing limitations, Mill proposes to restrain 'the accumulation of large fortunes in the hands of those who have not earned them by exertion', and to impose 'a limitation of the amount which any one person should be permitted to acquire by gift, bequest, or inheritance' (Mill, *CW, III*: 811).

One important point to note is that Mill's discussion of inheritance taxation is not only a manifestation of the second part of his difference principle (b), but also the first part (a). Even though he generally believes that it is appropriate for the state to impose heavy inheritance taxes, he is careful not to deprive the rights which belong to direct heirs in cases in which their guardians have failed, or been unable, to make sufficient provision before death. These include the right to be raised up properly until reaching adulthood, and the right to the means of subsistence. Mill stipulates the limitations on the government's power of taxing as follows:

> that if there are descendants, who, being unable to provide for themselves, would become burthensome to the state, the equivalent of whatever the state would accord to them should be reserved from the property for their benefit. [...] In case of intestacy, the whole property to escheat to the state: which should be bound to make a just and reasonable provision for descendants, that is, such a provision as the parent or ancestor ought to have made, their circumstances, capacities, and mode of bringing up being considered.
>
> (Mill, *CW, III*: 887)

It is worth mentioning that Mill's arguments for heavy inheritance taxation are also grounded on his observation of human behaviour and his theory of character. Mill believes that in most cases, leaving a moderate amount of property is more beneficial to the individual and the society than leaving a huge amount of property (Mill, *CW, II*: 221). It is Mill's view that other than for the purposes of ostentation or an improper exercise of power, no one needs enormous fortunes for any personal purpose (Mill, *CW, II*: 226). He believes that too much unearned property will usually have a negative impact on an individual's character, especially in the cases of those who know when they are young that they will inherit huge amount of property because they often incline to become idle and profligate people (Mill, *CW, III*: 893). Mill does not deny the truth that some obtain happiness after inheriting a huge amount of estate, but he believes these not to be the usual cases (Mill, *CW, II*: 221).[6] Mill's assertion regarding the formulation of character itself is not an ethical claim, but one concerning facts. Whether the claim is true or false cannot be affirmed a priori. Rather, empirical evidence and Mill's method of ratiocination are both essential for testing the soundness of the claim as a fact. If it indeed can be proved to be true, it would strengthen the scientific foundation of Mill's taxation theory. If the claim is proved to be false, we should consider how far it would put constraints on Mill's arguments for highly progressive inheritance taxation.

Is Rawls's theory of distributive justice superior to Mill's?

Despite its title, Rawls's *A Theory of Justice* is a book dealing with issues much broader than a theory of justice; it actually presents an old debate between deontology and teleology in the field of political and moral philosophy. A key difference between teleology and deontology lies in their views on the relationship between the right and the good. According to Rawls, deontological theories maintain that the right has priority over the good. For a deontologist like Rawls, this priority is very important because it does not allow the loss of freedom for some to be made for a greater good shared by others (Rawls, 1999, p. 25). In the mind of deontologists, it is a serious problem of teleological theory that it allows the judgement of goodness to be made without referring to what is right (Rawls, 1999, p. 22).

However, it is still debatable whether Rawls is successful in claiming that the right is prior to the good in his theory of justice. In contrast with teleological theories, deontological theories hold that 'something is good only if it fits into ways of life consistent with the principles of right already on hand' (Rawls, 1999, p. 347). Yet in order to establish those principles of the right, Rawls admits, 'it is necessary to rely on some notion of goodness, for we need assumptions about the parties' motives in the original position' (Rawls, 1999, p. 347). In other words, Rawls cannot avoid the problem of where the contents of the right come from.

To avoid jeopardizing the prior place of the concept of right, Rawls carefully proposes a thin theory of the good, in contrast to the full theory of the good, by restricting goods to the bare essentials (Rawls, 1999, p. 348). Nevertheless, Rawls's proposition of the thin theory of the good cannot be considered as offering the final vindication about the priority between the right and the good. In fact what it reflects is only the old debate between German metaphysics and English empiricism: can human beings form the idea of the right before they acknowledge what is good for them?

The probable conflict between basic rights is also a tough challenge for Rawls. Throughout his book he emphasizes the theme that justice does not allow the restriction of basic liberties for the sake of other benefits; they 'can be limited and compromised only when they conflict with other basic liberties' (Rawls, 1999, p. 54). Rawls's doctrine which ascribes priority to liberty over other values is appealing. Yet, 'the original position does not seem to contain enough information to allow one to sort out the priority of different liberties' (Mueller, 2003, p. 604). This problem becomes apparent, as Hart comments, 'when we consider [...] what the application of this doctrine would require in practice' (Hart, 1975, pp. 230–231).

On the conflict between different liberties, as shown in Chapter 5, Mill appeals to social utility as the final judge.[7] Admittedly, we have to interpret the idea of social utility very carefully when putting this philosophical idea into practice, yet at least the problem of conflict is not left unanswered in Mill's theory. This author believes that Chapter 5 has shown some examples of economic issues in which a possible way of reasoning leading to solutions for the conflicts are suggested. As to Rawls's theory of justice, it seems to lack a clear answer if conflicts occur between basic liberties. We can use Rawls's own example, the introduction of rules of order in debate, to show the difficulty. The rules of order in debate are introduced to restrict our liberty to speak from speaking whenever we want. Without this restriction, very often the liberty of speech will be hampered. Therefore, such rules of limiting the liberty to speak, Rawls believes, are necessary for 'profitable' discussion. Yet Rawls's illustration may not be as convincing as he thinks. Hart's comments are insightful:

> In this very simple case there seems to be a quite obvious answer to the question as to which of the two liberties here conflicting is more valuable since, whatever ends we are pursuing in debate, the liberty to communicate our thought in speech must contribute more to their advancement than the liberty to interrupt communication. It seems to me, however, misleading, to describe even the resolution of the conflicting liberties in this very simple case as yielding a 'greater' or 'stronger' total system of liberty, for these phrases suggest that no values other than liberty [...] are involved. Plainly what such rules of debate help to secure is not a greater or more extensive liberty, but a liberty to do something which is more valuable for any rational person than the activities forbidden by the rules, or, as Rawls himself says, something more 'profitable'. So some criterion of the value of different liberties must be involved in the resolution of conflicts between them; yet Rawls speaks as if the system 'of basic liberties' were self-contained, and conflicts within it were adjusted without appeal to any other value besides liberty and its extent.
>
> (Hart, 1975, pp. 239–240)

What Rawls tries to achieve in his theory of justice is to avoid an arbitrary and unstable balance between conflicting interests between different people. However, it seems that his principle still encounters a similar problem, which results from conflicting liberties. Since Rawls's theory of justice is merely a political theory rather than a comprehensive moral theory, it is possible that beyond the political domain there are some resolutions in his comprehensive theory which can solve the conflict between basic liberties. Nonetheless, since Rawls's moral system stands for a pluralistic value system, Rawls still has to solve the problem caused by the pluralism that is intrinsic in the first principle of morality.

For at least the two problems presented in this section, it is still premature to announce the absolute superiority of Rawls's deontological theory of justice over Mill's teleological one.

7 Sen versus Mill

Equal capability versus equal claim to happiness

In his seminal paper *Utilitarianism and Welfarism*, published in 1979, Sen asserts that utilitarianism is a philosophy comprising two distinct theories: consequentialism and outcome utilitarianism. The latter can be further decomposed into two elements, welfarism and sum-ranking. Welfarism and sum-ranking, Sen emphasizes, are characteristics which are not intrinsic components of consequentialism. Later, this view that utilitarianism is a combination of three independent requirements, is restated in an even clearer formulation in his book *On Ethics and Economics*:

> 1 welfarism, requiring that the goodness of a state of affairs be a function only of the utility information regarding that state;
> 2 sum-ranking, requiring that utility information regarding any state be assessed by looking only at the sum-total of all the utilities in that sense;
> 3 consequentialism, requiring that every choice, whether of actions, institutions, motivations, rules, etc., be ultimately determined by the goodness of the consequent states of affairs.
>
> (Sen, 1987, p. 39)

These three characteristics have become the accepted view of utilitarianism among economists and philosophers, and Sen's own criticisms of utilitarianism are also based on these. His capability approach can also be seen as a reaction to utilitarianism in the hope of remedying the problems caused by these three components.

As a moral theory, the version of utilitarianism in Sen's mind suffers at least three serious problems for him: first, it neglects rights, freedoms and other non-utility concerns; second, it is indifferent to the distribution of utilities among individuals; third, mental conditioning and adaptive attitudes make utility an unreliable basis for judging individual well-being (Sen, 1999, p. 62). Sen considers these three problems serious limitations for utilitarianism to serve as a theory of morality and, in particular, as a theory of justice.

According to Sen's analysis, neglecting rights, freedoms and other non-utility concerns is a problem arising mainly from the requirement of welfarism, a doctrine which judges the relative goodness of alternative states of affairs exclusively according to 'utility'. Perhaps influenced by the development of the notion of utility in economics,[1] Sen generally understands utility as 'desire-fulfilment', and considers it as pure mental state (e.g. Sen, 1987, p. 45; 1992, p. 53). Interpreting utility in this way, it is natural for Sen to claim that freedoms and rights are external to and independent from the concept of utility. Consequently, Sen believes that utilitarianism will inevitably deny the importance of rights and freedoms.

As to the problem of distributional indifference, Sen argues it to be the consequence of the requirement for sum-ranking because sum-ranking is insensitive to inequality of utilities (Sen, 1979, p. 468). Following Rawls, Sen also holds the view that for utilitarians 'equality of utility distribution between persons has no [...] intrinsic value' (Sen, 1979, p. 470).[2] Sen believes that 'maximizing the sum of individual utilities is supremely unconcerned with the interpersonal distribution of that sum' (Sen, 1973, p. 16). It follows that utilitarianism is very likely to produce 'strongly anti-egalitarian results' (Sen, 1973, p. 23).

According to Sen, the third limitation of utilitarianism as a standard of morality is due to his observation that people will become accustomed to their conditions and their mental states will adapt. The problem of adaptation will occur, Sen explains, no matter whether the idea of utility is defined as desire-fulfilment or happiness:

> A person who has had a life of misfortune, with very little opportunities, and rather little hope, may be more easily reconciled to deprivations than others reared in more fortunate and affluent circumstances. The metric of happiness may, therefore, distort the extent of deprivation, in a specific and biased way. The hopeless beggar, the precarious landless labourer, the dominated housewife, the hardened unemployed or the over-exhausted coolie may all take pleasures in small mercies, and manage to suppress intense suffering for the necessity of continuing survival, but it would be ethically deeply mistaken to attach a correspondingly small value to the loss of their well-being because of this survival strategy. The same problem arises with the other interpretation of utility, namely, desire-fulfilment, since the hopelessly deprived lack the courage to desire much, and their deprivations are muted and deadened in the scale of desire-fulfilment.
>
> (Sen, 1987, pp. 45–46)

Accordingly, Sen suggests that using mental metrics to guide public policy is unfair to those who are stuck in miserable situations. It has to be emphasized that the subjectivity of utility is not the target of Sen's critiques here. As Sen points out, his capability approach also relies on subjective mental evaluation. The key difference between his capability approach and utilitarianism is that the former is founded on *critical* evaluation, while the latter is not.[3]

Intriguingly, throughout his criticisms of utilitarianism in his various writings Sen rarely makes Mill a target for attack. In fact, in a special issue of *Utilitas* which collects five papers comparing Sen with Mill, Sen delightedly admits the direct influence of Mill's ideas on his thinking, particularly the idea of personal liberty. Even though Mill's influence may not be so direct in some other dimensions, Sen is still pleased with the attributed congruence in their theories, for he considers himself 'belonging to a tradition in which Mill is a towering figure' (Sen, 2006, p. 91). Even though Sen announces that he was influenced by Mill's thought, this does not imply that Sen would fully agree with Mill's utilitarianism as a moral theory. A possible reason why Sen does not directly criticize Mill's utilitarian theory is that there are in fact many similarities in their conclusions on some substantial issues such as individual liberty, education, gender equality, and so on. It is worth pointing out that on the rare occasions when Mill is mentioned in Sen's writing, the reference is usually made in a very general way and Sen does not often directly quote Mill's own words to support his arguments. In fact, a careful reading of Mill will enable us to see the significant similarities between Mill's utilitarianism and Sen's capability approach.

The remainder of this chapter will first summarize some important elements of Sen's capability approach. It will then relate these points to Mill's utilitarian theory of justice and show the similarities between Sen's and Mill's theories of justice. By so doing, we will see that Sen's criticisms of utilitarianism are actually inapplicable to Mill's utilitarianism and theory of justice. Moreover, this author argues that in some aspects Mill's utilitarian theory of justice is superior to Sen's capability approach.

Capability approach

Sen developed the capability approach as an evaluation system in order to offer an alternative scheme to the existing moral theories, including utilitarianism and Rawls' theory of justice, among others. Unlike Rawls's theory of justice, which is intended by Rawls to be solely a political theory, Sen's capability approach aims to be a theory both of personal morality and of public choice, with the latter including a theory of justice. Given that the focus of our study is the theory of justice, we will focus our attention on Sen's capability approach from this dimension. However, in order to interpret the capability account of justice correctly, it is first necessary to understand some key elements of Sen's capability approach as a general moral theory.

According to Sen, each evaluative approach of economic arrangements can be characterized by its 'informational base', which reflects the idea of justice underlying each approach (Sen, 1992, p. 73; 1999, p. 56). For instance, the informational base of standard utilitarianism, in Sen's view, 'is the utility sum total in the states of affairs'; it follows that the utilitarian view of injustice 'consists in aggregate loss of utility compared with what could have been achieved' (Sen, 1999, pp. 58–59). In contrast, Sen's capability approach uses 'capability' as the informational base for evaluating the states of economic arrangements.

One of the main reasons why Sen proposes the capability approach is his dissatisfaction with the notion of well-being widely used by contemporary economists. According to Sen, well-being in modern economics is defined as desire-fulfilment or preference satisfaction. Moreover, in order to make such a definition operative in practice, economists largely employ measures such as income or wealth as the indication of well-being. Sen rejects both the narrow concept of well-being and the limited measures of well-being. He argues that well-being is a far broader concept of how well a person lives as a being and hence introduces the concept of functionings to broaden the notion of human 'being':

> Living may be seen as consisting of a set of interrelated 'functionings', consisting of *beings* and *doings*. A person's achievement in this respect can be seen as the vector of his or her functionings. The relevant functionings can vary from such elementary things as being adequately nourished, being in good health, avoiding escapable morbidity and premature mortality, etc., to more complex achievements such as being happy, having self-respect, taking part in the life of the community, and so on.
>
> (Sen, 1992, p. 39, emphasis added)

In other words, functionings reflect 'the various things a person may value doing or being' (Sen, 1999, p. 75). For Sen, the advantage of functionings, in comparison with the traditional view of well-being, is their ability to cover broader and more concrete items. Since a human being's 'living' consists of a set of functionings, Sen suggests that it is necessary to take these constituent elements into account in order to evaluate a person's well-being (Sen, 1992, p. 39).

Capability, the core conception underlying Sen's capability approach, is itself built on a foundation of functionings. According to Sen, capability is 'a set of vectors of functionings', which represents 'the various combinations of functionings (beings and doings) that the person can achieve' (Sen, 1992, p. 40). It reflects a person's freedom to achieve these valuable functionings or a person's freedom to lead various lifestyles. In other words, while the idea of functionings stresses the diverse composition of well-being, the idea of capability to function extends to include the dimension of *freedom*. Sen's analogy between the economist's 'budget set' and his 'capability set' well illustrates this point: 'Just as the so-called "budget set" in the commodity space represents a person's freedom to buy commodity bundles, the "capability set" in the functioning space reflects the person's freedom to choose from possible livings' (Sen, 1992, p. 40).

One of Sen's main purposes in characterizing human well-being by functionings is to remedy the defective view of well-being in modern economics. Nonetheless, Sen does not think that an inclusive concept of well-being alone is sufficient to reflect the state of a person adequately. In addition to well-being, he believes that to evaluate a person's achievement, an 'agency aspect' is an indispensable element. In Sen's view, utility is only one element of well-being and well-being is only one element of a person's achievement. Therefore, the evaluation of personal achievements requires information regarding not only a person's well-being but also their agency aspect. Moreover, the evaluation of a person's well-being requires information not only on the utility they enjoy but also on other functionings.

Introducing this important distinction between the well-being and agency aspects of a person does not yet complete the whole picture of Sen's capability approach. According to Sen, a person's freedom has an intrinsic value, no matter whether it is conducive to achievements or not (Sen, 1987, p. 60). Even though, from the perspective of achievement, 'choosing *x* when *y* is available' eventually has the same result as 'choosing *x* when *y* is not available', Sen argues, these two cases should not be treated as the same because freedom is absent in the latter case. Sen takes fasting as an example (Sen, 1987, pp. 60–61). The outcome of fasting, if continued, is starving. However, continued fasting means something more than starving; it implies the existence of the option not to starve. Sen insists that freedom has to be given an independent weight irrespective of achievement, even if freedom to choose will not change the outcome. It follows that freedom represents an independent dimension from achievement in Sen's capability approach evaluation system.

Accordingly, there are two different lines of categorization in Sen's capability approach: well-being and agency, on the one hand; achievement and freedom, on the other. The combination of these two categories yields *four* distinct categories of relevant information regarding a person for Sen's evaluation system: (1) 'well-being achievement'; (2) 'well-being freedom'; (3) 'agency achievement'; (4) 'agency freedom'.[4] Each of these four categories, Sen emphasizes, has its own specific interest and significance (Sen, 2006, p. 91).

This brief sketch of Sen's capability approach provides a good starting point for us to examine how Sen grounds his theory of justice on the capability approach and why he believes that his capability approach to justice is superior to Mill's utilitarian account of justice.

Sen's critique of utilitarianism and Mill's utilitarianism compared

As mentioned, Sen considers welfarism, sum-ranking, and consequentialism to be the three key features of utilitarianism, and Sen's criticisms of utilitarianism as a theory of justice are largely based on these three components. However, since it is questionable whether Mill's utilitarianism and his theory of justice contain these three components, it is therefore questionable whether Mill's theory suffers the problems raised by Sen. For Sen, identifying the shortcomings of utilitarianism is important because 'for a long time welfare economics [has been] dominated by utilitarianism' (Sen, 2009, p. 272). Sen's claim regarding the status of utilitarianism in welfare economics is not wrong, but slightly misleading. We should not forget that the form of utilitarianism underpinning welfare economics has undergone significant transition in the first half of the twentieth century.[5] Since Sen's criticisms are specifically targeted at the modern variants of utilitarianism, it is questionable whether they are applicable to older theories, such as Mill's. Indeed, when identifying the three components, the variants of utilitarianism Sen has in mind are mainly act-utilitarianism and rule-utilitarianism, both of which were developed in the twentieth century (Sen,

1979). Mill is rarely if ever explicitly associated with these three components by Sen.

We have examined in the previous three chapters the predominant place of distribution within Mill's utilitarianism, both at the philosophical level and the level of practice. If our analysis is correct, it then answers Sen's second charge against utilitarianism, that the sum-ranking element makes utilitarianism indifferent to issues regarding distribution, so we will not discuss sum-ranking any further in this chapter. We will also postpone discussion of the third charge until the concluding chapter, so here we focus on the first charge Sen made against utilitarianism. We will demonstrate that Mill's utilitarian theory is resistant to this charge. Meanwhile, we will also argue that there are in fact significant similarities between the foundational elements of Mill's utilitarianism and Sen's capability approach. We will start our discussion by analysing Mill's idea of happiness. For this purpose, we will first introduce a classification which allows us to specify the aspect of happiness we are discussing.

Happiness can be used in a descriptive or normative sense. When used in the former sense, happiness usually refers to a psychological state. In this case, happiness means pleasure. For instance, when we say someone is happy, we often mean that the person is having pleasant feelings or experiencing other similar positive affections. We make a distinction between descriptive and normative, rather than a distinction between descriptive and evaluative, because evaluation is needed not only when happiness is used in a normative sense, but also in a descriptive sense. To judge whether someone is happy or not involves evaluating and judging the person's state.

In philosophy, happiness in the normative sense has more significance than in the descriptive sense. When philosophers claim that happiness is a concept of good or suggest that happiness should be the aim of life, this happiness is not always meant to imply having pleasures. The conflation of happiness in the descriptive and in the normative sense is one of the main sources of the confusion over happiness in philosophical studies. The conflation of the role of happiness with the contents of happiness is another important source. To make our discussion easy to follow, we can differentiate the role of happiness from the contents of happiness by following Rawls's distinction between 'concept' and 'conception'.[6] We use the concept of happiness to refer to the role, and the conception of happiness to refer to the contents. More specifically, the former relates to the status of happiness in a system of moral philosophy. The separation of the two is important because it is possible that the disagreement on the conception is related to the disagreement on the concept but it is also possible that there is agreement on the concept, which as a result cannot then account for the disagreement on the conception. We will first examine Mill's concept of happiness, that is, the status of happiness within his utilitarian moral philosophy. Then we will turn to examine Mill's conception of happiness, or what happiness comprises, after accepting happiness to be the aim of life.

Mill's concept of happiness

According to Mill, the 'theory of life' on which his utilitarian theory of morality is grounded is that

> pleasure, and freedom from pain, are the only things desirable as ends; and that all desirable things (which are as numerous in the utilitarian as in any other scheme) are desirable either for the pleasure inherent in themselves, or as means to the promotion of pleasure and the prevention of pain.
>
> (Mill, *CW, X*: 210)

This statement probably generated almost as much controversy as his notorious proof of the principle of utility as the first principle. In the controversial proof, Mill claims that happiness is the only thing desired and desirable as the 'end' and that other things are desired only as means, having no intrinsic value in themselves. The above statement and the proof are often rejected on the grounds that things other than happiness are also desirable for their own sake and have intrinsic value. Arguably, Sen has such a view in mind when arguing that

> There are other achievements that can figure in our evaluation [...] of what we regard as important (for example, violation of people's personal liberties can be judged to be more terrible than what is reflected in the calculus of pleasure or desire fulfilment).
>
> (Sen, 2006, p. 92)

However, it is evident that Mill's utilitarianism would not suggest that violating people's personal liberties is not important or less important than how people feel.[7] Sen's statement above suggests a conflation of treating happiness or utility as the *ultimate* end of all conduct, and thus as the *ultimate* test of moral standards, with using the feelings of pleasure as a direct criterion for making moral judgements.

Brown insightfully points out that Mill does not intend to formulate a criterion of right and wrong in *Utilitarianism*. Instead, Mill's focus is almost exclusively on happiness as the only desirable end.[8] It is often claimed that for Mill things other than happiness are not desirable for their own sake. This interpretation is mistaken. It is evident from the text of *Utilitarianism* that Mill does not deny the desirability of things other than happiness. What Mill really means is that they are desired and desirable not only for their own sake *but also for other goods*. Happiness is the only thing for which we cannot find a higher good, which partly motivates our desire for it. In other words, happiness is the only thing we pursue not for anything else but only for its own sake. This point is made clear in Chapter I of *Utilitarianism*, where Mill tries to explain why the ultimate ends cannot be proved:

> Questions of ultimate ends are not amenable to direct proof. Whatever can be proved to be good, must be so by being shown to be a means to something

> admitted to be good without proof. The medical art is proved to be good by its conducing to health; but how is it possible to prove that health is good? The art of music is good, for the reason, among others, that it produces pleasure; but what proof is it possible to give that pleasure is good?
>
> (Mill, *CW, X*: 207–208)

Mill's argumentation here clearly follows the Aristotlean tradition in the sense that he uses means and ends to articulate the concept of good. A contrast of Mill's argumentation of ultimate ends with Aristotle's discussion of goods and the final good shows a striking similarity between the two authors:

> [What the good is] seems different in different actions and arts; it is different in medicine, in strategy, and in the other arts likewise. What then is the good of each? Surely that for whose sake everything else is done. In medicine this is health, in strategy victory, in architecture a house, in any other sphere something else, and in every action and pursuit the end; for it is for the sake of this that all men do whatever else they do.
>
> (Aristotle, 1966, 1097a 16–23)

> Since there are evidently more than one end, and we choose some of these (e.g. wealth, flutes, and in general instruments) for the sake of something else, clearly not all ends are final ends; but the chief good is evidently something final [...] Now we call that which is in itself worthy of pursuit more final than that which is worthy of pursuit for the sake of something else, and that which is never desirable for the sake of something else more final than the things that are desirable both in themselves and for the sake of that other thing, and therefore we call final without qualification that which is always desirable in itself and never for the sake of something else.
>
> (Aristotle, 1966, 1097a 25–38)

> Now such a thing happiness, above all else, is held to be; for this we choose always for self and never for the sake of something else, but honour, pleasure, reason, and every virtue we choose indeed for themselves (for if nothing resulted from them we should still choose each of them), but we choose them also for the sake of happiness, judging that by means of them we shall be happy. Happiness, on the other hand, no one chooses for the sake of these, nor, in general, for anything other than itself.
>
> (Aristotle, 1966, 1097a 38–1097b 7)

If philosophers have no difficulties in understanding what Aristotle means by these passages, they should have no difficulty in understanding what Mill means by happiness as the ultimate end. What causes misgivings with Mill's treatment of happiness as the ultimate end, but not with Aristotle's, is the direct association of happiness Mill makes with pleasures and pains, which are usually deemed to be solely subjective feelings. However, taking the simple identification of happiness with pleasures and freedom from pain to be Mill's *concept* of happiness does not make much sense here because the identification only tells us what happiness *is*, but not what happiness *is about*. In the context of the final good or the end of life, a better interpretation of Mill's concept of happiness is defined in relation to 'existence'.

When explaining the ultimate end, Mill is specific in linking it with existence on several occasions. For instance, he writes:

> According to the Greatest Happiness Principle, [...] the ultimate end [...] is an *existence* exempt as far as possible from pain, and as rich as possible in enjoyments, both in point of quantity and quality.
>
> (Mill, *CW, X*: 214, emphasis added)

In addition, Mill defines the utilitarian standard of morality as

> rules and precepts for human conduct, by the observance of which an *existence* such as has been described [that is, an existence exempt as far as possible from pain, and as rich as possible in enjoyments, both in point of quantity and quality] might be, to the greatest extent possible, secured to all mankind; and not to them only, but, so far as the nature of things admits, to the whole sentient creation.
>
> (Mill, *CW, X*: 214, emphasis added)

In other words, it is the aim of utilitarian moral theory to secure *a certain type of existence* to as many sentient beings as possible. For Mill this type of existence is happiness, but what constitutes happiness still requires further exploration.

The strongest evidence for the existence explanation can be found when Mill, in the context of discussing happiness as the end of life, refutes the view that happiness means a continuity of pleasurable excitement (Mill, *CW, X*: 215):

> The happiness which they meant was not a life of rapture; but moments of such, in an *existence* made up of few and transitory pains, many and various pleasures, with a decided predominance of the active over the passive, and having as the foundation of the whole, not to expect more from life than it is capable of bestowing. *A life thus composed*, to those who have been fortunate enough to obtain it, has always appeared worthy of the name of happiness.
>
> (Mill, *CW, X*: 215, emphasis added)

It should be emphasized that these passages are to be read as Mill's concept of happiness, not his conception of happiness. He does not provide any discussion of the affirmative and comprehensive contents of pleasures and pains in these passages. After stating that by happiness is intended 'pleasure, and the absence of pain', Mill immediately gives a supplement to this definition:

> To give a clear view of the moral standard set up by the theory, much more requires to be said; in particular, *what things it includes in the ideas of pain and pleasure; and to what extent this is left an open question.*
>
> (Mill, *CW, X*: 210, emphasis added)

This means that accepting happiness to be the end of life does not exhaust the discussion of Mill's theory of life. The conception of happiness still needs to be fleshed out. The concept and the conception of happiness can and should be treated as two separate notions in Mill's utilitarianism, even though they are closely related. It is perfectly logical that we might agree with Mill that happiness, understood as an existence, should be the end of life but it does not follow that we must then agree with him on what such an existence called happiness should be like. A great many arguments against Mill's theory of life are in fact not rejections of his concept of happiness but of misinterpreted representations of his conception of happiness. Certainly, we might reject taking happiness to be the end of life because even the broadest conception of happiness may not appear adequate to be the ultimate end of life. However, any judgement should wait until we have a correct understanding of what Mill means by happiness.

Mill's conception of happiness

Mill claims that happiness means pleasures and absence of pains, but he also stresses that what pleasures and pains are requires further exploration. If Mill understood happiness to be simply a state of mind, this emphasis of the necessity of further exploration would appear redundant, if not odd.

There is an instance where Nussbaum argues that Mill falls between Aristotle and Bentham in the sense that his idea of happiness is different from Bentham's utility and has similarity with Aristotle's eudemonia (Nussbaum, 2004). There are also several other scholars arguing that Mill's idea of happiness is actually very similar to Aristotle's eudemonia.[9] Indeed, strong textual evidence can be found in Mill's *Utilitarianism* to support this claim. For instance, he writes:

> The ingredients of happiness are very various, and each of them is desirable in itself, and not merely when considered as swelling an aggregate. The principle of utility does not mean that any given pleasure, as music, for instance, or any given exemption from pain, as for example health, is to be looked upon as means to a collective something termed happiness, and to be desired on that account. They are desired and desirable in and for themselves; besides being means, they are a part of the end.
>
> (Mill, *CW, X*: 235)

For Mill, happiness is not an abstract idea but composed of a variety of elements, such as virtue, health, fame, power, money, dignity and so on. Individuality is one of the most well-known elements Mill identifies to be part of happiness and he gives extensive discussion to it in his *On Liberty*. According to Mill, the utilitarian doctrine does not mean that any given pleasure or any given exemption from pain is to be looked upon solely as means to a collective 'something' termed happiness, and to be desired only on that account. Many things are desired and desirable in themselves; besides being means, they are a part of the end. Mill maintains that things are rarely naturally or originally part of an end, but are capable of becoming so. Once they have become so, they are desired and cherished not merely as means to happiness, but as a part of that happiness. What was once desired as an instrument for the attainment of happiness has come to be desired for its own sake. In short, Mill's conception of happiness is broader than it used to be understood to be: it is not merely a feeling of pleasure; it comprises several additional elements, some being more concrete than others, including virtues, health, individuality, and so on.

The key step which allows Mill to move from happiness as pleasure to happiness as a multi-element whole is his theory of association. Psychology plays a fundamental role in Mill's utilitarianism and the theory of association is one of the keystones of Mill's psychology. As discussed in Chapter 1, Mill uses the theory of association to demonstrate that happiness is the only thing desired as the end and not for anything else. Note that Mill treats the claim that happiness is the end of all human conduct to be a claim regarding a fact, not a claim regarding an ethical value judgement. What he tries to demonstrate with his theory of association is whether this claim is true or false. How this claimed fact is related to the criterion of goodness and rightness is another question.

We have explored both the concept and the conception of happiness in Mill's utilitarianism. Now it is time to turn to Sen's first charge against utilitarianism and explain why Mill's theory is resistant to it. To counter the charge that utilitarianism neglects rights, freedoms and other non-utility concerns, we need to break down our argument into two parts. First, Mill's utilitarianism does not include any form of welfarism, which is identified by Sen as the main cause of the informational constraint problem. Second, Mill's utilitarianism does not neglect rights, freedoms, etc., although these concerns may have different significance in Mill's moral system. However, the fact that they have different moral values cannot be seen as a weakness of Mill's theory but, instead, a strength of his utilitarianism. In regard to the simultaneous and multidimensional value structure for diverse utilities, Mill's theory contains similarities with Sen's capability approach. We examine these two points in turn.

According to Sen's definition, welfarism requires that the evaluation of the goodness of a state of affairs depends solely on utility. Mill's utilitarianism is nowhere close to welfarism thus defined. It is actually arguable whether welfarism and Mill's utilitarianism are comparable at all. For Sen, welfarism is a theory stipulating utility to be the sole information base for judging *the goodness or badness of states of affairs*. That is to say, welfarism is not a theory concerning *the rightness or wrongness of actions*, which is the subject of Mill's utilitarian theory of morality, narrowly defined. It is true that Mill's utilitarianism, when perceived as a system of moral philosophy in a broader sense, is a theory regarding not only moral right and wrong, but also moral and non-moral goodness and wrongness.[10]

However, it does not make much sense for Mill to judge whether some state is good or bad without relating it to an end. Evaluating and comparing alternative states of affairs is a popular exercise in contemporary welfare economics, but the approach of the exercise is actually alien to Mill. Despite arguing that moral standards cannot be independent from consequences of conduct, Mill rarely if ever designated his moral theory as consequentialism. More often Mill associates his theory with teleology, but not consequentialism. Over-emphasizing consequentialism, the modern terminology for teleology, will underestimate the significant place of *telos* in teleology. *Telos* means 'end', 'purpose' or 'goal' and is the Greek root of the term teleology. For a teleologist like Mill, it does not make much sense to say one state is a better consequence than others if the assessment and comparison is done in isolation from the end, that is, the intended consequence. For teleologists, the good must be dependent on the end. For Mill happiness, despite being the ultimate end of all human conduct, is not the immediate end of every conduct. It follows that happiness, despite being the ultimate criterion of all human conduct, is not the direct criterion of goodness for everything. Given that various ends other than happiness are pursued, the criterion of goodness should not be restricted to happiness on every occasion.[11] When different secondary ends clash, the principle of utility should act as the umpire. Note that utility must not be interpreted as merely likings or dislikings, as Mill emphasizes: as the appeal to ethical questions, 'it must be utility in the largest sense, grounded on the permanent interests of man as a progressive being' (Mill, *CW, XVIII*: 224).

Mill's idea of happiness is much richer than it is usually thought to be. Things emphasized by Sen, such as rights and freedom, are all elements of happiness. Accordingly, Mill's conception of happiness is in fact close to Sen's notion of capability: the variety of ingredients of Mill's happiness is parallel to the diversity of functionings in Sen's capability set. Mill does not exhaust the constituents of happiness in his discussion. Similarly, Sen does not provide a comprehensive list of functionings. Moreover, as with Sen's capability approach in which different functionings have different importance, different utilities in Mill's utilitarianism also have different importance. For Mill, as the ingredients of happiness, 'some kinds of pleasure are more desirable and more valuable than others' (Mill, *CW, X*: 211). This point is in fact noticed and endorsed by Sen (Sen, 1980–1981). Similarly, there are also some kinds of utilities more desirable and more valuable than others. It is useful to recall a point made before: when Mill uses the term utility in a descriptive sense, utility refers to 'interests' of all human beings and sentient creatures. In this sense, utility is not meant to be a synonym for happiness as the end of life but the means or source of happiness. It follows that utilities are not homogeneous. Moreover, some utilities are more important than others and different utilities might conflict with one another. The conflict can be intrapersonal or interpersonal.

The difference in kind between utilities is crucial to Mill's utilitarianism, especially to his theory of justice. It is not always easy to tell which utility should be given more value in each circumstance, but it is not always necessary to know for practical purposes. It is sufficient at the theoretical level if we agree with Mill that human beings indeed have the ability to reflect on the difference of happiness of some utilities and to weigh one against another in any specific circumstances. In some cases, the comparison is straightforward. For example, human beings can recognize that the utility of potatoes in preventing starvation is more important than the utility of chocolate as a luxury. Even though a person may feel more pleasure eating chocolate than potatoes, the judgement remains obviously valid that utility derived from food for survival is more important and thus should be given more value than utility from food purely for enjoyment when physical nutriment is ensured. No matter how much utility luxury can produce, the utility is always lower in kind than that produced by the means of subsistence. Hence the universal need for food to prevent hunger gives justification to take away the resources of some for luxuries and transfer them to others for survival. Isn't this a very trivial example? Can luxury really have utility to someone who is dying? If one asks questions like these, he is thinking about intrapersonal comparison of utilities. However, the major role of Mill's argument of qualitative difference in utilities to his theory of justice is in interpersonal comparison of utilities. It is fair to say that the importance of the comparison between the above two types of utilities has not been taken seriously in current political and economic policy debates. Income taxation is one of the examples. It is a common phenomenon in many developed countries that the utility of income for subsistence is not given much more value than the utility of income for luxury.

In most cases, the comparison is less straightforward and that is where the controversies emerge and require our attention. It is impossible to make the discussion entirely comprehensive by giving examples but as Clark notices, Mill's general principle is that the assessment of utilities must be 'grounded on the permanent interests of man as a progressive being', in Mill's words (Clark, 2001 and Elliott, p. 474). It is important to underline that we should not strive to generate an exhaustive list stipulating a lexical order of the priorities of utilities. The judgement is highly sensitive to the specific circumstances, and relative priorities will be different in different contexts. When the context is personal business, people should be given absolute freedom of judgement for themselves.

Justice for real freedom

On several occasions Sen argues that the avoidance of making interpersonal comparison is one of the main factors leading to the impoverishment of welfare economics. Sen believes that interpersonal comparison is not only possible but also necessary for welfare economics, even though it involves value judgement. His capability approach can be deemed to be a reaction to the avoidance of interpersonal comparison in welfare economics, a fashion that the discipline started to develop in the 1930s. In order to make interpersonal comparison possible, an appropriate informational base for the comparison is needed. Providing such a base is an important goal that Sen tries to achieve with his capability approach.

In his book *Inequality Reexamined*, Sen points out that 'every normative theory of social arrangement that has at all stood the test of time seems to demand equality of something – something that is regarded as particularly important in that theory' (Sen, 1992, p. 12). Since every theory of justice is compatible with the idea of equality in some way, the crux of the debates about justice is not for or against equality, but 'equality of what?' (Sen, 1992, p. ix) Sen's answer to this question would be equality of 'the capability to achieve functionings'.

As mentioned in Chapter 4, substantive justice requires equality in one sense, which almost inevitably requires inequality in another sense. The equality Sen's theory of justice requires is the equality of capability. Since Sen's notion of capability represents 'the substantive freedoms' to choose a life one has reason to value (Sen, 1999, p. 74), we can say that the essence of Sen's theory of justice is 'equal real freedom for all'. 'Real' is a key word here.

In Sen's view, his concept of substantive freedom is different from the freedom advocated by Rawls and other libertarians and this concept plays a crucial role in his theory of justice. According to Sen's interpretation, Rawls's theory of justice concentrates on 'the means to achieve freedom'; by contrast, his own capability approach emphasizes 'the extent of freedom' (Sen, 1992, p. 8). Sen's reading of Rawls might not be entirely correct, but his arguments against Rawls's theory highlight the key points of his own theory.

In Sen's interpretation, Rawls's theory of justice requires equality in relation to primary goods. The main reason Sen argues against this requirement is that individuals differ in their capacities to transform resources into desirable achievements. Sen's objection is based on his observation of different individuals. According to Sen's observation, there are at least five different factors affecting people's ability to convert goods into functionings.[12] As a consequence, two different individuals with the same amount of resources may have very different levels of real freedom to lead lives they have reason to find valuable. For example, a person with physical disability will enjoy less freedom than a physically able person, assuming the two hold identical bundles of primary goods and other conditions are the same. (Sen, 1992, pp. 81–84) Therefore, Sen argues that equal means to freedom suggested by Rawls's principles of justice will not lead to equal extent of freedom due to the enormous differences in external and personal characteristics among human beings. In contrast, his capability approach aims to reflect the condition in terms of what people are actually able to be and do with the resources they have. Through this contrast, we can see that the essence of Sen's theory of justice is to ensure everyone's substantive freedoms.

Sen comments that 'someone's position in the alleged conflict between equality and liberty has often been seen as a good indicator of his or her general outlook on political philosophy and political economy' (Sen, 1992, p. 21). Indeed, the similarities between Sen's and Mill's political philosophy and political economy can also be observed through the relationship between equality and liberty in their views.

Unlike Sen, Mill does not give freedom an absolute weight independent from utility.[13] Yet their ideas of freedom share some important features. Among these, the material condition of freedom is particularly significant. It is the key factor which makes both their theories of distributive justice distinct from most libertarians' views of justice. Both Mill and Sen would support policies which give people who are in a disadvantaged position more resources because substantive justice requires treating different people differently, and the unequal treatment is to ensure everyone's minimum level of freedom.

In Mill's view, the means for subsistence is one of the most important utilities of human beings, having a paramount value over others. In the nineteenth century, facing the problem of poverty prevalent among the working class, Mill recognized that before the means of subsistence are assured human beings cannot have real freedom, even if sometimes it looks as if their actions are results of their own choices. For this reason, if the socio-economic arrangements of a society do not aim to ensure everyone's minimum subsistence, these arrangements cannot be considered just. Therefore, Mill would agree that some people's liberty of economic activities should give way to others' subsistence since this is a necessary condition for minimum substantive freedom for all. Nonetheless, it is important to note that Mill does not advocate radical measures to level all kinds of economic inequalities. Above the level of subsistence, the redistribution of wealth may be desirable for other reasons yet society does not have the duty to guarantee that everyone can have enough resources to reach their own goals.

In spite of their different socio-economic backgrounds, both Mill and Sen are concerned with the dignity of life, which is threatened by poverty. While people live in want and deprivation, the need for self-preservation will form an unavoidable constraint on human actions. This means that the realization of freedom is not always a problem of free will: it requires the prior fulfilment of certain conditions. This view plays a crucial role in their theories of distributive justice.

It is fair to say that the key reason leading to the congruence of their versions of substantive justice is their understanding of the inequalities between human beings. In the opening paragraph of *Inequality Reexamined*, Sen comes straight to the point that 'human diversity' is the core of his discourse on equality (Sen, 1992, p. 1). In spite of the acknowledgement of the differences in natural and social environments as well as external characteristics, Sen's capability approach is more concerned with the differences in personal characteristics, such as age, sex, and physical and mental abilities (Sen, 1992, p. 20). For Sen, human diversity is the origin of the issue of equality: if all people were exactly the same, 'equality in one space (e.g. incomes) would tend to be congruent with equalities in others (e.g. wealth, well-being, happiness)' (Sen, 1992, p. 20). Given the existence of human diversity, it seems unavoidable that equality in one space will go with inequality in another.

Sen complains that the rhetoric of 'all men are born equal' often tends to disguise the fact that human beings are in fact different, both in terms of external and personal characteristics (Sen, 1992, p. 1). As with Sen, Mill does not buy into this romantic view of equality of man, even though it prevailed among radical social reformers in the nineteenth century. Long before Sen, Mill already notes that human diversity would affect the degree of freedom people could really have. Therefore, one aspect of his theory of justice is based on levelling natural differences or inequalities between men and women, between the capable and the less capable.[14] Mill is aware that any pledge of equal opportunity or free competition is illusory if there is no initial attempt to level these inequalities caused by nature. Therefore, he claims that 'the true idea of distributive justice consists not in imitating but in redressing the inequalities and wrongs of nature' (Mill, *CW, III*: 808).

Challenges of the capability approach

Believing the utilitarian view of man to be deficient, Sen strongly advocates valuing both the well-being and agency aspects for a person in the perspective of both achievement and freedom. In view of this purpose, Sen's capability approach has been genuinely successful in drawing attention to the totality of a person as a human being. However, as a theory of justice, Sen's capability approach seems incomplete. It is not our purpose to give a full account of the challenges to Sen's capability approach as a theory of justice. Here we will focus on two points which are most relevant to this study: first, despite aiming at ensuring everyone equal substantive freedoms, the capability approach in its current form is not quite up to this task and further theoretical refinement is required; second, the capability approach as a theory of justice does not seem able to provide clear guidelines for economic policies and institutions at a practical level.

The tension between justice and liberty

To understand Sen's position concerning the relationship between justice and liberty, it is helpful to start from his critique of utilitarianism regarding the tension between justice and liberty. The utilitarian account of justice often causes misgivings among philosophers. One common charge is that utilitarianism cannot secure equal freedom for all since it is in principle ready to sacrifice the freedom of some for the interests of others. Rawls's criticism is a classic example.[15] Sen also criticizes utilitarianism for its threat to individual liberty. His critique shares some similarities with Rawls's views but has a different focus.

As early as 1970, Sen discusses the tension between social welfare considerations and commitment to individual liberty within utilitarianism. Sen's argument is well known as 'the impossibility of a Paretian Liberal' or 'the Paretian Liberal Paradox', which alleges that 'a principle reflecting liberal values even in a very mild form cannot possibly be combined with the weak Pareto principle, given an unrestricted domain' (Sen, 1970b). The conclusions from Sen's argument aroused wide debate among democratic political theorists, welfare economists and moral philosophers, for it implies the impossibility of integrating respect for liberty and respect for unanimity within the same social choice framework. It is obvious that the conflict in Sen's assertion is between Paretianism and individual liberty, and that what Sen argued against is the 'adherence to Pareto optimality' (Sen, 1970b, p. 157). However, because Paretianism is deemed to be a weak form of welfarism, which is thought to be one of the fundamental components of utilitarianism, the Paretian Liberal Paradox has been widely perceived to be a feature of utilitarianism (Sen, 1979, p. 479; Sen and Williams, 1982, pp. 3–4). For instance, based on Sen's conclusion, both Mirrlees and Hammond assert that utilitarianism conflicts with individual rights to free choice over private matters (Mirrlees, 1982, p. 82; Hammond, 1982, pp. 87–88).

Does Sen's capability approach do better than utilitarianism in terms of protecting individual liberty? Sugden (2006) suspects that when there is a divergence between what people actually desire and what they have reason to value, Sen's theory creates a possible danger of overriding individual liberties. In reply to Sugden, Sen rejects his interpretation of imposing collective judgements on individual choices. Sen emphasizes that either the imagined impartial observer, borrowed from Smith, or public reasoning, borrowed from Rawls, is for the exact purpose of assessing critically our own unscrutinized assessments (Sen, 2006, pp. 88–89). In a recent paper examining both Sugden's critique and Sen's reply, Qizilbash (2011) suggests that Sugden's reasoning does not establish that Sen's works are 'obviously illiberal or paternalistic in an objectionable way' (p. 50), but they do highlight a danger that some ways of applying Sen's works might be illiberal even though this is not Sen's intent.

This problem deserves attention because it is not a pure theoretical issue but one with practical implications, especially when the capability approach is used as the theoretical foundation for distributive policies to be put into practice. Every philosophical theory has the danger of being misused. No theorist should be held responsible for each misuse of their theory. However, if the likelihood of misuse is evident, due to the incompleteness or vagueness of the theory, then closing the theoretical loophole is undoubtedly the philosopher's job. However, it is not the purpose of our study to give a thorough investigation of such aspects of Sen's theory. Our focus here is to identify one cause of the flaws in Sen's theory which has not received much attention in the literature.

To a large extent, the unease of Sugden and Qizilbash, this author believes, is related to the fact that the line between moral and non-moral spheres is vague within Sen's capability approach and there seems to be no mechanism in Sen's theory to guide us on how to draw a clearer line.[16] If we examine the examples Sen uses to illustrate value judgement, we find that he rarely if ever differentiates moral from non-moral issues. For instance, Sen (1967) uses examples such as 'John should not dress like a beatnik' and 'On rainy days, I should carry an umbrella' for his discussion of prescriptive judgements. We do not deny that issues like dressing or bringing an umbrella may have importance in some circumstances and judgements regarding these issues can be prescriptive judgements. However, Sen's treatment tends to lead to mixing up moral and non-moral issues. If by prescriptive judgements Sen means moral judgements, it is questionable whether it is appropriate to discuss these rather personal issues as if they are moral questions. At best, it creates only mild conceptual confusion.

At worst, the realm of morality would be unduly expanded to cover issues for which individuals should have absolute freedom to decide what to do. Blurring the boundary between moral and non-moral may result in the threat of coercion to individual liberty since in theory if an affair falls within the realm of morality it should be subject to public interest and hence public opinion. Sen's invoking public reasoning does not seem to be able to give a clear answer on how individual liberties can be protected from social encroachment. Paradoxically, openness, a notable merit of Sen's theory in general, seems to become a weakness on this occasion.

Along with his analysis of Sen, Qizilbash (2011) also analyses Nussbaum's response to the paternalism accusation, a problem similar to the one raised by Sugden regarding Sen. According to Qizilbash, Nussbaum's solution is to appeal to Mill's harm principle. Nussbaum's solution implicitly indicates one merit Mill's utilitarian theory has over Sen's capability approach. We should not forget that the aim of Mill's *On Liberty*, where the so-called harm principle is proposed, is specifically to draw a line between the sphere in which one has absolute freedom to act and the sphere in which one's behaviour may need to be constrained for the general good. Most importantly, the derivation of the harm principle is grounded on the principle of utility. That is to say, in Mill's system, the principle of utility provides the guideline to draw the line between moral and non-moral spheres whereas in Sen's theory such a built-in mechanism is missing and hence he has to appeal to an external rule to secure individual liberties. The problem is that public reasoning, the mechanism Sen invokes to fend off the charge against his theory as being illiberal, indicates only the procedure to reach a solution but says little about the contents of any solution. Then how can we guarantee the outcome of public reasoning is indeed both desirable and liberal?

To sum up, distinguishing moral from non-moral should be one of the main tasks of moral philosophy, for non-moral issues should not be bound by public opinion. If unaware of the distinction, value judgements made by the public are very likely to creep into inappropriate spheres, thereby becoming a threat to individuality.

Pluralism and distributive justice

We discuss pluralism and distributive justice together because the former tends to generate challenges to Sen's capability approach being a theory of distributive justice. Let us first briefly review the policy implication of Sen's theory for the distribution of wealth. Sen believes that his 'capability-centred view gives us a better understanding of what is involved in the challenge of poverty' (Sen, 1992, p. 151). In Sen's view, poverty in a modern sense is not just about low income, but also 'the lack of substantive freedom' (Sen, 1992, p. 151). The key idea in Sen's argument is real freedom, with the most important policy implication Sen intends being: in order to ensure everyone's equal real freedom, the distribution of goods should be unequal, rather than equal. This is due to individuals' differing abilities at converting goods to functionings. For example, Sen explains, 'a disabled person cannot function in the way an able-bodied person can, even if both have exactly the same income' (Sen, 1992, p. 20). Accordingly, distributive justice, for Sen, would give people who have physical or mental disadvantages more commodities than those without such disadvantages.

Sen's account of freedom marks a significant advance for the idea of freedom in economics and economic policy. It turned the attention of economists and policy-makers from treating economic growth as the sole goal of economic activities towards other humane aspects. However, Sen's capability approach as a theory of justice is not free from difficulties at the practice level. The challenges are related to the pluralism of values and methods embedded in Sen's capability approach. The problem is twofold: one relates to the competing functionings; the other to the competition between well-being and agency.

Since Sen's notion of well-being is composed of various functionings, it is natural to ask whether these functionings have equal importance. Charles Beitz, for instance, considers it is a serious problem for Sen's theory that 'not all capabilities stand on the same footing' (Beitz, 1986, p. 287). For example, the capability to move about has a different level of importance to the capability to play basketball. With regard to this challenge, Sen does not think it is a problem for his concept of capacity at all. On the contrary, for Sen, it is an essential part of his theory that different functionings and therefore different capabilities have different significance. It is not his intention, Sen explains, to argue that everything that can be put into the set of capabilities must be important or have equal significance. Instead, what he intends to achieve by proposing a capability-based evaluation is to identify the relevant *dimensions* for evaluation (Sen, 1992, pp. 45–46).

It is true that there is no need to rank the various functionings with a complete and inflexible order. In fact, it is impossible to do so. But it is also true that, in practice, we do need to make a decision about which functioning has more importance and hence should be accorded higher value, especially for policy-making involving allocating resources and transferring pecuniary means. Despite Sen's rejection of ranking the importance of different functionings, it is worth noting that a great number of examples of capability given by Sen relate to people's lives: for instance, being adequately nourished, being in good health, avoiding escapable morbidity, premature mortality, and so on. Sen's long-term observations on poverty in developing countries lead him to remark that 'economic unfreedom, in the form of extreme poverty, can make a person a helpless prey in the violation of other kinds of freedom' (Sen, 1999, p. 8). It is no exaggeration to say that if it lacked the emphasis on these fundamental needs, Sen's capability approach would not be as important as it is.

In addition to ranking functionings, another challenge for the capability approach comes from Sen's distinction between the 'well-being aspect' and the 'agency aspect' of a person when evaluating their achievement. Of these two aspects, Sen considers the well-being aspect more relevant to assessing issues of distributive justice (Sen, 1987, pp. 58–59). However, if Sen insists on the moral importance of both agency and well-being aspects, it requires some principle for determining their relative weight in relation to distributive justice. Otherwise, using Sen's plural framework to provide principles for distributive justice will create various problems in practice, as Arneson notices (Arneson, 1998, pp. 192–195). For instance, if a girl wants to become a musician, to what degree should the government transfer resources from other people to this person to enlarge her set of capabilities? In Sen's capability approach, it seems unclear whether it is the duty of society to help people to reach every goal they value, by means of economic redistribution. If Sen's answer to this would be that radical redistribution of wealth will be required, then it is highly questionable that such redistribution could really be just. The expansion of the capability set of one person usually involves the reduction of the capability sets of others. In the long term, this transfer might result in the enlargement of the sum of all capability sets through some reciprocal process and virtuous circle but, in the short term, the immediate reduction of some people's capability sets is almost inevitable. To be a sensible theory of justice, the capability approach needs to provide some principle to reconcile the conflict between different people's capability sets. It is also possible that Sen does not consider that a government has any duty to guarantee people the resources necessary for the lives they have reasons to value. If so, then the question remains: what is the criterion within the capability approach which enables us to draw the boundary between the capabilities that should and should not be guaranteed by society?

8 Hayek versus Mill

Equality before the law versus equal real freedom for all

While criticizing the utilitarian theory of justice, Rawls and Sen rarely refer to Mill. When mentioning Mill, both are usually sympathetic with him. By contrast, Hayek is specifically critical of Mill. Despite their generally favourable stance, Rawls and Sen seem to believe that Mill's utilitarianism, like all other variants, is indifferent to distribution, while Hayek blames Mill for his advocacy of distributive justice. The reasons behind Hayek's criticism of Mill's theory of justice are very different to those behind Rawls's and Sen's criticisms of utilitarianism: hence they deserve separate examination.

Hayek on social justice

Hayek is well known for his hostility towards the notion of social justice. There are two main reasons why Hayek argues against the idea: first, he believes that the idea of social justice is meaningless in a market economy; second, he considers that the pursuit of social justice threatens individual liberty.

To understand why Hayek is against the idea of social justice, it is necessary to understand his idea of justice. It is important to note that Hayek does not reject the *concept* of justice, despite being critical of the idea of social justice. On the contrary, justice plays an essential role in his social theory, since Hayek considers that 'justice in the sense of rules of just conduct is indispensable for the intercourse of free men' (Hayek, 1982, vol. 2, p. 97). A chief function of justice as rules of conduct is to secure the protected domains in which individuals can pursue their own purposes (Hayek, 1982, vol. 2, p. 37; Mack, 1983, p. 571). This is the essence of Hayek's advocacy of 'the rule of law': these domains preserve individual liberty by preventing individuals from the intervention enforced by other's will. In other words, justice plays a significant role in Hayek's social theory because justice is the consistent application of a set of end-independent rules of conduct which serve 'the formation of a spontaneous order', the core of Hayek's social theory (Hayek, 1982, vol. 2, p. 31).

For Hayek, the idea of justice in this sense characterizes the condition for the idea of justice to be applicable, that is, there must be someone who can be assigned responsibility for the intended or foreseeable results of human action (Hayek, 1982, vol. 2, p. 70). In short, 'justice presupposes the deliberate agency of a person or persons' (Lukes, 1997, p. 69).[1] It follows that justice is an attribute of human actions.

With this concept of justice in mind, it is not difficult to understand why Hayek believes that it does not make sense at all to apply the notion of justice to the market-determined distribution. For Hayek, 'just' and 'unjust' can be used to describe 'the actions of individuals or the concerted actions of many individuals, or the actions of organizations', but not 'a factual situation' or 'a state of affairs' unless someone is 'responsible for bringing it about or allowing it to come about' (Hayek, 1982, vol. 2, pp. 31–32). Given that there is not a single designer or planner in market order, it is simply 'a category mistake' to refer to the distribution caused by the market order as a matter of justice or injustice (Hayek, 1982, vol. 2, p. 31; Lukes, 1997, p. 71). Consequently, the market-determined distribution must be '*neither* just *nor* unjust', and judgements about its justice 'meaningless'. This is the major point of Hayek's argument in the second volume of his book *Law, Legislation and Liberty – The Mirage of Social Justice* (Hayek, 1982, pp. xv–xvi; MacLeod, 1983b, p. 579; Feser, 1997, p. 595).

Although, using Hayek' the idea of social justice is meaningless for a market outcome, social justice can be meaningful for an outcome provided there is someone who can be held 'responsible for bringing it about or allowing it to come about' (Hayek, 1982, vol. 2, pp. 31–32). Accordingly, the idea of social justice does make sense in certain conditions, such as within an organization or within a centralized or command economy (Hayek, 1982, vol. 2, p. 69; Lukes, 1997, pp. 67–68; Feser, 1997, pp. 585–586). Moreover, in these circumstances social justice means distributing income according to some moral standard, such as according to merit or need, or to achieve equality of holdings (Feser, 1997, p. 591). If social justice means distributing income according to merit or deserts of services 'to society', then, in order to meet the aim, in Hayek's view, there must be an authority to judge each person's merit (Hayek, 1982, vol. 2, p. 85). Once this principle is accepted as *the* principle of distribution, Hayek insists, it has to be carried out precisely (Johnston, 1997b, p. 608). Consequently, the authority will acquire dominant power in the procedure of distribution and will inevitably influence people's choices of activities. Because people then make choices based not on their own knowledge but on others' will, their seeming choices, according to Hayek's definition of liberty, are not really free ones. If social justice is equated with distributing income or wealth equally among people, the government will interfere with people's decisions and economic activities even more gravely.

Mill's influence on the formulation of Hayek's views on social justice should not be neglected, given that Hayek frequently referred to Mill in his discussion of social justice. It is no exaggeration to say that Hayek's conception of social justice is founded on Mill's idea of social justice, even though the version in Hayek's mind is in reality a distortion of Mill's theory.

One of the main themes that is repeated in Hayek's works and speeches throughout the 1970s and 1980s is that 'Mill, by trying to defend "social justice", had fostered socialism' (Légé, 2008, p. 212). Hayek's reproach against Mill for the prevalence of the idea of social justice in the twentieth century appears frequently in his work, yet two instances where Hayek cites Mill very clearly demonstrate the strong influence of Mill's theory on Hayek's views of social justice. The first appears in *The Mirage of Social Justice*, where Hayek cites Mill's statements on social and distributive justice and remarks that it is the origin of the contemporary conception of social justice which 'leads straight to full-fledged socialism' (Hayek, 1982, vol. 2, pp. 63–64). The two excerpts quoted by Hayek are:

> society should treat all equally well who have deserved equally well of it, that is, who have deserved equally well absolutely. This is the highest abstract standard of social and distributive justice; towards which all institutions, and the efforts of all virtuous citizens should be made is the utmost degree to converge.
>
> (Mill, *CW, X*: 257; cited by Hayek, 1982, vol. 2, p. 63)

and

> it is universally considered just that each person should obtain that (whether good or evil) which he deserves; and unjust that he should obtain a good, or be made to undergo an evil, which he does not deserve. This is perhaps the clearest and most emphatic form in which the idea of justice is conceived by the general mind. As it involves the idea of desert, the question arises of what constitutes desert.
>
> (Mill, *CW, X*: 242; cited by Hayek, 1982, vol. 2, p. 63)

According to Hayek, the above two quotations from Mill are responsible for the modern meaning of social justice, namely, 'the treatment by society of the individuals according to their deserts', or to achieve 'a particular pattern of distribution' (Hayek, 1982, vol. 2, p. 64). Further, deserts can mean either 'performance or merit' or 'needs' assessed by an authority.

The other argument of Hayek shows that Mill's significant influence on Hayek relates to Mill's famous distinction between the laws of production and distribution. According to Légé, Hayek believes that Mill's persistence in the absurd notion of social justice is partly due to his erroneous distinction between the laws of production and the laws of distribution.[2] In his article *The Muddle of the Middle*, Hayek quotes Mill's distinction between the production and distribution:

> 'The laws and conditions of the production of wealth,' he argued, 'partake of the character of physical truth.... It is not so with the Distribution of Wealth. That is a matter of human institutions only. *The things once there* [!] Mankind, individually and collectively, can do with them as they like. They can place them at the disposal of whoever they please and on whatever terms' (P.O.P.E., II, 1, §1). To rub it in he repeats later, 'Of the two

> great departments of Political Economy, the production of wealth and its distribution, the consideration of values has to do with the latter only' (ibid. III, 1, §1).
>
> (Hayek, 1983, pp. 92–93, emphasis in original)

An important motive for Hayek to cite Mill in the article is to argue that Mill should be blamed for smuggling socialist ideas into economics by inventing a new notion of social justice (Hayek, 1983, pp. 91–92). This suggests that Hayek's interpretation of Mill's distinction between the laws of production and distribution closely relates to his opposition to social justice. Hayek considers Mill's distinction false, and therefore that his idea of social or distributive justice, grounded on this distinction, is also false.

Hayek's hostility towards social justice can be seen as partly the result of misreading Mill's discussion of social justice. In particular, his argument that the demand for social justice threatens individual liberty is largely related to his reading of Mill's conception of social justice as distributing income in accordance with merits or needs. The following section will analyse Hayek's reading of Mill and demonstrate why Hayek's criticisms do not in fact undermine Mill's theory of justice.

Evaluating Hayek's reading of Mill

In Chapter 4, we noticed that the statement 'society should treat all equally well who have deserved equally well of it, that is, who have deserved equally well absolutely' is a formal and abstract standard of social and distributive justice. The standard itself does not stipulate desert to be merit or need, nor does it require 'material equality' as Hayek suggests. In fact, Mill often considers that absolutely equal distribution of income is unjust.

Another important reason underlying Hayek's opposition to Mill's idea of distributive justice is his objection to Mill's distinction between the laws of production and those of distribution. Hayek is undoubtedly right in claiming that production and distribution are not unrelated aspects of the economic process in a market economy.[3] Even the defenders of Mill's distinction do not deny this.[4] Hayek is also right in disputing the conventional view of social justice as simply pursuing a particular result of distribution. Nonetheless, it is arguable whether Mill's distinction between laws of production and distribution actually contains those errors which Hayek imputes to it.

Hayek's reading of Mill's distinction suggests a combination of three factors: first, that the activities of production and distribution are totally unrelated in Mill's economic theory; second, that Mill's distinction between the laws of production and distribution is a distinction between technological matters and moral ones; third, that for Mill, the issue of distribution is to choose a particular pattern of distribution of income or wealth, rather than to choose a system of rules for distribution. This triple combination is the target of Hayek's criticisms of the distinction between the laws of production and distribution. Hayek's arguments are compelling, yet they seem to be targeted at an apocryphal version of Mill.

First, Mill's claim that the laws of production have a different nature from that of the laws of distribution does not imply that the activities of production are unrelated to those of distribution. In spite of some misleading statements within Mill's own arguments,[5] it would be rash to suggest that 'Mill divorced distribution from production as if these two aspects of the economic process were separate realms' (Smith, 1985, pp. 267–268).[6] In fact, it is hard to deny that Mill recognizes the importance of the system of distribution on individual incentives and consequently on production. His advocacy for abolishment of cottier tenancy in Ireland and his concerns about slavery and communism are all related to his full realization of the impact of distribution on production.[7]

Second, the contrast between the laws of production and the laws of distribution is not a contrast between rules of technology and rules of morality, but between the laws of production, derived from 'collocations of both the laws of matter and those of mind', and the laws of distribution, which are solely 'dependent upon the laws of mind' (Smith, 1985, pp. 278–279). However, Mill's discussions, as Hollander comments, do not make the purpose of his distinction evident; as a result, Mill's distinction, understood literally, becomes a brittle one (Hollander, 1985, pp. 222–223). A major confusion about Mill's distinction is caused by the fact that Mill stresses the malleability of distribution in his *Principles of Political Economy*, where the set of rules of distribution should be treated as given, according to the scope of political economy confined by Mill. According to Vardaman Smith's analysis,

> [the] flexibility Mill associates with distribution is located in the inherent indeterminacy of the opinions and feelings of the ruling porting of society, which gives rise to rules and customs […] However, the laws that generate these opinions and feelings are […] *outside* the purview of political economy […] In marked contrast to the examination of the laws that actually generate the rules and customs found in a particular society, it is the consequences which follow once a particular set has been chosen (and the particular initial conditions identified) which Mill argues political economy should examine.
>
> (Smith, 1985, pp. 280–281, emphasis original)

Hollander shares a similar view and his argument goes further (Hollander, 1985, p. 222). If the above interpretation of Mill's distinction is indeed valid

> there seems no reason to treat the laws of distribution any differently from the laws of production: Given the state of opinion – and the corresponding distributive system – there will be certain results which follow and which are as much 'immutable' as are the laws of production. This is indeed precisely what Mill proceeds to say: 'We have here to consider, not the cause, but the consequences, of the rules according to which wealth may be distributed.

Those, at least, are as little arbitrary, and have as much the character of physical laws, as the laws of production' (200).

(Hollander, 1985, p. 222)

Accordingly, it is reasonable to conclude that Mill's distinction between the laws of production and distribution is invulnerable to Hayek's criticisms if considered in context. It follows that Hayek's opposition to Mill's idea of distributive justice needs to be reconsidered, since Hayek's opposition is partly grounded on his objection to his own interpretation of Mill's distinction between production and distribution. Nevertheless, it has to be admitted that Mill's distinction is confusing, or even unnecessary, from the perspective of political economy *alone*.

Distributive justice and economic freedom

In Chapter 5, we saw that in Mill's system the pursuit of distributive justice does not threaten individual freedom. It instead aims to protect real freedom for all. This view contrasts with Hayek's assertion that the pursuit of social justice will endanger individual freedom. In addition to the difference between Mill's and Hayek's ideas of social justice, the difference between their ideas of liberty also explains why the relationship between distributive justice and economic freedom diverges in their theories.

At the beginning of the *Constitution of Liberty*, Hayek clearly defines liberty and freedom for his discourse:

> We are concerned in this book with that condition of men in which coercion of some by others is reduced as much as is possible in society. This state we shall describe throughout as a state of liberty or freedom [...] The state in which a man is not subject to coercion by the arbitrary will of another or others is often also distinguished as 'individual' or 'personal' freedom, and whenever we want to remind the reader that it is in this sense that we are using the word 'freedom,' we shall employ that expression.
>
> (Hayek, 1960, p. 11)

In short, for Hayek, liberty means the absence of coercion by others. According to this definition, Hayek's conception of liberty is a negative one, namely, freedom from others' coercion.[8] Yet it is important to note that the liberty Hayek advocates is not unlimited liberty, but 'liberty under the law', for he is clearly aware that there must be conflicts between unregulated liberties. What he means by the law here is not legality, but general, abstract rules regarding what the law ought to be.

In his well-known book *On Liberty*, Mill does not start his discourse by giving a similarly exact but abstract definition of liberty as does Hayek. Instead, Mill begins with the distinction between liberty from the suppression of the ruling class and liberty from the interference of the public. He then confines his discussion to the latter. Nevertheless, we can consider the following to be Mill's definition of liberty:

> The only freedom which deserves the name, is that of pursuing our own good in our own way, so long as we do not attempt to deprive others of theirs, or impede their efforts to obtain it.
>
> (Mill, *CW, XVIII*: 226)

At first glance, Mill's definition looks similar to Hayek's. Yet the precondition required by his conception of liberty differentiates his theory from Hayek's.

The traditional dichotomy between positive and negative freedoms has a strong impact on views of the relationship between freedoms and material conditions. Generally speaking, people who support unconstrained capitalism tend to think in terms of *negative* freedom, 'the freedom *from* interference by other people', while people who are sympathetic with strongly regulated capitalism or with socialism value *positive* freedom, 'the actual *ability to do* things that we want to do' (Nathanson, 1998, p. 69, emphasis in original). Those who think in terms of negative freedom usually deny there is any relationship between freedoms and the possession of goods, while those who think in terms of positive freedom normally assert a proportional correlation between freedoms and the amount of possessions.

Hayek is a representative of the former view and unreservedly denies that the range or eligibility of an agent's options will affect their individual freedom:

> Whether he is free or not does not depend on the range of choice but on whether he can expect to shape his course of action in accordance with his present intentions, or whether somebody else has power so to manipulate the conditions as to make him act according to that person's will rather than his own.
>
> (Hayek, 1960, p. 13)

With this point of view, Hayek argues that 'we may be free and yet miserable' (Hayek, 1960, p. 18). According to Hayek's definition of liberty, as long as there is no coercion from the will of others, we are free, even if we have so few choices open to us that we are unable to avoid starving (Hayek, 1960, p. 18).

Nevertheless, it is interesting to note that Hayek once claimed that a man's freedom may be curtailed by others' withdrawal of their services if these are crucial to his existence (Hayek, 1960, pp. 135–136; Gray, 1989, p. 101).[9] Such a claim in fact implies that to be free requires more than just the absence of coercion. Human existence is not merely a phenomenon of spirit, but also requires a minimum of material conditions for physical survival. It follows that Hayek's assertion that we may be free and yet starving makes sense only if we can choose to starve or choose *not* to.

Unlike Hayek's, Mill's conception of liberty cannot easily be categorized either as positive or as negative freedom. On the one hand, in Mill's mind more wealth does not always lead to more freedoms. On the other hand, without a certain amount of materials, complete independence is also unlikely to be achieved. The first point is supported by Mill's uncompromising position on liberty:

> The perfection both of social arrangements and of practical morality would be, to secure to all persons complete independence and freedom of action, subject to no restriction but that of not doing injury to others: and the education which taught or the social institutions which require them to exchange the control of their own actions for any amount of comfort or affluence, or to renounce liberty for the sake of equality, would deprive them of one of the most elevated characteristics of human nature.
>
> (Mill, *CW, II*: 208–209)

Generally speaking, more wealth implies more choices to exercise the power of satisfying desires, but it does not imply more freedoms in other aspects. If Mill believed that more wealth always leads to more freedoms, exchanging liberty for affluence would not be an issue for him. Mill's worries regarding the sacrifice of liberty as the price for greater wealth imply that, in his view, there is no proportional correlation between the amount of wealth and the degree of liberty.

However, for Mill, the idea of liberty cannot be completely cut off from the issue of material conditions either. Due to their physical constitutions, human beings need a minimum level of means to survive. Therefore, they should not be considered entirely free if they face a threat to this minimum level of subsistence. Sufficient means for survival consequently should be deemed to be a precondition of liberty. 'After the means of subsistence are assured', Mill wrote in *the Principles of Political Economy*, 'the next in strength of the personal wants of human beings is liberty' (Mill, *CW, II*: 208). The same idea is expressed even more explicitly in *The Subjection of Women*: 'After the primary necessities of food and raiment, freedom is the first and strongest want of human nature' (Mill, *CW, XXI*: 336). This idea constitutes one of the foundations of his economic theory. Nevertheless, once beyond this threshold for survival, there is no necessarily correlative relationship between liberty and possessions.

The limitation of Hayek's theory of justice and liberty

So far we have seen that Hayek's criticisms cannot defeat Mill's theory of justice. The rest of this chapter will argue that Hayek's theory of justice and liberty is in fact less comprehensive than Mill's. It will first show the deficiency in Hayek's idea of equality and then show the limitation of his theory of liberty in providing policy guidance.

In spite of Hayek denouncing the pursuit of equality as being the enemy of liberty in most cases, it should not be neglected that equality in fact plays a crucial role in his theory of justice. It is Hayek's view that equality before the law has been the great aim of the struggle for liberty in human history and that the extension of this principle of equality to the rules of moral and social conduct constitutes the chief part of democratic spirit (Hayek, 1960, p. 85). Not only is equality before the law compatible with liberty, it is also conducive and necessary to liberty. Nevertheless, for Hayek, equality before the law is the only type of equality that is compatible with a free society, in which individual liberty is 'bound to produce inequality in many respects' (Hayek, 1960, p. 85).

We can use the distinction between the practice and the concept of justice introduced in Chapter 4 to analyse Hayek's notion of equality. Equality before the law concerns mainly the practice of justice: the government has to enforce the law impartially, and this requires ignoring information which is irrelevant to the law. In regard to the concept of justice, Hayek believes that equality before the law means that the *content* of the law has to be set up in accord with the idea that 'people should be treated alike in spite of the fact that they are different' (Hayek, 1960, p. 86). However, equality before the law in this sense concerns only the formal part of the concept of justice. It provides no information on the substantive content of the law. In fact, Hayek recognizes the necessity of treating people differently as part of substantive justice:

> From the fact that people are very different it follows that, if we treat them equally, the result must be inequality in their actual position, and that the only way to place them in an equal position would be to treat them differently.
>
> (Hayek, 1960, p. 87)

Nevertheless, his description of equality before the law is unable to provide the criteria to judge in which case different people should be treated differently and in what way, and in which case differences between people should be ignored.

In contrast to equality before the law, equal material benefits and distribution in accordance with equal proportion to merit or exertion – which Hayek considers to be so-called social justice – are the substantive part of the concept of justice. Strictly speaking, equality before the law and equality of materials or equal distribution in proportion to merit are two *incomparable* ideas because they are concepts belonging to two different levels. Since they are not comparable, there is no problem of incompatibility. Nonetheless, it is worth noting that despite failing to differentiate equality before the law in the sense of practice from that of concept, Hayek does acknowledge the distinction, though rather vaguely, by stating that equality before the law means *more* than that any law should apply equally to all (Hayek, 1960, p. 209). If so, what is that 'more'? Hayek is not satisfied with the two criteria that 'law must not make irrelevant distinctions' and that 'it must not discriminate between persons for reasons which have no connection with the purpose of the law', but nor can he find a better one (Hayek, 1960, p. 209). In fact, equal treatment is merely an empty form of justice. It says nothing about how to make the laws. Once we turn to giving the laws some content, we create artificial categorization for the purpose of equal treatment within the same category. However, because of the fear that 'classification in abstract terms can always be carried to the point at which [...] the classes singled out consist only of particular known persons or even a single individual', it is impossible for Hayek to accept the idea of substantive justice (Hayek, 1960, p. 209). In the end, he can only insist that the ideal of equality before the law is not meaningless, while admitting that it is solely an ideal, 'without fully determining the goal' (Hayek, 1960, p. 209).

In addition to the deficiency in Hayek's idea of equality in providing guidance for policy or content for law, his theory of justice, fundamentally grounded on his theory of liberty, suffers similar problems. We can use Mill's and Hayek's contrasting positions on inheritance taxation as an example to support this claim. Mill advocates highly progressive inheritance taxation, whereas Hayek argues against it.

It is important to note that Mill's advocacy of a high tax rate on inheritance is not based on the socialist ideal of justice, but on the spirit of the institution of private property. Mill invokes the opinion of supporters to define the true meaning of the institution of private property within capitalism. 'The institution of Property', Mill remarks, 'is upheld and commended principally as being the means by which labour and frugality are insured their reward, and mankind enabled to emerge from indigence' (Mill, *CW, V*: 712). In other words, private property is meant to be a promising scheme for providing 'the guarantee to individuals of the fruits of their own labour and abstinence' (Mill, *CW, II*: 208). Therefore, Mill considers it to be violating the spirit of private property if the law allows the main source for obtaining huge amounts of property to be gifts or inheritance, rather than people making their own effort. Moreover, when inequality reaches a certain degree, it not only fails to promote the aim of the institution of private property but also provokes conflict (Mill, *CW, II*: 208).

It needs to be stressed that advocating highly progressive inheritance taxation does not mean Mill prefers absolute equality of wealth. On the contrary, Mill never believed absolutely equal distribution of wealth to be a desirable pattern of distribution. In fact, he believes that if we accept the institution of private property, then we have to accept the unequal result as well, as mentioned in Chapter 6.

However, the acceptance of inequality requires a commitment from government to diminish the inequality of opportunities either by instruction or by legislation (Mill, *CW, III*: 811). The limitation on the amount of inheritance suggested by Mill can be considered as a means to provide *ex ante* equality or equal opportunities (Ekelund and Walker, 1996, p. 575). This is to ensure a minimum level of liberty rather than those egalitarian demands which, as Hayek claims,[10] stem from 'envy'. Since Mill believes that the spirit of private property is to protect the fruit of one's labour then, for the public good, what needs to be restrained is 'not the fortunes which are earned, but those which are unearned' (Mill, *CW, II*: 225). It follows that though everyone should have the right to dispose of their own properties, as part of the institution of private property, they are not entitled to a right 'to lavish it in enriching some one individual, beyond a certain maximum' (Mill, *CW, II*: 225).

Nevertheless, given that the right of bequest is considered to be part of people's right of property, certain rules are needed to regulate government's power to impose inheritance taxation to ensure that the right of bequest is properly protected. For this reason, Mill proposes one restriction on government interference on freedom of bequest, that is, in the case that descendants are unable to provide for themselves, the government's power of taxing should be bound to make a reasonable provision of them (Mill, *CW*, *III*: 887).

This condition is crucial to the scheme of inheritance taxation which Mill advocates. It demonstrates the integrity of Mill's thinking. It was mentioned earlier that the principle behind high levels of inheritance tax is for equality of opportunities and therefore for the freedom of everyone. This condition is also for the freedom, but not for the freedom of uncertain persons but of inheritors. Hence, it would not be a complete understanding of Mill's theory of inheritance taxation if we only see the idea of justice without paying attention to the principle of freedom within it.

In contrast to Mill, the unearned nature of inheritance is not the main concern in Hayek's discussion of inheritance taxation (Hayek, 1960, pp. 90–91). Hayek believes that inheritance, even though being unmerited, can sit comfortably with the institution of private property. His view reflects the nature he attributes to the market. That the market can reward people according to their merit is a popular justification among advocates of the free market. It may surprise some people that Hayek, a defender of the free market system, in fact strongly disputes this belief. Hayek does not consider that the market provides any guarantee of reward in accord with exertion or performance at all. Therefore, he does not think inheritance is inconsistent with the market system, even though it is unearned income.

Nevertheless, neither does Hayek dismiss inheritance taxation because he believes it may in fact have positive functions, even claiming that

> inheritance taxes could, of course, be made an instrument toward greater social mobility and greater dispersion of property, and consequently, may have to be regarded as important tools of a truly liberal policy.
>
> (Hayek, 1949, p. 118)

However, once he affirms that inheritance taxation is a desirable institution, Hayek has to face the problem of what kind of scheme would be best. This is an inevitable question, even though Hayek disputes the intention of *designing* social institutions.

Modern laws on inheritance taxation are the result of human deliberation, even though there may remain some inexplicable historical elements which are inherited from the customs in the past. If we think the present law on inheritance needs amendment, we are actually appealing to our intelligence and rationality. Hayek evades the question 'whether liberty demands unlimited freedom of bequest' when he tries to prove that 'people ought to be free to pass on to children or others such material possessions' (Hayek, 1960, p. 91). Yet nowhere does he show the attempt to answer this question. If we try to answer the question for Hayek, we will encounter serious difficulty for it is impossible to find his limitation on the freedom of bequest from his idea of liberty or his rule of law. There are more problems about the design of inheritance taxation. For instance, how much inheritance can be exempted from tax? Should a minor be treated differently from adult children? Should the law give them more allowances? If yes, to what extent, and what is the rationale? Moreover, what is the optimal structure for tax rates? It seems the same logic as income tax is not applicable. Since inheritance is not earned income, a progressive tax rate will not affect the relative rates of rewards from different kinds of work. Hayek would need other reasons to justify proportional tax rates. All these are questions we cannot escape if we intend to introduce or maintain an inheritance taxation system in a society. Considering these practical difficulties, which are largely ignored in Hayek's theory of liberty, it is perhaps fair to claim that Mill's utilitarianism, which takes happiness as the ultimate test of all human conduct, is a more complete theory to secure real freedoms in real life.

Conclusions

Prospect – the continuing relevance of Mill's utilitarianism today

For a long time, John Stuart Mill has been portrayed by many philosophers as self-contradictory and incompetent in his construction of a unified system of philosophy. His *Utilitarianism* is widely read but often used as a negative demonstration. Despite the wide recognition of his contribution to political and social reform in such issues as suffrage and women's rights, Mill won respect mostly as a liberal activist, but not so much as a coherent philosopher whose theory can consistently support liberty. In the concluding chapter of his *Liberalisms*, Gray writes: 'Mill can for the most part be only an eminent Victorian' and 'Mill's project of a radical revision in liberalism is a failure, and his predominant liberalism has as little to say to us as it did to his contemporaries' (Gray, 1989, p. 229). Gray is an outstanding scholar and much of his analysis of Mill is groundbreaking and insightful, but this book argues that his verdict of Mill as being outmoded is premature.

Contrary to many commentaries, this book is devoted to demonstrating that Mill's utilitarianism coherently supports justice and liberty and it seeks to explain why the common charges levied against utilitarianism are inapplicable to Mill. So far, we have analysed and reinterpreted Mill's moral philosophy by contextualizing his writing and arguments, re-examining them in the context of the intellectual and historical background. To a large extent, the reading of Mill in the previous chapters is retrospective. In this concluding chapter, the author wishes to demonstrate that Mill's philosophy is not only an enlightened theory in retrospect, but also a progressive theory even from today's point of view. We will first discuss the implications of recent advances in science for Mill's foundational theories of epistemology and psychology from the theoretical perspective, before turning to the significance of his utilitarianism as a moral philosophy to today's real world.

A forward-looking moral philosophy

In many ways, Mill's construction of his system of knowledge allows his moral philosophy to be a forward-looking theory. Above all, his separation of art and science plays a fundamental role in his system of knowledge and the merit of this distinction becomes clear when applied to practical reasoning. We discussed in Chapter 2 how the art and the science have distinctive natures and tasks and how each one cannot work properly without the assistance of the other.

Knowledge has always been an important foundation of human actions, both individual and collective. The advance of science equips us to better understand the world. Science itself cannot tell us how to act, but it provides important information which enables us to make a better decision about how to act. The cooperation of science and art is hence essential to the progress of moral philosophy. The development of neuroscience in recent years deserves some special attention here, since how it influences, or claims to be able to influence moral philosophy appears to be unique in the sense that it might enable philosophers to answer the long-lasting debate between teleologists and deontologists over the first principle of morality.

Neuroscience and Mill's theories of epistemology and psychology

In the last decade or so, the booming study of neuroscience and moral psychology has opened a new window into ethical studies. With the aid of technology, scientists are now able to use equipment such as functional magnetic resonance imaging (fMRI) machines to examine neural activities in the human brain while moral judgments are being made. Neuroscientific research is groundbreaking and, it has been suggested, may have significant normative implications.

The dual-process theory of moral judgement, a theory proposed by Joshua Greene, a Harvard psychologist, is particularly relevant to our discussion here. Greene makes an illuminating analogy with the dual-mode of a camera to illustrate how the human brain works. According to Greene, the human brain has the same general dual-mode design as dual-mode cameras: on the one hand, humans have a variety of automatic settings in the sense that we rely on reflexes and intuitions to guide our behaviour; on the other hand, our brains also have a manual mode in the sense that there is a reasoning system which allows us to guide our behaviour by formulating behavioural plans based on detailed knowledge of the specific situations and general knowledge about the world: in short, we have the capacity to think and to reason. Moreover, the automatic settings occur in the area of brain that governs emotion, while the manual mode is processed in the area of brain that governs cognition. Note that the view that human brains have a dual-process phenomenon itself is not new to scientists or psychologists.[1] The original contribution of the experiments done by Greene and his colleagues is to demonstrate that the act of making moral judgements shares this same feature: moral judgement is influenced by both automatic emotional responses and conscious reasoning. Moreover, Greene's dual-process theory of moral judgement suggests that 'characteristically deontological judgments are preferentially supported by automatic emotional responses, while characteristically consequentialist judgments are preferentially supported by conscious reasoning and allied processes of cognitive control'. He calls this proposition the 'Central Tension Principle' (Greene, forthcoming).

Not surprisingly, the implications of this revolutionary approach to ethics are controversial. One of the most notable criticisms rejecting the significance of neuroscience to normative ethics is made by Harvard philosophers Selim Berker (2009) and Frances Kamm (2011). Joshua Greene, one of the leading scholars in the field of moral psychology, has become the key target of Berker and Kamm. According to Berker (2009), it is Greene's view that if his empirical hypothesis regarding dual neural processes and moral judgements is true, it would give us good grounds to privilege our utilitarian/consequentialist intuitions and to discount our deontological intuitions. Echoing Berker, Kamm (2011) also suggests that the findings of Greene's experiments have led some to believe that 'consequentialist moral reasoning is more likely to produce correct moral judgments than forms of reasoning that involve deontological constraints' (Kamm, 2011, p. 331). If what Berker and Kamm attributed to Greene was indeed what Greene claimed, then Greene would be wrong for conflating what is and what ought to be. However, there seem to be misunderstandings in both Berker's and Kamm's articles regarding the purpose of Greene's experiments and the conclusion Greene drew from the applications of his experiments. Greene indeed suggests that neuroscientific evidence can help us make better moral judgments, but he does not claim that we can derive normative conclusions *solely* from experimental findings. On this specific point, the author is by Greene's side even though this does not imply any endorsement of Greene's reasoning and his normative conclusions based on his experiments. Here we do not intend to enter the debate between Berker, Kamm and Greene, nor will we explore the normative significance or insignificance of neuroscience. For the purpose of our study, we will focus on the relevance of Greene's work to an old philosophical debate in which Mill was engaged. In a nutshell, Greene's research suggests that 'moral psychology looks much like the rest of judgments and decision-making'. If the process of making moral judgements is indeed indifferent from other judgements, as Greene demonstrates, then one of the most important debates between Mill and British ethical intuitionists has been answered by Greene's research.

In Chapter 1, we saw how fighting against ethical intuitionism was one of Mill's main aims throughout his life and it is an important theme in his ethical writings. The purpose of fighting against ethical intuitionism was not purely for his intellectual interest. On the contrary, Mill believes that the ethics advocated by the influential intuitionists in his time had become a powerful weapon of reactionaries to oppose progressive social and political reforms. Among these forces, the sense of justice was one of the strongest forces used by intuitionists to oppose utilitarianism. They argued that utilitarianism cannot possibly be the theory of morality because our sense of justice is so distinct and different from the feeling we have towards utility. Justice must be a command given by the divine being. Such a view was often invoked to justify the denial of women's and the poor's claim to happiness in nineteenth-century England. In order to fight against this reactionary force, Mill considered it necessary to eradicate the false epistemological belief on which ethical intuitionism was grounded.

According to eighteenth- and nineteenth-century intuitionists like Sedgwick and Whewell, moral sense is a distinct innate faculty. Human beings make moral judgements by appealing to their moral sense and conscience. For Whewell, morality is rested on innate conscience. Note that the way these philosophers used the term intuition is not exactly the same as moral intuition in modern psychological experiments. Unlike the former, the latter does not necessarily suggest that the intuition is inbuilt as a distinct faculty. For instance, Greene argues that intuitions 'need not be "innate" or "hard-wired". They can be acquired or modified through cultural learning [...] and through individual experiences' (Greene, forthcoming). The phrases 'need not be' and 'can be' may give an impression that it is still possible for intuitions to be innate. However, Greene's 'cognitive miracle' argument excludes this possibility. According to Greene, for our automatic settings to function well, their design must be shaped by trial-and-error experience. 'Genetic transmission', 'cultural transmission' and 'learning from personal experience' are the only three mechanisms known to endow human automatic cognitive processes with the information needed for them to function well.[2] It would be a cognitive miracle if any of our automatic settings were to function well without the information provided through these three mechanisms. In other words, according to Greene, cognitive science suggests that intuitions with automatic settings must come from experience; if it does not come from our own personal experience, it must come from someone else's experience. For that reason, Greene uses the term moral 'intuition' in the sense that it does not require a deliberate cognitive process, but it does not follow from this that moral intuitions are innate. The contents of moral intuitions must come from experience.

Greene's research shows that making moral judgements, like making other types of judgement, requires various faculties: there is no specific faculty that is distinctively responsible for making moral judgements. If Greene's research on how human beings formulate their moral judgements is correct, it proves that there is no innate moral sense which tells us what is right and what is wrong. It follows that human beings have no a priori moral knowledge. If so, the ground of ethical intuitionism which Mill fought against will collapse and Mill would be the winner of the old philosophical debate between him and moral intuitionists over the source of moral senses. It is important to emphasize that this in no way suggests that utilitarianism as a moral theory is the winner of the debate. What we say is that as far as the scientific evidence can demonstrate, the psychological and epistemological theory on which Mill's utilitarianism is grounded is closer to the truth than the one upon which ethical intuitionism was grounded. If the scientific evidence of neuropsychology has proved something, it is the soundness of the scientific foundation of Mill's moral theory, not the rightness or desirability of his moral theory per se.

In one of his most recent articles, Greene (forthcoming) opens the article with the following thesis which he intends to defend:

> Science can advance ethics by revealing the hidden inner workings of our moral judgments, especially the ones we make intuitively. Once those inner

> workings are revealed we may have less confidence in some of our judgments and the ethical theories that are (explicitly or implicitly) based on them.

It is impressive to see that the boom of the cognitive science of ethics today was anticipated by Mill's work more than 150 years ago. More remarkably, when psychology was still struggling for its scientific status as an independent discipline, Mill had grounded his moral philosophy on the psychological and epistemological foundation which is demonstrated to be correct by the latest evidence of neuroscience and psychology. Mill's thought would be no doubt an invaluable source for researchers who share similar goals to Greene. In return, scientists and philosophers will be able to answer many questions which Mill was unable to answer due to the limited understanding of human nature, partly as a consequence of the backward state of science at his time.

Recent research into happiness and Mill's utilitarianism

Mill's philosophy has more than this to offer in advancing the cooperation between science and moral philosophy. Here the author proposes one possible way forward. Science can help us analyse Mill's idea of happiness in a way that traditional philosophy and psychology could not, and in particular his distinction between higher and lower pleasures. This in turn can help us appreciate the strengths and shortcomings of the current studies of well-being and happiness.

Today utilitarianism often encounters the challenge that happiness as a state of mind is not an appropriate criterion of morality due to the subjectivity of feelings and the fact that pleasure may be obtained via the desiring of something not truly desirable. Such challenges are not entirely new. Utilitarianism, by taking happiness as the end of life, has been criticized as 'a doctrine worthy only of swine' (Mill, *CW, X*: 210) for a long time. In response to this criticism, Mill makes a distinction between higher and lower pleasures. Mill's distinction did not quell the objections to utilitarianism; on the contrary, it generated even more controversy. On the one hand, it is argued that people do not always desire higher pleasures more than lower pleasures in the way Mill suggests. On the other hand, it is argued that Mill's distinction of higher and lower pleasures renders his theory elitist or even paternalistic because he suggests that which pleasures are more valuable should be determined by 'competent judges'. These criticisms partly result from the fact that Mill's discussion of the distinction is sometimes vague, but it is also fair to say that a great many of the criticisms result from misreading his intention and arguments. We have analysed Mill's distinction of higher and lower pleasures in Chapter 3 from a purely theoretical perspective. Here we will supplement the analysis with empirical evidence. Before we start to examine how empirical evidence supports Mill's distinction, it is worth emphasizing again the difference between treating the distinction of higher and lower pleasures as a fact and treating it as a moral value judgement.

As pointed out in Chapter 3, a key source of confusion regarding Mill's distinction resides in the fact that his discussion mixes arguments of facts with arguments of moral values. On the factual side, Mill believes that various pleasures differ not only in quantities, but also in qualities. The claim that pleasures differ in quality concerns facts and the claim per se does not involve moral value judgement. In this context, higher pleasures are merely intended by Mill as those pleasures derived from exercising faculties unique to human beings. It is a separate question what normative implications we can obtain from the qualitative difference in pleasures if the difference indeed exists. We may choose to give higher pleasures greater value, like Mill does. Alternatively, we may choose not to grant the qualitative difference any moral significance if there is no good reason in moral terms to justify differential treatment. Before we can argue that pleasures derived from exercising higher faculties are more valuable in moral terms, we need to prove that there is indeed qualitative difference between different pleasures. Science alone cannot tell us whether higher pleasures are more valuable than lower pleasures. Nevertheless, science can help us better understand the nature of pleasures. The more we know about the nature of pleasures, the better our judgement on whether qualitative differences exist between different types of pleasures. If the qualitative difference can be affirmed, science can also help us assess whether higher pleasures deserve to be granted greater value than lower pleasures.

If so, what have we learnt from science about pleasures? In the last two decades, a flood of studies exploring people's subjective well-being has led the study of happiness and pleasures to enter a new era. It is not our purpose to give a full account of the findings of this line of research. Our focus here is to demonstrate how scientific evidence supports Mill's theory of happiness and pleasures in terms of facts and to suggest how this can further support his utilitarianism as a moral philosophy. We will illustrate how different scientific evidence supports Mill's view that happiness consists of various pleasures and that there is a qualitative difference between higher and lower pleasures. Our contention is that the qualitative difference can be articulated as the different impact of higher and lower pleasures to happiness, despite it being arguable that this might not be exactly the same as what Mill means by the difference between higher and lower pleasures. In addition, we have to admit that the results of the scientific happiness research still require further test to verify their validity. In particular, it requires careful reasoning to suggest the causal relation between variables in the correlation. Nevertheless, the prima facie evidence is consistent with Mill's theory of happiness and some puzzling phenomena, such as the so-called paradox of happiness, can be explained by Mill's distinction of higher and lower pleasures.

Income and happiness

First of all, abundant empirical investigations have shown that there is a strong positive correlation between income and happiness in poor countries, whereas the correlation is unclear in rich countries.[3] We can investigate the relevance of this finding to Mill's distinction of higher and lower pleasures from two aspects. First, we can infer from the positive correlation between income and happiness in poor countries a proposition that people generally feel happier when they have more pecuniary means to satisfy their basic needs. This proposition is consistent with Mill's view of human nature that the utilities attached to a minimum subsistence are paramount to happiness. Grounded on this view of human nature, Mill's utilitarian moral theory grants an overriding value to securing people's minimum subsistence and this is a major guiding principle of his socio-economic policies. The second proposition derived from empirical evidence is that once people are able to afford the necessities of life, increasing levels of affluence matter little to happiness. This indicates that after basic needs are satisfied, the gratification of lower pleasures can no longer make a significant contribution to happiness. This is consistent with Mill's view of human nature that for a human being to be happy it is not just an issue of satisfying the needs required by their lower faculties. It also supports Mill's argument of qualitative differences amongst pleasures in the sense that the pleasure from exercising the higher faculties can bring human beings more lasting happiness.

'Fellow-feeling' and other higher pleasures in relation to happiness

Various researches also support Mill's views regarding how specific higher pleasure promotes happiness. Take fellow-feelings as an example. Fellow-feeling is classified as a higher pleasure by Mill because it requires cultivation by exercising not only the capacity of sympathy but also intellectual capacity. In Mill's view,

> When people who are tolerably fortunate in their outward lot do not find in life sufficient enjoyment to make it valuable to them, the cause generally is, caring for nobody but themselves. To those who have neither public nor private affections, the excitements of life are much curtailed, and in any case dwindle in value as the time approaches when all selfish interests must be terminated by death: while those who leave after them objects of personal affection, and especially those who have also cultivated a fellow-feeling with the collective interests of mankind, retain as lively an interest in life on the eve of death as in the vigour of youth and health.
>
> (Mill, *CW, X*: 215)

In short, for Mill selfishness is one of the most important reasons preventing people from finding happiness and the cultivation of fellow-feeling enhances happiness. In the past, such a view has often been considered merely as the value judgement issuing from a philosopher's pure speculation, even though Mill insists on building his moral philosophy on the science of man. Today we can say that empirical evidence, although still inconclusive, is consistent with Mill's factual judgement that selfishness tends to prevent people from being happy.

According to the contemporary psychological and sociological study of subjective well-being, happy people are indeed less self-focused, more loving, forgiving, trusting, helpful and sociable (e.g. Myers, 1993; Myers and Diener, 1995; Seligman, 2011). If more studies can show this to be true, then we will have more confidence in Mill's moral judgement that selfishness is not conducive to happiness.

Next to selfishness, Mill identifies 'want of mental cultivation' to be the principal cause which makes life unsatisfactory (Mill, *CW, X*: 215). By a 'cultivated mind', Mill does not refer to 'that of a philosopher, but any mind to which the fountains of knowledge have been opened, and which has been taught, in any tolerable degree, to exercise its faculties' (Mill, *CW, X*: 216). Mill believes that a cultivated mind which exercises higher human faculties 'finds sources of inexhaustible interest in all that surrounds it' (Mill, *CW, X*: 216). This view is consistent with the findings of modern happiness research, in particular the study of 'eudaimonic well-being', a part of the mainstream of happiness research initiated by Ryff (1989).

Science, politics, and philosophy of happiness

The scientific research of happiness today shows the continuing relevance of Mill's theory of happiness and pleasures. Moreover, political movements such as those strengthening the legal status of human rights and those developing such concepts as Human Development Index (HDI) and happiness index do not really go beyond what Mill has achieved in his utilitarian philosophy. To a large extent, they are equivalent to the institutionalization of Mill's utilitarianism. In comparison with Rawls's theory of justice and Sen's capability approach, the value of Mill's moral philosophy has been underestimated by many philosophers. Deontological moral and political theories like Rawls's theory of justice are usually believed to be a sounder philosophical foundation for human rights than utilitarianism. In reality, so-called human rights are nothing but what has been recognized as important almost universally to human beings in today's world. In Mill's language, a human right is just the name given to those utilities which are most imperative for everyone, and hence are those for which it is in everyone's interest that they be protected by the rules of society as a matter of justice.[4]

It is said that Sen's capability approach offers a better understanding of human well-being than does utilitarianism. Indeed, it is Sen's capability approach not utilitarianism that inspires and underpins the HDI developed by the United Nations Development Programme (UNDP) and the Equality Measurement Framework (EMF) developed by the British Equality and Human Rights Commission (EHRC) and Government Equalities Office (GEO). However, it is no exaggeration to say that these 'new' concepts of human development are in effect a modern manifestation of Mill's conception of happiness presented in a more systematic and compressed way.[5] A key difference between Mill's conception of happiness and the modern concept of human development is the method of identifying what aspects of life are central to human lives universally or almost universally. Mill mainly relies on observation and introspection, while the modern approach largely relies on survey and consultation. Despite differing in methods, Mill's idea of happiness and the modern theories of human development converge on contents.

The HDI is a measure of human development developed by the UNDP in order to overcome the deficiency of using income, the traditional measure of well-being, to assess the level of people's long-term well-being. The HDI measures the achievements in a country in three basic dimensions of human development, namely, a long and healthy life (health), access to knowledge (education), and a decent standard of living (income).[6] In fact, these are also three fundamental components of happiness identified by Mill. In his view, 'poverty' and 'disease' are the two grand sources of human suffering, the removal of which is essential for the aim of pursuing happiness (Mill, *CW, X*: 216–217). In addition, education is also indispensable for pursuing happiness. As mentioned above, in Mill's view, 'want of mental cultivation' is the second principal cause, next to selfishness, which makes life unhappy (Mill, *CW, X*: 215–216).[7]

Note that the above discussion does not claim that the modern concepts of human development are exactly the same as Mill's conception of happiness. In fact, there are some differences which should not be neglected. For instance, Mill gives income for subsistence paramount weight while giving income beyond subsistence level much less importance. When the amount of income of an individual goes beyond a certain point, Mill assumes that the income will have a negative impact on the individual's happiness. In comparison, the HDI also takes into account the diminishing importance of income by using the logarithm of income for calculating the income index, which is one of the components of the HDI. Nevertheless, the formula of the HDI still suggests a clear positive correlation between income and human development given that the higher level of gross national income (GNI) per capita will always lead to a higher value of HDI.

Moreover, security and subsistence are the two utilities which Mill identifies as universally needed by everyone; hence they are the universal components of happiness. It is intriguing although not surprising to see the similarities between the components which are deemed by Mill as the most fundamental to human happiness and the indicators of 'the central and valuable things in life' selected for the EMF developed by the EHRC and GEO. The first five domains listed by the EMF as the central and valuable freedoms for adults are life, health, physical security, legal security, and education and learning. These are in essence equivalent to the fundamental components of happiness identified by Mill, namely security, subsistence, the removal of disease and poverty, and education. The other five are mostly the higher pleasures, the importance of which are recognized and emphasized by Mill.[8] These include the capability 'to be knowledgeable to understand and reason, and to have the skills to participate in society' and the capability of 'being and expressing yourself, and having self-respect'. Naturally, the detailed contents of these capabilities have to accommodate the needs for living in a modern society. Nevertheless, the core ideas of these two capabilities are nearly identical to two fundamental elements of happiness highlighted by Mill: the capability to be knowledgeable, to understand and reason, and to have the skills to participate in society is the capability that Mill's proposal of universal education aims to ensure that everyone in the society can obtain; the capability of being and expressing yourself, and having self-respect is the capability that Mill's *On Liberty* aims to protect.

What we have shown is that Mill's utilitarianism is a forward-looking philosophy: it has anticipated much of the later development in putting human rights, capabilities and happiness on the political agenda which aims to institutionalize the protection of the most essential interests of human beings. Given that we have these modern developments, do we still need Mill? The answer is simple: yes, we do. A lot of pending work at both theoretical and practical level still requires the contribution of a unified and comprehensive philosophy like Mill's.

In recent years, whether the pursuit of happiness should be on the political agenda has been hotly debated. Further research and debate on philosophical and moral questions is needed in order to know whether it is desirable to promote happiness by political means and which form this should take, as Valérie De Prycker (2010) comments. Mill's utilitarianism, as a philosophy of happiness, naturally stands out as one of the best candidates for the task of bridging the gap between the science of happiness and the politics of happiness. Unfortunately, Mill's utilitarianism is often misunderstood by moral philosophers, and in consequence the reference to Mill in modern happiness research is usually superficial. An area where Mill's theory is capable of making significant contribution is the discussion on how we can move from facts to norms. Three characteristics identified in the previous chapters of this book highlight how his theory can help. First, Mill's moral philosophy is an integral part of his system of knowledge. As demonstrated in Chapter 2, his system of knowledge is comprehensive and well structured. Science and art are like the two pillars holding the whole system together; they are separate but not independent. The way science and art could interact and support each other, as illustrated in Mill's writings, is valuable when developing sophisticated methods of reasoning to connect scientific results with normative rules. Moreover, Mill's utilitarianism has a clear first principle, the operation of which can reconcile competing values in a consistent manner. Lastly, Mill explicitly separates the realm of morality from the realm of prudence and that of aesthetics. This distinction plays a crucial role in preventing utilitarianism from being a paternalistic doctrine.

How are the above features of Mill's theory supposed to work to improve the application of the scientific study of happiness for policy-making? The findings of the new science of happiness have been used widely to suggest how to live a happy life. In essence, this type of application is oriented more towards an individual's private life. This is also a main reason why the application causes misgivings in regard to its potential for paternalism. The structure of Mill's theory provides a mechanism to prevent this problem. If we follow the division of Mill's art of life, at present many of the applications concern matters belonging to the division of prudence and aesthetics. According to Mill, on issues which do not affect others people should have absolute freedom to decide for themselves.

The science of happiness may suggest what factors are likely to lead to happy life, but nobody should be forced to lead a life which is believed to be happy by others. On the other hand a scientific study, if done properly, could also provide reliable information to complement purely introspective philosophical speculation in finding what the essential elements of happiness are. If something is universally or almost universally needed by everyone for their happiness, the protection of this element of happiness is a legitimate subject of morality and some form of coercion such as laws or moral rules will usually be desirable to ensure the effectiveness of the protection.

The study of happiness as the totality of a human being: a way forward

Happiness research suggests a new approach to understanding human well-being, but not all philosophers are comfortable granting to happiness such a vital role in moral philosophy. For instance, Griffin argues that happiness is not an important notion in ethics. In Griffin's view, happiness is important only if one thinks that happiness is the only thing that contributes to well-being or if one uses happiness to mean the same thing as well-being (Griffin, 1998, p. 227). Sen also argues that happiness cannot be a reliable indicator of the quality of people's life, because the mental state of those who live in deprived conditions will adapt. Neither Griffin nor Sen denies the value of happiness to well-being. However, they seem to be reluctant to give happiness such a primary role when it is understood as a state of mind. Such reluctance is understandable but arguably tends to underestimate the close and probably inseparable connection between the mental and the physical states.

The human being has hardly been tackled in moral philosophy as a complete entity, at least not in Western moral philosophy. This tends to downplay the value of mental state in moral philosophy. More knowledge of the natural constitution of human beings, especially the relationship between physical and psychic being, is important for us to better understand the nature of happiness. In light of this, using the problem of adaptation in order to reject utilitarianism, as Sen does, is based on a problematic observation of human beings. According to Sen, people in a miserable situation will get used to it. This is like saying that if slaves were unaware of their lot or not pained by it, utilitarianism would justify slavery in the name of happiness. Objections to utilitarianism such as this ignore the fact that happiness and unhappiness are more than a state of mind: they are 'expressions of the state of the entire organism, of the total personality', as Fromm spelled out a long time ago. Fromm's view of happiness in relation to the totality of a human being deserves quoting in length here because few utilitarian philosophers have ever made this point as lucidly as Fromm did, even though his view is not that unfamiliar today, especially to psychologists and physicians:

> Happiness and unhappiness are so much a state of our total personality that bodily reactions are frequently more expressive of them than our conscious feeling. The drawn face of a person, listlessness, tiredness, or physical

> symptoms like headaches or even more serious forms of illness are frequent expressions of happiness [...] Likewise, the functioning of our mental and emotional capacities is influenced by our happiness or unhappiness. The acuteness of our reason and the intensity of our feelings depend on it. Unhappiness weakens or even paralyzes all our psychic functions. Happiness increases them. The subjective feeling of being happy, when it is not a quality of the state of well-being of the whole person, is nothing more than an illusory thought *about* a feeling and is completely unrelated to genuine happiness.
>
> (Fromm, 1986 [1947], p. 185)

If we use the contemporary terminologies of happiness research, Fromm's passage can be reinstated as a claim that hedonic well-being is closely associated to eudaimonic well-being. Mill's theory of happiness contains the characteristic elements of both hedonic and eudaimonic well-being. The further exploration of his theory is promising in shedding new light on the future study of happiness by suggesting the possible connection between the two.

The objective conditions and functions of happiness are not fully recognized by scientists, and they are clearly underestimated by those philosophers who treat happiness as a purely subjective mental state. In the past, when explaining why happiness is good for human beings, philosophers like Aristotle and Mill have to stop at the point where people desire happiness for its own sake and no further reason can be found to explain why happiness is good. Today we are still far from having a full knowledge of why people naturally desire being happy, namely pursuing pleasures and avoiding pains. Nevertheless, science has suggested a highly sensible biological explanation: human beings tend to desire pleasures and to avoid pains because it is crucial for the survival and procreation of the human race (Berridge and Kringelbach, 2011, p. 26). Therefore, happiness is desirable not only because it is desired as an end but also because it is vital to the existence of the human race. In a similar way, science may one day provide more evidence for us to assess the value of higher pleasures to happiness. Based on the empirical evidence available so far, we have a relatively steady ground to suggest the answer to be that exercising higher faculties is crucial for humans to flourish. If this can be proved to be true and if human beings are the purpose of morality, then our confidence in the principle of utility to be the first principle of moral philosophy is justified.

It should be emphasized that the above discussion of how science can improve our decision as to how we should act is by no means an assertion that we can make better judgements simply by obtaining more scientific knowledge. Whatever knowledge we have about the world cannot discharge us from the responsibility of making judgements on what we ought to do.

A modern theory for true happiness, justice and liberty

In this last section of the book, we will explore Mill's relevancy today by considering some pressing issues in political and economic debates. The focus will be the idea of economic freedom and its relation to other freedoms as well as Mill's views on the equality of wealth distribution in relation to liberty.[9] The problem of inequality of wealth distribution has been a long-lasting issue in the history of philosophy. It is a core subject of the theory of justice and liberty. The financial crisis and the consequent economic instability in recent years have made it more hotly debated than ever. Many reasons have been proposed to argue against the current status of inequality in wealth distribution.[10] There is also a lot of discussion put forward to dispute these arguments.[11] To stay close to the subject matter of this book, we will investigate extreme inequalities from the philosophical perspective.

It is a common belief for both critics and defenders of unequal distribution of wealth that social justice and liberty are two incompatible ideals. For the former, in order to promote social justice, it is tolerable to give up some degree of liberty and it is reasonable to ask some to give up their liberty for others. For the latter, the pursuit of social justice is a big threat to individual liberty. Contrary to the common view, this book has argued that for Mill, Rawls and Sen, social justice does not necessarily clash with liberty. In fact, the theories of justice of these three authors all aim to protect individual liberty. Even Hayek, who denies the idea of social justice, believes that justice is required by a society to protect individual liberty. The review of these authors' theory of justice and liberty in this book suggests that we need a more refined philosophical theory for the current political and economic debates. In particular, we need to reflect more deeply on the meaning of liberty and the relationship between liberty and pecuniary means.

Economic freedom: what freedom? Whose freedom?

Economic freedom is a key reason why people have misgivings about pursuing equal wealth distribution. Most scholars who are in favour of inequality of wealth distribution believe that inequality is a natural result of the free market and the pursuit of equality in the name of social justice will inevitably impair economic freedom. What is economic freedom then? The definition provided by The Heritage Foundation is perhaps one of the most prominent today in terms of influence:

> The highest form of economic freedom should provide an absolute right of property ownership; fully realized freedoms of movement for labor, capital, and goods; and an absolute absence of coercion or constraint of economic liberty beyond the extent necessary for citizens to protect and maintain liberty itself.[12]

To assess to what extent this idea of economic freedom is achieved at a national level, the Foundation created the Index of Economic Freedom in 1995 and since then publishes the index annually jointly with the *Wall Street Journal*. The index scores a country's economic freedom from ten separate dimensions, and these ten areas of economic freedoms can be grouped into four categories: first, rule of law, including property rights, and freedom from corruption; second, limited government, including fiscal freedom,[13] and government spending; third, regulatory efficiency, including business freedom, labour freedom, and monetary freedom; and fourth, open markets, including trade freedom, investment freedom, and financial freedom. It is claimed that most of the measured aspects are meant to assess 'the liberty of individuals to use their labour or finances without undue restraint and government interference'. In essence, the index is concerned with the degree of government interference: the less restraint from the government, the more economic freedom.

Do people really have more economic freedom when the government has less involvement in the economy and when there are less governmental restraints on economic activities? The answer to this question depends on several factors. Most importantly, it depends on how we define economic freedom. The answer to the above question would be positive if economic freedom simply means less government restraints. However, it is debatable whether this is the only meaning of economic freedom. An important question deserving deep reflection is whether someone can be considered to have economic freedom if they have to choose between unemployment and extremely low payment.

Moreover, it is problematic to equate economic freedom with liberty. Even the experts of the Heritage Foundation would not deny this: according to them, economic freedom is 'an essential aspect of human liberty'. This implies that economic freedom is only one aspect of human liberty. Hardly anyone can deny the paramount value of liberty in economic aspect of one's life. However, economic freedom in the sense of free markets is not the whole story when considering the concept of liberty. Much has been said about the importance of economic freedoms, but little has been said about the tension between economic freedoms and other aspects of liberty. There are still many political and economic problems related to the idea of liberty and freedom waiting for further philosophical exploration. For instance, when the different dimensions of the liberties of different individuals clash, how should the conflict be reconciled? How can we clearly identify which freedoms and whose freedoms are under consideration? How do we prioritize different freedoms of different individuals?

Liberty is often believed by moral and political philosophers to be a clearer and more reliable goal than utility for a society to pursue. Yet this is not always true. For instance, there is an obvious tension between some people's freedom of selling and possessing firearms and others' freedom from being hurt by gunshots. On the surface, the conflict is about whether people have the right to gun ownership for self-defence and how important this right is to protect a 'free' state. In effect, despite sometimes being unspeakable, the truth is that the idea of economic freedom is no less influential than the right to gun ownership in the gun lobby which plays an important role in shaping gun regulations. For some, the freedom of selling guns is part of economic freedom and is also related to the freedom of working in the gun industry. Indeed, constraining one's freedom of producing and selling guns implies the limitation on their freedom of making money from one type of production and transaction. In the debate of firearm regulations, which freedom should be prioritized is by no means an easy question, at least not to people who live in the United States. Tensions between different freedoms are not always so apparent or straightforward, but this does not mean that they do not exist. For instance, there is a tension between the freedom of media mergers and acquisitions and the freedom of accessing diverse information. It is difficult to identify a clear threshold beyond which the activities of merger and acquisition of media will start to impair the public's freedom in accessing information. However, it is not difficult to expect a threat to the freedom of accessing diverse information if there was no constraint at all on the freedom of enterprise mergers and acquisitions. Again, the latter is an important type of economic freedom in some people's view. It is by no means an easy question to strike a balance between the freedom of merger and acquisition and the freedom of information. It does not seem to be possible for those political and moral theorists who give liberty paramount value (e.g. Hayek and Milton Friedman) to provide a consistent principle at the theoretical level to reconcile different people's different freedoms. We need an alternative philosophy to provide a consistent principle to assess and judge the importance of different freedoms when they clash. It is one of the key arguments of this book that Mill's utilitarianism has the potential to offer such an alternative.

Equal wealth distribution: a trade-off between social justice and liberty?

In addition to the meaning of liberty and freedom and how to reconcile different freedoms, the relationship between pecuniary means and liberty is another pressing issue which needs to be explored by contemporary philosophers. Traditionally, libertarians believe that an individual's freedom is independent from the resources they have, which implies that there is no positive correlation between wealth and liberty. In contrast, socialists generally believe that the degree of freedom one can have is related to resources, which implies that there is a positive correlation between wealth and liberty. This contrast between libertarian and socialist views might be useful in grasping quickly the key disagreement of the two views, but this is an oversimplified distinction, which cannot fully characterize the subtle relationship between wealth and liberty. A refined argument is needed.

This book has argued that Mill's position is in-between the above two opposite standpoints. On the one hand, before minimum subsistence is satisfied one's freedom of choice is constrained, especially choices regarding employment. For this reason, we can say that there is a positive correlation between pecuniary means and freedom before one's basic needs are satisfied. On the other hand, once the minimum subsistence is satisfied, the correlation between pecuniary means and freedom is less obvious. According to this view of relationship between pecuniary means and freedom, redistributive policies which aim to provide everyone minimum subsistence can be seen as policies pursuing real freedom for all. This policy implication of securing subsistence contains an element of equality, which is termed by Berger a 'baseline conception of equality' (Berger, 1984, pp. 159–166). In Berger's words, 'inequalities must not be permitted to push anyone below a certain "baseline"', that is, equal status as a fully-fledged participant in the common social life must be guaranteed to everyone to preserve dignity and independence (Berger, 1984, p. 160).

Clearly, arguing for the provision or protection of minimum subsistence, either in an absolute or relative term, is not the same thing as arguing for a more equal wealth distribution. First of all, it does not require a huge amount of money to satisfy a person's basic physical needs and hence in theory the scale of redistribution should not be great if the goal of redistribution is only to satisfy everyone's basic physical needs.[14] Even if the consideration is about the level of minimum subsistence in a relative term to accommodate the continuingly rising living standard of a society, the scale of redistribution will not be radical because the minimum subsistence for social life does not require a huge amount of material goods, if we constrain the needs into the scope of *basic* ones, such as basic needs for transportation and resources for information and communications technology (ICT). Therefore, if Mill prefers more equal distribution of wealth to a less equal one, he must have reasons other than that everyone's minimum subsistence should be satisfied. Similarly, for a society to favour a more equal distribution of wealth, it needs reasons other than securing everyone's subsistence.

Equal distribution of income and wealth is believed by many to be an important goal that any just society would pursue. A related but not identical belief is that economic justice is equivalent to equality in income or wealth distribution. We discussed in Chapter 4 that the relationship between equality and economic justice in Mill's utilitarianism is far more complicated than these popular views. The idea of equality is indeed an essential element of Mill's idea of economic justice, but Mill's theory of economic justice cannot be reduced to equality of something in one single dimension.

Is Mill committed to equality? Is he an egalitarian? These questions have been addressed by several scholars.[15] There is no received answer. The difficulty of answering them is partly due to the vagueness of the questions. Both the dimension of equality and the meaning of commitment in the questions are unclear. When dealing with these questions, the equality in the mind of most commentators is equality of income or wealth. This is one crucial dimension of equality in Mill's idea of economic justice, as the following passage shows:

> equality, though not the sole end, is one of the ends of good social arrangements; and that a system of institutions which does not make the scale turn in favour of equality, whenever this can be done without impairing the security of the property which is the product and reward of personal exertion, is essentially a bad government – a government for the few, to the injury of the many.
>
> (Mill, *CW, XX*: 354)

Mill sees equality of wealth distribution itself as an important end, but it is only one of the many secondary ends which are subordinate to the ultimate end, that is the greatest happiness of all concerned. The value of equality in wealth is not absolute. When the pursuit of equality threatens other values that have greater importance to social utility, equality has to give way to other more imperative values. Mill's utilitarian philosophy is clear on the point that the principle of utility is needed for reconciling conflicting dimensions of equality, just as it is needed for reconciling conflicting utilities and conflicting freedoms.

For what reason would Mill's philosophy consider unequal wealth distribution undesirable? Mill did not deal with this problem directly. Yet based on the analysis of his idea of justice presented in earlier chapters, it is fair to venture Mill's answer as follows: an extremely unequal wealth distribution tends to threat individual liberty, an essential element of every individual's happiness. This is because an extremely unequal wealth distribution tends to result in unequal dominant relations between human beings. It sounds paradoxical, but the liberty of the majority today is under threat in the name of economic freedoms. However genuine the advocates' love of economic freedom was, the love of freedom is becoming the best disguise of the appetite for power. Economic freedom is an essential component of a free society, but if left unattended and unmitigated by considerations of the aggregate happiness of the whole of society, it gives rise to a dynamic process whereby the effective liberty of many will be curtailed through the top 'winners' ability to use wealth to exercise power over others and change the 'rules of the game' in their favour.

Here we need to be very careful with the relationship between pecuniary means and liberty. It is true that more wealth does not necessarily lead to more freedom. It is also true that more wealth does not necessarily lead to more happiness. But when the distribution of material resources reaches a status where the top 1 per cent of households own a third of the wealth of a country and the bottom 80 per cent share only around 10 per cent of it,[16] there is another factor coming into the picture and it complicates the relationship between wealth, freedom and happiness. The factor we are referring to is power. It might not be clear whether the super-rich become happier when getting richer, but they certainly get more power. This power might not allow them to enjoy more liberty as a whole, but it certainly helps them obtain more freedom in some dimensions. Take the above conflicting freedoms as examples. The super-rich in the USA have the power to lobby Congress and to support legislations which are in favour of the types of freedoms they desire. When the social and political institutions allow the super-rich to exercise their power in this way, there is a threat to the individual liberty of the majority. The traditional concept of negative freedom is inadequate to indentify such a problem because it is often grounded on an individualistic view of society, which usually emphasizes individuals' responsibilities for their successes or failure and neglects that it is inevitable, as a consequence of the evolution of human society, that some will win and some will lose irrespective of their personal merits.

As a civilization progresses, every part of the society becomes more and more interdependent:

> As civilization advances, every person becomes dependent, for more and more of what most nearly concerns him, not upon his own exertions, but upon the general arrangements of society. In a rude state, each man's personal security, the protection of his family, his property, his liberty itself, depend greatly upon his bodily strength and his mental energy or cunning: in a civilized state, all this is secured to him by causes extrinsic to himself.
>
> (Mill, *CW, XVIII*: 129)

This description of the interdependent connection between the members of the society remains accurate today. In particular, the deep financialization of human exchange activity that occurred in the last few decades has increasingly tied the string of everyone's life to the financial markets.

It has become a universal fact that hardly anyone in a modern society where financial markets are highly developed can entirely detach their life from financial markets. How this would affect people's liberty is a question new to moral philosophy and deserves a careful investigation. One's connection to financial markets is different from the connection to good markets. If one does not like the new devices of technology such as mobile phones, digital cameras or computers, they can choose not to use them and still live well. However, it is not quite the same for someone to reject financial innovation. The absence of coercion, the traditional definition of negative freedom, is insufficient to secure people's economic freedom. For instance, before the wave of financial deregulation that set in after 1980 starting from countries like the USA and the UK, the retirement of those who lived on their own savings was not affected by the financial markets as much as today. In contrast, today even if one prudentially saves money for retirement, by the retirement date the value of the savings may have shrunk much more considerably than before. At first glance, everyone who saves for their retirement is affected by the dilution caused by inflation. The real impacts on those who are super-rich and on those who can save only from their moderate salaries differ significantly. Today one could hardly live on their savings when retired if they reject any type of financial investment apart from putting their savings in the bank, a major way for ordinary people to keep the fruit of their labour. One might argue that access to financial markets today is very simple for everyone, through no-fee mutual fund platforms, discount brokers, exchange traded funds, etc. Accordingly, one has absolute freedom to choose to invest or not. If one does not invest money in the financial markets, they should be responsible for failing to maintain the value of their own savings. One can say that the innovation of financial products is necessary to the capitalist economy and that the volatility of the markets is inherent to the nature of the financial systems. One can also say, as Hayek did, that who benefits more from financial markets is irrelevant to justice or injustice because the outcome of the financial markets is nobody's fault.[17] However, this is only one possible perspective. Mill's philosophy offers us an alternative perspective: if the financial markets are indispensable to our civilization, we can choose to work collectively to tamper the volatility or, if that is not possible, to share that risk in more deliberate ways rather than leaving it to the operation of those same markets to decide on whom the risk falls. Mill reminds us that a major feature of civilization is the increasing interdependence of every member in the community, and utilitarian moral philosophy is meant to provide rules to maintain and advance the civilization by taking into everyone's interest into account.

Mill once issued a warning against confounding the love of liberty with the love of power. While the warning of conflation was given in a political context against centralization, Mill's differentiation of the love of liberty from the love of power is equally enlightening in the context of the economic world today:

> The love of liberty, in the only proper sense of that word, is unselfish; it places no one in a position of hostility to the good of his fellow-creatures; all alike may be free, and the freedom of one has no solid security but in the equal freedom of the rest. The appetite for power is, on the contrary, essentially selfish; for all cannot have power; the power of one is power over others, who not only do not share in his elevation, but whose depression is the foundation on which it is raised.
>
> (Mill, *CW, XIX*: 610)

For Mill power and liberty are not synonyms, especially when power refers not only to the power over oneself but also to the power over others. 'The only freedom which deserves the name', Mill wrote in his *On Liberty*, 'is that of pursuing our own good in our own way, so long as we do not attempt to deprive others of theirs, or impede their efforts to obtain it' (Mill, *CW, XVIII*: 226). The proviso should not be neglected because it suggests that the power over other people does not deserve the name of freedom.

Five decades ago when Milton Friedman, the leading exponent of post-World War Two neo-liberalism, was writing his famous book *Capitalism and Freedom*, the political power of the state was the predominant source of the threat to individual freedom. 'By removing the organization of economic activity from the control of political authority', Friedman believed, 'the market eliminates this source of coercive power' (Friedman, 2002, p. 15). Friedman wished to liberate economic activities in the hope that dispersed economic strength would be 'a check to political power rather than a reinforcement' (Friedman, 2002, p. 15). In retrospect this appears to be a naive view, especially in contrast to his clear awareness that 'there is an intimate connection between economics and politics' (Friedman, 2002, p. 8). Friedman is absolutely right in that 'the great threat to freedom is the concentration of power' (Friedman, 2002, p. 2). Indeed, the concentration of economic power today has become a great threat to freedom and this is exactly why we need to be cautious with the concentration of power. The neo-liberal world that was born out of the fight against dictatorial government power and its control over the individual has ended up replacing that threat with a different one: a minority of people and the corporations they own are acquiring the ability of using their disproportionate share of wealth to exercise undue influence over the lives of the majority. The result of practicing Friedman's liberal philosophy in the USA and in many other countries for more than 30 years seems to suggest that the belief that economic freedoms guarantee the dispersal of power is a myth. An alternative philosophy is needed urgently before more people's liberty has to be surrendered to the power of the minority.

Those philosophical theories that elevate individual liberty to the absolutely supreme status will inevitably encounter difficulty in prioritizing competing liberties. This incompleteness in theory leaves no ambiguity in practice however: in today's world it is the super-rich that have the real power to decide whose liberty is more important. At this point, one cannot help but recall Madame Roland's infamous quote: 'O Liberty, O Liberty, what crimes are committed in thy name!' (Lamartine 1847, p. 774).

As a counterpoint to the dominant political and economic thinking in practice, here is the relevance of Mill's thought to today's world: Mill's utilitarianism, if understood properly, can serve as a philosophical foundation of contemporary moral and political theory guiding us to seek a just society in which the happiness and freedom of everyone is truly respected. For Mill, social justice and liberty are not two incompatible ideals as is commonly believed. It is Mill's view that social justice must secure real liberty for all. If social justice is incompatible with liberty, it is because the liberty that has been pursued is not liberty for all, but only for the power of those whose liberty is already secured. Utilitarian philosophy is one of the most important legacies Mill leaves to us: it is a theory that promises human beings a world of true happiness, justice and liberty. For this reason alone, Mill deserves to be recognized as one of the greatest thinkers in human intellectual history.

Notes

1 Epistemological and psychological foundations of Mill's utilitarian moral philosophy

1 According to W. D. Hudson, there are two schools in British intuitionism: one claims that it is moral sense which discerns moral properties; the other believes that it is reason that plays this role (Hudson, 1967, p. 1). Nonetheless, according to Mill's discussion, it seems that all the opponents in Mill's mind hold only the first view.

2 These two types of intuitionism are related, but have different focuses. Methodological intuitionism focuses on the plurality of first principles and epistemological intuitionism focuses on the view that certain moral propositions are self-evident so that they can be perceived directly by intuition (Stratton-Lake, 2002, p. 2). For Williams's discussion of the distinction and the relationship between methodological intuitionism and epistemological intuitionism, see B. Williams, 'What does Intuitionism Imply?', in his Making Sense of Humanity and Other Philosophical papers 1982–1993, pp. 182–191.

3 Logic is a discipline of proof or evidence, rather than the theory of epistemology. Interestingly, Mill wrote the System of Logic as a challenge to the epistemological grounds of mathematics and physical sciences. For instance, he wrote

> In attempting to clear up the real nature of the evidence of mathematical and physical truths, the System of Logic met the intuitive philosophers on ground on which they had previously been deemed unassailable; and gave its own explanation, from experience and association, of that peculiar character of what are called necessary truths, which is adduced as proof that their evidence must come from a deeper source than experience.
>
> (Mill, CW, I: 233)

For further discussion on this viewpoint, see, McRae, 1973, pp. xxiii–xxiv.

4 In *Utilitarianism* where he discusses the sentiment of justice, Mill repeats a similar view: there is no necessary connection between the question of the origin of moral sentiments and that of their binding force. See, Mill, CW, X: 240.

5 The question of how to form moral rules according to utilitarian moral reasoning will be discussed in later chapters.

6 For this purpose, Mill believes that 'a rigid adherence to the canons of inductive proof must be insisted on' (Mill, XXXI: 239).

7 For instance, E. Halevy, among others, holds this view. See Kelly 1990, pp. 15–16.

8 Mill does not think that this is a reasonable attempt because the motives of human conduct are far too many to exhaust. Some scholars defend Bentham's listing of motives against Mill's criticism by arguing that it is Bentham's intention to offer legislators a guide about how the laws can be used to direct human behaviour, rather than embracing all the motives on the list. However, this defence does not affect the validity of Mill's arguments about the defects of Bentham's approach.

9 Since Mill's discussion includes the properties of virtues, it is clear that when making comments on Bentham's moral theory, he uses the word 'moral' in a broad sense, including the areas of both moral obligation and moral value. It is very important to note that Mill does not always use the word 'moral' in this broad sense. Sometimes he uses the term when discussing only moral obligation. For further discussion, see Chapter 2.

10 As David Collard among others notices, it is Mill's hope to reach the 'ideal perfection of utilitarian morality' through the process of education and learning (Collard, 1978, p. 58). This implies that Mill's utilitarianism will not be a sustainable doctrine if the cultivation of social feelings is impossible by virtue of human nature.

11 In his discussion of motives, Mill does not include unconscious motives, or, in Freud's term, base motives. Although base motives are important to explain human behaviour, the mechanism they spring on human actions is different from that of those motives which are recognized by the agent. They should be treated differently.

12 For instance, Hoffman *et al.* 1996; Smith 1998; Sally 2001.

13 According to Mill, the fundamental phenomena of mind can be studied only by experiment or observation (Mill, CW, VIII: 853); therefore, psychology is an experimental science (Mill, CW, VIII: 872).

14 This view has important implications for the development of economics. If the assumption of rational choice in modern economics is a positive statement, then this statement seems to miss a considerable part of human behaviour. If the assumption implies normative command, then it will prevent people from behaving virtuously. Nevertheless, it must be admitted that even if we accept that a confirmed character can be more influential than rational deliberation in determining behaviour, it is still arguable how human character can be or should be moulded in a particular direction.

15 Some key viewpoints here benefited from Berger's insightful analysis on Mill's view of the relationship between social feelings and moral sentiments. See Berger, 1984, pp. 19–23. Donner's analysis on the same topic is also illuminating: Donner, 1991, pp. 112–117.

2 Mill's utilitarianism as a system of moral philosophy

1 In MacIntyre's view, G. E. Moore (1873–1958) is the one accountable for intuitionism's flourishing in Cambridge circles in the early twentieth century. As for Scarre, H. A. Prichard (1871–1947) and W. D Ross (1877–1971) were the two most representative figures among others (Scarre, 1996, p. 122). For the development of emotivism as a successor theory of intuitionism in early twentieth-century England, see MacIntyre, 2007, pp. 11–18.

2 For a fuller account of the background of the emergence of rule-utilitarianism, see Scarre, 1996, pp. 122–123.

3 According to John C. Harsanyi, Harrod was the first to point out the advantages of rule-utilitarianism over act-utilitarianism, but he did not actually use this terminology. The terms 'act-utilitarianism' and 'rule-utilitarianism' were actually introduced by R. Brandt (1959). See Harsanyi, 1977, p. 41.

4 Here the term moral philosophy indicates an idea similar to Mill's moral arts as a whole, which covers fields broader than morality. This use is close to Smith's use of the term moral philosophy, which includes ethics and jurisprudence. However, the realm of Mill's morality is smaller than that of Smith's ethics. This point will become clearer as the arguments develop. For Smith's notion of moral philosophy, see Smith, 2002, p. 420.

5 It seems uncontroversial that there is a matching relationship between art and science. Yet it is open to the question whether the relationship is a coupling one as Donner suggests in her claim that 'every moral art is coupled with *a* corresponding moral science' (Donner, 1991, p. 132, emphasis added). This author believes that the interpretation here is closer to Mill's text.

6 It is important to note that moral judgement is not equivalent to normative judgement; it is only one type of normative judgement. According to Frankena's classification, normative judgement includes moral judgement and non-moral judgement; the former can be further divided into judgements of moral obligation and of moral value in general. For further explanations of the distinction between moral and non-moral normative judgements and examples for each type of judgements, see Frankena, 1963, pp. 8–10 and Su, 2012, pp. 379–382.

7 Mill's response to this misunderstanding can shed light on Sen's capability theory, which is based on a similar objection to the utilitarian approach of judging rightness and wrongness. For further discussion, see Chapter 7.

8 On this account, Larmore's accusation that modern moral philosophy has been dominated by the 'imperative' conception of morality cannot be applied to Mill. Although Mill's morality stresses duty and obligation, he does not overlook the values of virtues. We should not forget that his morality is only a department within the complete structure of his moral arts. It follows that the starting point of the revival of virtue ethics in recent decades is highly questionable because it is largely based on the assumption that modern morality neglects the values of virtues. The movement towards virtue ethics in moral philosophy is largely influenced by the arguments of Anscombe (1958) and MacIntyre (2007; first published in 1981). Larmore, perhaps misled by Anscombe and MacIntyre, is just a typical example of the confusion between the idea of morality and virtue, see Larmore, 1998. Also see Slote, 2005b.

9 According to Frankena, 'Not everything that is right is just or vice versa, and not everything that is wrong is unjust or vice versa' (Frankena, 1963, p. 36). Without 'vice versa', the author would agree with Frankena.

10 Before Fuchs, who sees Mill's utilitarianism as an ideal moral code form of rule-utilitarianism, R. Brandt had proposed the ideal moral code theory and used it to interpret Mill's theory of morally correct actions (Brandt, 1967). We focus on Fuchs's version here because it provides a fuller account of Mill as a result of taking into consideration the new development in Mill scholarship since the first time Brandt proposed the ideal moral code form of rule-utilitarianism.

11 The term 'indirect utilitarianism' can be found in Gray's *Hayek on Liberty* which was first published in 1984. Gray continues using this term in his later works to interpret Mill's utilitarianism. For Gray's argument that Mill's utilitarianism is an indirect version, see Gray, 1995, pp. 52–53; 1996, pp. 12–13.

12 For instance, Smart and William (1973) and M. Slote (2005a).

13 For further discussion of Mill's idea of happiness, see Chapter 7, pp. 142–148.

14 The status and meaning of this 'highest abstract standard of social justice' will be further expounded in Chapter 4.

3 Mill's utilitarianism as a theory of morality

1 Brown (2010) acknowledges Schaller's article and considers his exploration of the difficulties faced by inner sanction arguments impressive. Brown did not utilize Schaller's analysis to support his own argument, however. It is not too surprising that Brown did not do so, because his interpretation, also grounded on the appropriateness of punishment, cannot entirely escape the same problem.

2 See the editor's note in footnote 12, Mill, *CW*, *XV*: 650.

3 See also the discussion of Mill on Bentham's human nature and motives of human conduct in Chapter 1.

4 For further discussion of Mill's concept of happiness, see Chapter 7, pp. 142–145 and Conclusions, pp. 172–178.

5 See Conclusions, pp. 172–175.

6 Riley wrote substantively on this topic. See Riley 1988, 1993, 2003, 2008, 2009, 2010. Brink (1992) and Millgram (2009) are examples of this category; Crisp may be classified

as in this group. He believes that Mill accepts the lexical priority of higher pleasures, although he thinks that Mill is wrong on this point. See Crisp, 1997, pp. 40–41.

7 For Donner's discussion on this topic, see Donner 1998, particularly pp. 268–273; 2009, Chapter 1. Despite being diverse in details, Schmidt-Petri (2003, 2006) and Saunders (2010) can be allocated within this category.

4 Reconstructing Mill's theory of justice

1 See Chapter 2, pp. 45–49.

2 For instance, Berger claims that Mill has a strong commitment to 'a substantive conception of equality' (Berger, 1984, p. 158), while others like Gray do not consider that Mill entailed overriding commitment to equality (Gray, 1979b).

3 A. K. Sen has a similar argument:

> A common characteristic of virtually all the approaches to the ethics of social arrangements that have stood the test of time is to want equality of something—something that has an important place in the particular theory [...] To see the battle as one between those 'in favour of' and those 'against' equality [...] is to miss something central to the subject.
>
> (Sen, 1992, p. ix)

4 The disappointment prevention principle is a term used by Bentham himself in 'Pannomial Fragments' (Bentham 1843c, pp. 226–227). It does not appear in Principles of the Civil Code, though it is strongly implied there (Bentham 1843a, p. 341). This author is grateful to Michael Quinn for his valuable comments on the discussion of Bentham in this chapter and his assistance with the references to Bentham's work in this book.

5 Note that Bentham himself imposes a cognitive qualification on the franchise: if one cannot read, one cannot vote. Hence, strictly speaking, it is not quite universal suffrage. This qualification should not be seen as an exclusion, however, because Bentham argues that anyone who wants to can become literate fairly quickly. Therefore, in Bentham's view, the cognitive qualification on the franchise is not a defalcation from equality at all.

6 John Rawls, for one, holds this view. See Rawls, 1999, p. 185.

7 Since security and subsistence are universal human interests and hence the indispensable components of happiness, it is perfectly sensible and logical for a utilitarian to reconcile the equal distribution of security and subsistence with the maximization of total happiness. It is less clear that abundance is indispensable to one's happiness, however. Kelly, Postema and Quinn are all aware of this and do not pretend that abundance and equality are as fundamental as security and subsistence to happiness. In their view, Bentham is utterly consistent in saying first that security and subsistence are more important than abundance and equality, and second, that whenever equality conflicts with security, equality loses. See Kelly (1990, 1998), Postema (2006), and Quinn (2008).

8 Ethical relativism holds the view that 'moral values cannot be justified *in any way*' (Angeles, 1992, p. 204, emphasis added). A milder form of relativism considers morality as merely an expression of arbitrary and capricious behaviour, while relativism taken to an extreme is nihilism: moral inquiry is simply a mistaken project, because it is worthless and meaningless (Yeager, 2001, p. 39).

9 For further explanation of relativism in this sense, see Hare, 1991, p. 131.

10 This partly explains why Mill never explicitly endorses any specific principle as the principle of justice in economic issues.

11 Rawls' definition of institution may help to understand the idea of institution indicated here:

> By an institution I shall understand a public system of rules which defines offices and positions with their rights and duties, powers and immunities, and the like

> [...] An institution exists at a certain time and place when the actions specified by it are regularly carried out in accord with a public understanding that the system of rules defining the institution is to be followed.
>
> (Rawls, 1999, pp. 47–48)

In short, the existence of an institution is invisible; its existence is recognized only by its rules being understood and carried out.

12 For instance, Richard and Peggy Musgrave take this approach. See R. Musgrave and P. Musgrave, 1989, pp. 223–231.

13 This sentence is quoted from the first edition of Mill's *Principle of Political Economy*. It was removed in the final edition published in 1871. In spite of the removal, this passage is consistent with Mill's standpoint in the final edition.

14 For a further discussion of how Mill's distinction of higher and lower pleasures supports this statement, see Chapter 5.

15 Arguing against a common impression that Mill's economic theory is inconsistent with his philosophy, this author demonstrates in a previously published paper that Mill's discussion on income and inheritance taxation is more comprehensive and more coherent than Hayek's. See Su, 2009.

16 Much attention has been paid to tax rate structure in today's political debate in most Western countries. The strong emphasis on the burden imposed by the highest tax rate tends to disguise the injustice of a tax system, or at least its injustice from Mill's point of view. For instance, in April 2012, the UK parliament past the budget plan proposed by the coalition government to freeze age-related tax allowances for pensioners. To its critics, it is a 'granny tax'. According to the new scheme, the personal allowances for those who are aged over 65 and over will be frozen at the same levels as 2012–2013 and the allowances for those who turn 65 after April 2013 will not increase in relation to their ages. A personal allowance for these people in 2013 will be £9,205. This is actually a very moderate amount for a person living in the country to support minimum subsistence. It can barely cover the expense for the minimum level of food, shelter, and house fuel to meet the basic needs. On the other hand, the top rate of tax is to be reduced from 50p to 45p in 2013. It is clear that every penny of income is 'equally' treated by the coalition government no matter whether it is a pensioner's income for subsistence, or the income of someone who earns more than £150,000 per year. Chancellor George Osborne defended the cut by arguing that the 50p rate was a 'tax con', because the money it raised is insufficient to justify the 'enormous damage' it was doing to the economy. According to the HMRC's estimation, the amount of increase in revenue by the 50p rate started in 2010 is £1.1bn, and amount that is pathetic in George Osborne's view. Ironically, the money the government is going to save from the granny tax is estimated to be £1bn by 2015, which is just about enough to pay for the loss of cutting the 50p rate. Chancellor George Osborne defended the new scheme as a simplification in a complex tax system. According to Mill's views, we can say that the old system indeed could be simpler: it could drop the complicated age-related tax allowances simply by raising the personal allowances for all to a decent amount for subsistence.

17 In spite of the disparity about the origin of exchange value among different economic theories of value, it seems that most economists will agree that in a capitalist society an exchange of commodities is just, as long as the exchange is a voluntary transaction. Even a communist like Marx would not deny that it is a just rule according to the logic of capitalism:

> The justice of the transactions between the agents of production rests on the fact that these transactions arise as natural consequences from the conditions of production. The juristic forms, in which these economic transactions appear as activities of the will of the parties concerned, as expressions of their common will and as contracts which may be enforced by law against some individual party, cannot

> determine their content, since they are only forms. They merely express this content. This content is just, whenever it corresponds, and is adequate, to the mode of production. It is unjust, whenever it contradicts that mode.
>
> (Marx, 1909, p. 399)

5 Economic justice, liberty and utilitarianism

1 In a review of Gray's and Berger's work on Mill, Robert Hoag (1986) summarizes these three attributes as their characterization of Mill's idea of happiness.

2 For instance, D. Ricardo, *On Principles of Political Economy and Taxation* (Cambridge, 1953 [1821]), p. 93.

3 The 1871 edition, which is cited here, actually postdates Mill's recantation of the wages-fund doctrine in a review of a book by Thornton in the *Fortnightly Review* in 1869. However, it is not clear whether he abandoned the whole theory or merely a part of it. If the chief part of the wages-fund theory is the claim that wages depend on the proportion between the number of the labouring population and the capital devoted to the purchase of labour, what Mill abandoned is not the entire theory but the presumption that the fund is a predetermined amount at any given moment. In his 1869 review, Mill argued that the fund is not a fixed amount even in the short run. It can be augmented by the reduction of capitalists' personal expenditure. This alteration enabled the trade unions to affect the level of wages. However, Mill thought it was still too early to evaluate the influence of trade unions on wages, in a general treatise on Political Economy (Mill, *CW*, *II*: xciv); therefore, the wages-fund theory survived unchanged in his final (1871) edition of the *Principles*.

4 From the following statement, we can infer that Mill considered the claim for the protection of subsistence from society as labourers' moral right:

> Society mainly consists of those who live by bodily labour; and if society, that is, if the labourers, lend their physical force to protect individuals in the enjoyment of superfluities, they are entitled to do so, and have always done so, with the reservation of a power to tax those superfluities for purposes of public utility; among which purposes the subsistence of the people is the foremost.
>
> (Mill, *CW, II*: 357)

6 Rawls versus Mill: deontological versus teleological theory of justice

1 This proposition is important in the sense that it reminds us to look into the conflicts and compromises between distributive justice and commutative justice in Mill's theory of justice. A further investigation on this issue will shed new light on the old issue of how to strike a balance between efficiency and equality. Nevertheless, for the purpose of this chapter, we will sidestep this issue and only emphasize that Rawls's two principles of justice are not the corresponding principles to the principle of utility in Mill's theory of justice.

2 In *Political Liberalism* (1993), Rawls replaces 'the most extensive scheme' in the first principle with 'a fully adequate scheme'. There are also several forms of Rawls's second principle in his discourse. Here we quote the one which is best known. In comparison, on page 53 where Rawls makes his statement of the two principles for the first time, the second principle is proposed as follows: 'social and economic inequalities are to be arranged so that they are both (a) reasonably expected to be to everyone's advantage, and (b) attached to positions and offices open to all' (Rawls, 1999, p. 53).

3 It is controversial on what grounds Rawls can claim that it is just to eliminate the influence of the uneven distribution of natural abilities and talents. Here we are not going to judge whether mitigating the influence of natural fortune is a suitable element for the

principle of justice, since it is a question belonging to another debate. However, it is important to understand it plays an important role in Rawls's idea of justice.

4 Another interpretation, which is less popular, suggests that Rawls's principles are absolutely egalitarian. It follows that the more even the final outcome is, the better the redistribution. For example, A. M. Okun holds this type of interpretation (Okun, 1975, pp. 92–94). Another interpretation is held by Sen, who thinks that Rawls's principles of justice are about the equal distribution of primary goods.

5 It seems reasonable to suggest that Rawls considers the theory of ordinal utility to have won the debate, with the theory of cardinal utility, about whether different person's utilities are comparable in welfare economics in the early twentieth century.

6 Andrew Carnegie once proposed a claim similar to Mill's in 1891. He argued that 'the parent who leaves his son enormous wealth generally deadens the talents and energies of the son, and tempts him to lead a less useful and less worthy life than he otherwise would', which has been called 'Carnegie conjecture'. In 1993, the research of Holtz-Eakin, *et al.* shows that the 'Carnegie conjecture' does contain some truth, since they found that 'the likelihood that a person decreases his or her participation in the labour force increases with the size of the inheritance received'. See Sawyers (2001), p. 581.

7 It is worth emphasizing again that social utility does not mean summing up everyone's utility without regarding the quality of the utility. For the detailed discussion, see Chapter 4.

7 Sen versus Mill: equal capability versus equal claim to happiness

1 See Chapter 6, pp. 115–117.

2 This sentence, quoted from Sen's paper, originally appeared in Rawls' book *A Theory of Justice*. According to Sen, he is indebted to Rawls' analysis even though there is a crucial difference between their views about distributive justice (Sen, 1992, p. 8).

3 For detailed arguments of the 'uncriticality' of utility, see Sen's reply to Sumner's critiques in Sen, 2006, pp. 90–94.

4 For the arguments of this four-category distinction, see, Sen, 1985; 1987, pp. 60–61; 2006, p. 91.

5 See the discussion in Chapter 6, pp. 115–119.

6 See the discussion in Chapter 6, p. 120.

7 See, for instance, Riley, 1998, Chapter 7.

8 Although Brown might have gone too far to claim that the principle of utility is not a principle to be able to provide a test on what right and wrong is, his analysis regarding the focus of Mill's *Utilitarianism* is accurate. See Brown, 1972, 2010.

9 See, for instance, Uyl and Machan (1983) and Kreider (2010).

10 For the difference between moral philosophy and theory of morality, see, Chapter 2.

11 For the discussion of the role of secondary ends in Mill's utilitarianism, see Chapter 2, pp. 45–46. For the relationship between the end and the criterion of good, see Chapter 3, pp. 61–63.

12 The five factors identified by Sen are 'personal heterogeneities', 'environmental diversities', variations in social climate', 'differences in relational perspectives', and 'distribution within the family'. See Sen, 1999, pp. 70–71.

13 Recall Mill's famous declaration that

> I forego any advantage which could be derived to my argument from the idea of abstract right, as a thing independent of utility. I regard utility as the ultimate appeal on all ethical questions; but it must be utility in the largest sense, ground on the permanent interests of a man as a progressive being.
>
> (Mill, *CW*, *XVIII*: 224)

14 For example, when discussing the reform of inheritance law, Mill makes such a consideration:

> Some of the children may, without fault of their own, be less capable than others of providing for themselves: some may, by other means than their own exertions, be already provided for: and impartiality may therefore require that the rule observed should not be one of equality, but of compensation.
>
> (Mill, *CW*, *III*: 894)

15 See Chapter 6.

16 To some extent, the problem raised by Sugden and partly endorsed by Qizilbash is similar to the one noticed by Frances Kamm, a Harvard philosopher, in her recent review essay of Sen's book *The Idea of Justice*. According to Kamm (2011), it is not clear that Sen distinguishes issues of justice from other important moral matters despite the title of his book. In contrast, it is Mill's intention to draw the formal line between justice and other non-justice moral obligations. See Chapter 2.

8 Hayek versus Mill: equality before the law versus equal real freedom for all

1 This condition sometimes is labelled as the 'intention or foresight dictum'. Strictly speaking, this is not a comprehensive understanding of Hayek's requirement, because there are actually two elements to this condition: first, an assignable agency of person or persons; second, acting intentionally and with foresight. According to Feser's analysis it is the first element, rather than the second, that is the key reason why the concept of justice is not applicable to market-determined distribution, because a market is an impersonal process and there is no such agency that can be responsible for its results. See Feser (1998).

2 According to Légé, Hayek considers that there are two more errors, in addition to the distinction between the laws of production and distribution, which blinded Mill to the absurdity of the notion of social justice, and they reinforced one another:

> 1) the utilitarian doctrine, which according to Hayek, assumed that individuals were omniscient; 2) the classical theory of value, which Hayek considered as an inversion of the true functional relationship of value.
>
> (Légé, 2008, p. 212)

3 It is not difficult to find literature that supports Hayek's view regarding the inseparable interrelationship between production and distribution in a market economy. For instance, in his article 'The market economy and the distribution of wealth', Lachmann successfully demonstrates that the distribution of wealth is not an 'independent variable' of the market process, but 'continuously subject to modification by the market forces' (Lachmann, 1956, p. 177).

4 See, for instance, Smith, 1985.

5 For example, Mill writes, '[the Distribution of Wealth] is a matter of human institutions only. *The things once there*, mankind, individually and collectively, can do with them as they like. They can place them at the disposal of whoever they please and on whatever terms' (Mill, *CW*, *II*: 199–200, emphasis added). This statement, as Smith comments, 'is somewhat misleading because it suggests a degree of flexibility in distributing an *existing* social product which Mill only partially intended' (Smith, 1985, p. 280, emphasis added). Nevertheless, it is unfair to interpret Mill solely on the basis of a few unclear sentences and take them in isolation from their context. By reading in context, Smith discovers that the malleability Mill intends to associate with distribution is not in relation to an already produced social product, but mainly 'the opinions and feeling of the ruling class of society, which may differ across space and time' (Smith, 1985, p. 280).

6 In his paper 'John Stuart Mill's famous distinction between production and distribution', Vardaman Smith argues against this common view shared by Joseph Schumpeter, Mark Blaug, and Maurice Dobbs, among others. See Smith, 1985, pp. 267–284.
7 For Mill's discussion on different systems of distribution in relation to production, see, for instance, Mill, *CW, II*, Bk II, ch. 5, sect. 2 and ch. 10; Mill, *CW, V*.
8 Hayek himself also considers his concept of liberty as a negative one. Nevertheless, it is arguable whether Hayek's own recognition is consistent with his arguments. For instance, in *Law, Legislation and Liberty*, Hayek writes, freedom is a 'state in which each can use his own knowledge for his purposes' (Hayek, 1982, pp. 55–56). John Gray also argues that on balance Hayek's conception of liberty is a positive one. See Gray, 1989, Chapter 6.
9 Gray suggests that Hayek did this mistakenly. For Gray's explanation, see Gray, 1989, p. 101.
10 For Hayek's connection of envy, egalitarianism, and inheritance taxation, see Hayek, 1960, Chapter 6.

Conclusions: prospect – the continuing relevance of Mill's utilitarianism today

1 See, for instance, Daniel Kahneman 2003, 2011.
2 Here, genetic transmission seems to leave a possibility for moral faulty or moral sense to be innate. However, even if moral knowledge can be passed on from ancestors to the future generation, according to Greene's cognitive miracle argument, it remains valid to claim that the materials of moral knowledge come from experience. However, it is highly questionable whether moral knowledge can pass from one generation to the other through genes like physical reflexes and intuitions.
3 See Layard (2011) Chapter 3 for a brief summary of findings in the literature on this point.
4 For a more detailed discussion of the idea and status of right in Mill's utilitarianism, see Chapter 3.
5 For the argument of the multidimensional nature of Mill's conception of happiness, see Chapter 7, pp. 145–148.
6 http://hdr.undp.org/en/statistics/hdi/.
7 Equality is one of the key values emphasized by the Equality Measurement Framework (EMF). The three aspects of inequality which the EMF aims to address are: inequality of outcome, inequality of process and inequality of autonomy. Equality, both as the conception of justice and the practice of it, is also an essential element of Mill's utilitarian theory of justice. There are also significant overlaps between the EMF and Mill's theory of justice in the dimension of equality. However, the similarities between the two are less straightforward than the similarities in the dimension of well-being (i.e. happiness for Mill and capabilities for the EMF). For the idea of equality in relation to Mill's theory of justice, see Chapter 4.
8 See Equality and Human Rights Commission, n.d., 'Equality Measurement Framework', available at www.equalityhumanrights.com/key-projects/equality-measurement-framework/.
9 The focus here will be on the distribution of wealth, which is not the same as the distribution of income.
10 See for instance, Galbraith (2002), Wilkinson and Pickett (2009) and Stiglitz (2012).
11 See for instance Snowdon's (2010) reply to Wilkinson and Pickett (2009).
12 The Heritage Foundation, n.d. Defining Economic Freedom, www.heritage.org/index/book/chapter-7
13 According to the Heritage Foundation, fiscal freedom is 'a direct measure of the extent to which individuals and businesses are permitted by government to keep and control their income and wealth for their own benefit and use'. Put simply, the more

taxes the government imposes and the more debt the government owes, the less fiscal freedom individuals and businesses have.

14 This assertion should hold in an economy where most people make their own contribution to the production of the economy. If it does not hold, it implies that there is something wrong with the mechanism of distribution of collective production in the first place.

15 For instance, Pedro Schwartz (1972), John Gray (1979b), and Berger (1984).

16 These data reflect the situation of the USA in 2010. See Edward N. Wolff (2012).

17 For Hayek's arguments, see Chapter 8.

Bibliography

Adler, M. J. (1981), *Six Great Ideas: Truth, Goodness, Beauty, Liberty, Equality, Justice*. New York: Macmillan Publishing Co., Inc.

Angeles, P. A. (1992), *The HarperCollins Dictionary of Philosophy*. New York: HarperCollins Publishers.

Anscombe, G. E. M. (1958), 'Modern Moral Philosophy', *Philosophy*, 33:124, pp. 1–19.

Aristotle (1940), 'Metaphysica', in W. D. Ross (ed. and trans.), *Works of Aristotle*, vol. VIII. London: Oxford University Press.

Aristotle (1966), 'Ethica Nicomachea', in W. D. Ross (ed. and trans.), *Works of Aristotle*, vol. IX. London: Oxford University Press.

Arneson, R. (1998), 'Real Freedom and Distributive Justice', in Jean-Francois Lasier, et al. (eds), *Freedom in Economics: New Perspectives in Normative Analysis*, pp. 165–196. London: Routledge.

Arneson, R. J. (2002), 'Why Justice Requires Transfers to Offset Income and Wealth Inequalities', *Social Philosophy and Policy*, 19:1, pp. 172–200.

Arrhenius, G. and W. Rabinowicz (2005), 'Millian Superiorities', *Utilitas*, 17:2, pp. 127–146.

Arrow, K. J. (1951), *Social Choice and Individual Values*. New York: John Wiley & Sons, Inc.

Backhouse, R. E. and T. Nishizawa (2010), 'Introduction: Towards a Reinterpretation of the History of Welfare Economics, in R. E. Backhouse and T. Nishizawa (eds), *No Wealth but Life: Welfare Economics and the Welfare State in Britain, 1880–1945*, pp. 1–22. Cambridge: Cambridge University Press.

Barry, N. P. (1979), *Hayek's Social and Economic Philosophy*. London: The MacMillan Press Ltd.

Beitz, C. (1986), 'Amartya Sen's Resources, Values and Development', *Economics and Philosophy*, 2: 282–291.

Bentham, J. (1843a), *Principles of the Civil Code*, in J. Bowring (ed.), *The Works of Jeremy Bentham*, vol. 1, pp. 297–364, Edinburgh: William Tait.

Bentham, J. (1843b[1795]), 'Supply without Burden; or Escheat vice Taxation', in J. Bowring (ed.), *The Works of Jeremy Bentham*, vol. 2, pp. 585–598. Edinburgh: William Tait.

Bentham, J. (1843c), 'Pannomial Fragments', in J. Bowring (ed.), *The Works of Jeremy Bentham*, vol. 3, pp. 211–230, Edinburgh: William Tait, pp. 211–230.

Bentham, J. (1843d[1817]), 'Plan of Parliamentary Reform', in J. Bowring (ed.), *The Works of Jeremy Bentham*, vol. 3, pp. 433–557. Edinburgh: William Tait.

Bentham, J. (1843e[1830]), 'Constitutional Code', in J. Bowring (ed.), *The Works of Jeremy Bentham*, vol. 9. Edinburgh: William Tait.

Bentham, J. (1970[1789]), *A Fragment on Government and An Introduction to the Principles of Morals and Legislation*, ed. by J. H. Burns and H. L. A. Hart. London: Athlone.

Bentham, J. (1989), 'Supreme Operative', in P. Schofield (ed.), *First Principles Preparatory to Constitutional Code*, pp. 149–222. Oxford: Clarendon Press.

Berger, F. R. (1984), *Happiness, Justice, and Freedom: The Moral and Political Philosophy of John Stuart Mill*. Berkeley, CA: University of California Press.

Berker, S. (2009), 'The Normative Insignificance of Neuroscience', *Philosophy and Public Affairs*, 37:4, pp. 293–329.

Berridge, K. and M. Kringelbach (2011), 'Building a Neuroscience of Pleasure and Well-Being', *Psychology of Well Being*, 1:1 pp. 1–3.

Blackburn, S. (2005), *The Oxford Dictionary of Philosophy*. Oxford: Oxford University Press.

Boettke, P. (2001), 'F. A. Hayek as an Intellectual Historian of Economics', in S. G. Medema and W. J. Samuels (eds.), *Historians of Economics and Economic Thought: The construction of Disciplinary Memory*, pp. 117–128. London and New York: Routledge.

Brandt, R. B. (1959), *Ethical Theory*. Englewood Cliffs, NJ: Prentice-Hall. Inc.

Brandt, R. B. (1967), 'Some Merits of One Form of Rule-Utilitarianism', University of Colorado Studies 3, pp. 39–65. Later reprinted in his *Morality, Utilitarianism and Rights*. Cambridge: Cambridge University Press (1992).

Brennan, G. and J. M. Buchanan (1985), *The Reason of Rules: Constitutional Political Economy*. Cambridge: Cambridge University Press.

Brink, D. (1992), 'Mill's Deliberative Utilitarianism', *Philosophy and Public Affairs*, 21:1, pp. 67–103.

Broome, J. (1991), 'Utility', *Economics and Philosophy*, 7: pp. 1–12.

Brown, D. (1973), 'What is Mill's Principle of Utility?', *Canadian Journal of Philosophy*, 3:1, pp. 1–12.

Brown, D. G. (1972), 'Mill on Liberty and Morality', *The Philosophical Review*, 81:2, pp. 133–158.

Brown, D. G. (1974), 'Mill's Act-Utilitarianism', *The Philosophical Quarterly*, 24:94, pp. 67–68.

Brown, D. G. (2010), 'Mill's Moral Theory: Ongoing Revisionism', *Politics, Philosophy and Economics*, 9:1, pp. 5–46.

Brscic, B. (2007), 'On the Hayekian Impossibility of Social Justice – A Critique', Conference paper presented at the ESHET annual conference in Strasbourg, France (unpublished).

Caldwell, B. (2008), 'Hayek on Mill', *History of Political Economy*, 40:4, pp. 689–704.

Clark, B. S. and Elliott, J. E. (2001), 'John Stuart Mill's Theory of Justice', *Review of Social Economy*, 59:4, pp. 467–490.

Collard, D. A. (1978), *Altruism and Economy: A Study in Non-selfish Economics*. Oxford: Martin Robertson.

Copp, D. (1979), 'The Iterated-Utilitarianism of J. S. Mill', *New Essays on John Stuart Mill and Utilitarianism, Canadian Journal of Philosophy*, Supp. vol. 5, pp. 75–98.

Crisp, R. (1997), *Mill on Utilitarianism*. London: Routledge.

De Prycker, V. (2010), 'Happiness on the Political Agenda? PROS and CONS', *Journal of Happiness Studies*, 11, 585–603.

Dent, N. J. H. (2005), 'Good', in T. Honderich (ed.), *The Oxford Companion to Philosophy*, pp. 348–349. Oxford: Oxford University Press.

Donner, W. (1991), *The Liberal Self: John Stuart Mill's Moral and Political Philosophy*. New York: Cornell University Press.

Donner, W. (1998), 'Mill's Utilitarianism', in John Skorupski (ed.), *The Cambridge Companion to Mill*), pp. 255–292. Cambridge: Cambridge University Press.

Donner, W. (2006), 'Mill's Theory of Value', in Henry R. West (ed.), *The Blackwell Guide to Mill's Utilitarianism*, pp. 117–138. Malden, MA and Oxford: Blackwell Publishing Ltd.

Donner, W. (2009), Part I, 'Mill's Moral and Political Philosophy', in W. Donner and R. Fumerton, *Mill*, pp. 13–143. Chichester: Wiley-Blackwell.

Donner, W. (2010), 'John Stuart Mill and Virtue Ethics', in G. Varouxakis and P. Kelly (eds), *John Stuart Mill: Thought and Influence*, pp. 84–98. London: Routledge.

Dryer, D. P. (1969), 'Mill's Utilitarianism', in J. Robson (ed.), *Collected Works of J. S. Mill*, vol. 10, pp. lxiii–cxiii. Toronto: University of Toronto Press.

Ekelund, R. B. Jr. and D. M. Walker (1996), 'J. S. Mill on the Income Tax Exemption and Inheritance Taxes: The Evidence Reconsidered', *History of Political Economy*, 28:4, pp. 559–581.

Equality and Human Rights Commission (n.d.), *Equality Measurement Framework*, available at www.equalityhumanrights.com/key-projects/equality-measurement-framework/ (accessed 28 March 2013).

Feser, E. (1997), 'Hayek on Social Justice: Reply to Lukes and Johnston', *Critical Review*, 11:4, pp. 581–606.

Feser, E. (1998), 'Hayek, Social Justice, and the Market: Reply to Johnston', *Critical Review*, 12:3, pp. 269–281.

Frankena, W. K. (1963), *Ethics*. Englewood Cliffs, NJ: Prentice-Hall, Inc.

Friedman, M. (1962), *Capitalism and Freedom*. Chicago, IL: University of Chicago Press.

Fromm, E. (1986), *Man for Himself: An Inquiry into the Psychology of Ethics*. New York: Ballantine Books.

Fuchs, A. (2006), 'Mill's Theory of Morally Correct Action', in Henry West (ed.), *The Blackwell Guide to Mill's Utilitarianism*, pp. 139–158. Malden, MA, Oxford and Victoria, Australia: Blackwell Publishing.

Galbraith, J. K. (2002), 'The Importance of Being Sufficiently Equal', *Social Philosophy and Policy*, 19:1, pp. 201–224.

Gray, J. (1979a), 'John Stuart Mill: Traditional and Revisionist Interpretations', *Literature of Liberty*, 2:2, pp. 7–37.

Gray, J. (1979b), 'John Stuart Mill on the Theory of Property', in A. Parel and T. Flanagan (eds), *Theories of Property: Aristotle to the Present*, pp. 257–280. Ontario: Wilfred Laverier University Press.

Gray, J. (1984), *Hayek on Liberty*. Oxford: Basil Blackwell Publishers Ltd.

Gray, J. (1989), *Liberalisms: Essays in Political Philosophy*. London: Routledge.

Gray, J. (1995 [1986]), *Liberalism*. Milton Keynes: Open University Press.

Gray, J. (1996 [1983]), *Mill on Liberty: A Defence*, 2nd edn. London: Routledge.

Greene, J. (forthcoming), 'Beyond Point-and-Shoot Morality: Why Cognitive (Neuro) Science Matters for Ethics'.

Griffin, J. (1986), *Well-Being*. Oxford: Clarendon Press.

Griffin, J. P. (1998), 'Happiness', in Edward Craig (General Editor), *Routledge Encyclopedia of Philosophy*, vol. 4, pp. 226–229. London: Routledge.

Hamilton, A. (forthcoming), *The Self in Question*. Palgrave.

Hammond, P. J. (1982), 'Uncertainty and information', in A. K. Sen and B. Williams (eds), *Utilitarianism and Beyond*, pp. 85–102. Cambridge: Cambridge University Press.

Hare, R. M. (1981), *Moral Thinking: Its Levels, Method and Point*. New York: Oxford University Press.

Hare, R. M. (1991), 'Justice and Equality', in John Arthur and William H. Shaw (eds), *Justice and Economic Distribution*, pp. 118–132. Englewood Cliffs, NJ: Prentice-Hall, Inc.

Harrison, J. (1975), 'The Right, the Just and the Expedient in Mill's Utilitarianism', in T. Penelhum and R. A. Shiner (eds), *New Essays in the History of Philosophy, Canadian Journal of Philosophy*, suppl. 1, pp. 93–107.

Harrod, R. F. (1936), 'Utilitarianism Revised', *Mind, New Series*, 45:178, pp. 137–156.

Harsanyi, J. C. (1953), 'Cardinal Utility in Welfare Economics and in the Theory of Risk-Taking', *Journal of Political Economy*, 61:5, pp. 434–435.

Harsanyi, J. C. (1955), 'Cardinal Welfare, Individualistic Ethics, and Interpersonal Comparisons of Utility', *The Journal of Political Economy*, 63:4, pp. 309–321.

Harsanyi, J. C. (1977), 'Morality and the Theory of Rational Behaviour', *Social Research*, 44:4, pp. 623–656, reprinted in A. K. Sen and B. Williams (eds), *Utilitarianism and Beyond*, pp. 39–62. Cambridge: Cambridge University Press (1982).

Hart, H. L. A. (1975), 'Rawls on Liberty and its Priority', in Norman Daniels (ed.), *Reading Rawls: Critical Studies on Rawls' A Theory of Justice*, pp. 230–252. Oxford: Basil Blackwell.

Hart, H. L. A. (1982), 'Natural Rights: Bentham and John Stuart Mill', in H. L. A. Hart, *Essays on Bentham: Studies in Jurisprudence and Political Theory*, pp. 79–104. Oxford: Oxford University Press.

Hayek, F. A. (1949), *Individualism and Economic Order*. London: Routledge & Kegan Paul.

Hayek, F. A. (1960), *The Constitution of Liberty*. London: Routledge & Kegan Paul Ltd.

Hayek, F. A. (1982), *Law, Legislation and Liberty: A New Statement of the Liberal Principles of Justice and Political Economy*, vols 1–3, new edn. London: Routlegde & Kegan Paul Ltd.

Hayek, F. A. (1983), 'The Muddle of the Middle', in Svetozar Pejovich (ed.), *Philosophical and Economic Foundations of Capitalism*, pp. 89–100. Lexington, MA: Lexington Books.

Hayek, F. A. (1988), 'The Fatal Conceit: the Errors of Socialism', in W. W. Bartley, III (ed.), *The Collected Works of F. A. Hayek*. London: Routledge.

Held, V. (1989), *Rights and Goods: Justifying Social Action*. Chicago, IL: University of Chicago.

Heritage Foundation, 'About the Index', www.heritage.org/index/about?src=home, accessed 28 November 2012.

Heritage Foundation entry here, highlighted to move from p.206.

Heritage Foundation, (n.d.), *Defining Economic Freedom*, www.heritage.org/index/book/chapter-7 (accessed 28 March 2013).

Hoag, R. W. (1986), 'Happiness and Freedom: Recent Work on John Stuart Mill', *Philosophy and Public Affairs*, 15:2, pp. 188–199.

Hoffman, E., K. McCabe and V. L. Smith (1996), 'Social Distance and Other-regarding Behavior in Dictator Games', *American Economic Review*, 86, pp. 653–660.

Holdsworth, W. (1940), 'Bentham's Place in English Legal History', *California Law Review*, 28: 5, pp. 568–586.

Hollander, S. (1985), *The Economics of John Stuart Mill*, vol. 1. Toronto: University of Toronto Press.

Holtz-Eakin, D., D. Joulfaian and H. S. Rosen (1993), 'The Carnegie Conjecture: Some Empirical Evidence', *The Quarterly Journal of Economics*, 108:2, pp. 413–435.

Hudson, W. D. (1967), *Ethical Intuitionism*. London: Macmillan and Company Limited.

Hume, D. (1975), *Enquiries Concerning Human Understanding and Concerning the Principles of Morals*, 3rd edn. Reprinted from the 1777 edition with Introduction and Analytical Index by L. A. Selby-Bigge. Oxford: Oxford University Press.

Ikeda, Y. (2007), 'Friedrich Hayek on Social Justice: Taking Hayek Seriously', Conference paper presented at the ESHET annual conference in Strasbourg, France (unpublished).

Jackson, T. (2009), *Prosperity Without Growth: Economics for a Finite Planet*. London: Earthscan.

Johnston, D. (1997a), 'Hayek's Attack on Social Justice', *Critical Review*, 11:1, pp. 81–100.

Johnston, D. (1997b), 'Is the Idea of Social Justice Meaningful?', *Critical Review*, 11:4, pp. 607–614.

Kahneman, D. (2003), 'A Perspective on Judgment and Choice: Mapping Bounded Rationality', *American Psychologist*, 58:9 697–720.

Kahneman, D. (2011), *Thinking, Fast and Slow*. Harmondsworth: Penguin Books.

Kamm, F. M. (2009), 'Neuroscience and Moral Reasoning: A Note on Recent Research', *Philosophy and Public Affairs*, 37:4, pp. 330–345.

Kamm, F. M. (2011), 'Sen on Justice and Rights: A Review Essay', *Philosophy and Public Affairs*, 39:1, pp. 82–104.

Kelly, P. J. (1990), *Utilitarianism and Distributive Justice: Jeremy Bentham and the Civil Law*. New York: Oxford University Press.

Kelly, P. J. (1998), 'More on Bentham on Utility and Rights', *Utilitas*, 10:2, pp. 165–166.

Kreider, S. E. (2010), 'Mill on Happiness', *Philosophical Papers*, 39:1, pp. 53–68.

Kringelbach, M. and K. Berridge (2010), 'The Functional Neuroanatomy of Pleasure and Happiness', *Discovery Medicine*, 9: 579–587.

Kymlicka, W. (1988), 'Rawls on Teleology and Deontology', *Philosophy & Public Affairs*, 17:3, pp. 173–190.

Lachmann, L. M. (1956), 'The Market Economy and the Distribution of Wealth', in Mary Sennholz (ed.), *On Freedom and Free Enterprise: Essays in Honor of Ludwig von Mises*, pp. 175–187. New York: The Foundation for Economic Education.

Lamartine, Alphonse de (1847), *Histoire des Girondins*. Bruxelles: Meline, Cans et cie.

Lambert, P. J. (1993), *The Distribution and Redistribution of Income: A Mathematical Analysis*. Manchester: Manchester University Press.

Larmore, C. (1998), 'Right and Good', in Edward Craig (General Editor), *Routledge Encyclopedia of Philosophy*, vol. 8, pp. 322–325. London: Routledge.

Layard, R. (2011), *Happiness: Lessons from a New Science*. London: Penguin.

Légé, P. (2008), 'Hayek's Readings of Mill', *Journal of the History of Economic Thought*, 30:2, pp. 198–215.

Lukes, S. (1997), 'Social justice: The Hayekian challenge', *Critical Review*, 11:1, 65–80.

Lyons, D. (1976), 'Mill's Theory of Morality', *Noûs*, 10: 101–120; reprinted in his *Right, Welfare, and Mill's Moral Theory*. New York: Oxford University Press (1994).

Lyons, D. (1994), *Right, Welfare, and Mill's Moral Theory*. New York: Oxford University Press.

MacCallum, Jr. Gerald C. (1967), 'Negative and Positive Freedom', *The Philosophical Review*, 76:3, pp. 312–334.

MacIntyre, A. (2007), *After Virtue: A Study in Moral Theory*, 2nd edn. Indiana, IN: University of Notre Dame Press.

Mack, E. (1983), 'Hayek on Justice and the Market: A Reply to Macleod', *Canadian Journal of Philosophy*, 13:4, pp. 569–574.

MacLeod, A. M. (1983a), 'Justice and the Market', *Canadian Journal of Philosophy*, 13:4, pp. 551–561.

MacLeod, A. M. (1983b), 'Hayek on Justice and the Market: A Rejoinder to Cragg and Mack', *Canadian Journal of Philosophy*, 13:4, pp. 575–584.

Macleod, C. (in press), 'Was Mill a Non-Cognitivist?', *Southern Journal of Philosophy*.

McCloskey, H. J. (1957), 'An Examination of Restricted Utilitarianism', *The Philosophical Review*, 66:4, pp. 466–485.

McCloskey, H. J. (1965), 'A Non-Utilitarian Approach to Punishment', *Inquiry*, 8: 249–263.

McRae, R. F. (1973), 'Introduction' to Mill's *System of Logic*, in John M. Robson (ed.), *The Collected Works of John Stuart Mill, vol. VII*, pp. xxi–xlviii. Toronto: University of Toronto Press.

Marx, K. (1909), *Capital: A Critique of Political Economy*, vol. 3, ed. by Frederick Engels and translated from the first German edition by Ernest Untermann. Chicago, IL: Charles H. Kerr & Company.

Mill, J. S. (1963–1991), *The Collected Works of John Stuart Mill*, ed. by John M. Robson. Toronto: University of Toronto Press.

Miller, D. (2010a), *J. S. Mill*. Cambridge, UK and Malden, MA: Polity Press.

Miller, D. (2010b), 'Brown on Mill's Moral Theory: A Critical Response', *Politics, Philosophy and Economics*, 9:47, pp. 47–66.

Millgram, E. (2009), 'Liberty, The Higher Pleasures, And Mill's Missing Science Of Ethnic Jokes', *Social Philosophy and Policy*, 26: pp. 326–353.

Mirrlees, J. A. (1982), 'The economic uses of utilitarianism', in A. K. Sen and B. Williams (eds.), *Utilitarianism and Beyond*, pp. 63–84. Cambridge: Cambridge University Press.

Mueller, D. C. (2003), *Public Choice III*. Cambridge: Cambridge University Press.

Musgrave, R. A. and P. B. Musgrave (1989), *Public Finance in Theory and Practice*. New York: McGraw-Hill Book Company.

Myers, D. G. (1993), *The Pursuit of Happiness*. New York: Avon Books.

Myers, D. G. and E. Diener (1995), 'Who is Happy?', *Psychological Science*, 6:1, pp. 10–19.

Nathanson, S. (1998), *Economic Justice*. Englewood Cliffs, NJ: Prentice-Hall., Inc.

Nathanson, S. (2012), 'John Stuart Mill on Economic Justice and the Alleviation of Poverty', *Journal of Social Philosophy*, 43:2, pp. 161–176.

Nussbaum, M. C. (2004), 'Mill between Aristotle and Bentham', *Daedalus*, 133:2, pp. 60–68.

Okun, A. M. (1975), *Equality and Efficiency: The Big Tradeoff*. Washington, DC: The Brookings Institution.

Pattanaik, P. K. (2008), 'Social Welfare Function', in S. N. Durlauf and L. E. Blume (ed.), *The New Palgrave Dictionary of Economics*, 2nd edn, vol. 7, pp. 662–627. Basingstoke: Palgrave Macmillan

Pellissier-Tanon, A. and J. M. Moreira (2007), 'Can Social Justice Be Achieved? From Aristotle to Friedrich Hayek', *Journal of Markets & Morality*, 10:1, pp. 143–155.

Perelman, C. (1980), *Justice, Law, and Argument*. Dordrecht: D. Reidel Publishing Company.

Phelps, E. S. (1987), 'Distributive Justice', in John Eatwell, M. Milgate, and P. Newman (eds), *The New Palgrave: A Dictionary of Economics*, pp. 886–888. London: Macmillan Press Limited.

Pigou, A. C. (1932 [1920]), *The Economics of Welfare*. London: Macmillan and Co.

Postema, G. J. (1998), 'Bentham's Equality-sensitive Utilitarianism', *Utilitas*, 10:2, pp. 144–158.

Postema, G. J. (2006), 'Interests, Universal and Particular: Bentham's Utilitarian Theory of Value', *Utilitas*, 18:2, pp. 109–133.

Qizilbash, M. (2011), 'Sugden's Critique of the Capability Approach', *Utilitas*, 23:1, pp. 25–51.

Quinn, M. (2008), 'A Failure to Reconcile the Irreconcilable? Security, Subsistence and Equality in Bentham's Writings on the Civil Code and on the Poor Laws', *History of Political Thought*, 29:2, pp. 320–343.

Rabinowicz, W. (2003), 'Ryberg's Doubts About Higher and Lower Pleasures – Put to Rest?', *Ethical Theory and Moral Practice*, 6: 231–237.

Rae, D. (1981), *Equalities*. Cambridge, MA: Harvard University Press.

Raphael, D. D. (1994), *Moral Philosophy*. Oxford: Oxford University Press.

Rawls, J. (1971), *A Theory of Justice*, 1st edn. Oxford: Oxford University Press.

Rawls, J. (1993), *Political Liberalism*. New York: Columbia University Press.

Rawls, J. (1999), *A Theory of Justice*, 2nd edn. Oxford: Oxford University Press.

Rawls, J. (2001), *Justice as Fairness: A Restatement*. Cambridge, MA: Harvard University Press.

Ricardo, D. (1953 [1821]), *On the Principles of Political Economy and Taxation*, in Piero Sraffa (ed.), *The Works and Correspondence of David Ricardo*, vol. I. Cambridge: Cambridge University Press.

Riley, J. (1988), *Liberal Utilitarianism: Social Choice Theory and J. S. Mill's Philosophy*. Cambridge: Cambridge University Press.

Riley, J. (1993), 'On Quantities and Qualities of Pleasure', *Utilitas*, 5, pp. 291–300.

Riley, J. (1998), *Mill on Liberty*. London: Routledge.

Riley, J. (2003), 'Interpreting Mill's Qualitative Hedonism', *Philosophical Quarterly*, 53:212, pp. 410–418.

Riley, J. (2008), 'Millian Qualitative Superiorities and Utilitarianism, Part I', *Utilitas*, 20:3, pp. 257–278.

Riley, J. (2009), 'Millian Qualitative Superiorities and Utilitarianism, Part II', *Utilitas*, 21:2, pp. 127–143.

Riley, J. (2010a), 'Justice as Higher Pleasure', in G. Varouxakis and P. Kelly (eds), *John Stuart Mill: Thought and Influence,* pp. 99–129. London: Routledge.

Riley, J. (2010b), 'Mill's Extraordinary Utilitarian Moral Theory', *Politics, Philosophy and Economics*, 9:1, pp. 67–116.

Robson, J. M. (1969), 'Textual Introduction', in *Collected Works of John Stuart Mill, vol. X*, pp. cxv–cxxxix. Toronto: University of Toronto Press.

Rosen, F. (1983), *Jeremy Bentham and Representative Democracy: A Study of the Constitutional Code*. Oxford: Oxford University Press.

Rosen, F. (1997), 'Utilitarianism and the Punishment of the Innocent: The Origins of a False Doctrine', *Utilitas*, 9:1, pp. 23–37.

Rosen, F. (1998), 'Individual Sacrifice and the Greatest Happiness: Bentham on Utility and Rights', *Utilitas*, 129–143, reprinted in his *Classical Utilitarianism from Hume to Mill*. London: Routledge (2003).

Ryan, A. (1974), *J. S. Mill*. London: Routledge & Kegan Paul.

Ryan, A. (1987 [1970]), *The Philosophy of John Stuart Mill*, 2nd edn. London: Macmillan.

Ryan, A. (1991 [1965]), 'J. S. Mill's Art of Living', *The Listener*, 74; reprinted in J. Gray and G. W. Smith (eds), *On Liberty in Focus*, pp. 162–1668. London: Routledge (1991).

Ryff, C. D. (1989), 'Happiness is Everything, or is it? Explorations on the Meaning of Eudaimonic Well-being', *Journal of Personality and Social Psychology*, 57, 1069–1081.

Sally, D. (2001), 'On Sympathy and Game', *Journal of Economic Behavior and Organization*, 44, pp. 1–30.

Saunders, B. (2010), 'J. S. Mill's Conception of Utility', *Utilitas*, 22:1, pp. 52–69.

Sawyers, R. B. (2001), 'Restructuring Estate and Gift Taxes', *National Tax Journal*, LIV:3, pp. 570–612

Scarre, G. (1996), *Utilitarianism*. London: Routledge.

Schaller, W. E. (1991), 'Punishment and the Utilitarian Criterion of Right and Wrong', *Southern Journal of Philosophy*, 29:1, pp. 109–125.

Schofield, P. (2009), *Bentham: A Guide for the Perplexed*. London: Continuum International Publishing Group.

Schmidt-Petri, C. (2003), 'Mill on Quality and Quantity', *Philosophical Quarterly*, 53:210, pp. 410–418.

Schmidt-Petri, C. (2006), 'On an Interpretation of Mill's Qualitative Utilitarianism', *Prolegomena*, 5: 165–177.

Schwartz, P. (1972), *The New Political Economy of J. S. Mill*. London: Weidenfeld and Nicolson.

Seligman, M. (2011), *Flourish: A New Understanding of Happiness and Well-being – and How to Achieve Them*. London: Nicholas Brealey Publishing.

Sen, A. K. (1967), 'The Nature and Classes of Prescriptive Judgements', *Philosophical Quarterly*, 17, pp. 46–62.

Sen, A. K. (1970a), *Collective Choice and Social Welfare*. San Francisco, CA: Holden-Day.

Sen, A. K. (1970b), 'The Impossibility of a Paretian Liberal', *Journal of Political Economy*, 78, pp. 152–157.

Sen, A. K. (1973), *On Economic Inequality*. Oxford: Oxford University Press.

Sen, A. K. (1979), 'Utilitarianism and Welfarism', *The Journal of Philosophy*, 76:9, pp. 463–489.

Sen, A. K. (1980–81), 'Plural Utility', *Proceedings of the Aristotelian Society*, 81, pp. 193–215.

Sen, A. K. (1985), 'Well-being, Agency and Freedom: the Dewey Lectures 1984', *The Journal of Philosophy*, 82:4, pp. 169–221.

Sen, A. K. (1987), *On Ethics and Economics*. Oxford: Basil Blackwell.

Sen, A. K. (1992), *Inequality Reexamined*. Oxford: Oxford University Press.

Sen, A. K. (1999), *Development as Freedom*. New York: Alfred A. Knopf, Inc.

Sen, A. K. (2006), 'Reason, Freedom and Well-being', *Utilitas*, 18:1, pp. 80–96.

Sen, A. K. (2009), *The Idea of Justice*. Cambridge, MA: Harvard University Press.

Sen, A. K. and B. Williams (1982), 'Editors' Introduction', in A. K. Sen and B Williams, *Utilitarianism and Beyond*, pp. 1–21. Cambridge: Cambridge University Press.

Skorupski, J. (2007), 'The Philosophy of John Stuart Mill', *British Journal for the History of Philosophy*, 15:1, pp. 181–197.

Slote, M. (2005a), 'Utilitarianism', in T. Honderich (ed.), *The Oxford Companion to Philosophy*, pp. 936–939. Oxford: Oxford University Press.

Slote, M. (2005b), 'Virtues', in T. Honderich (ed.), *The Oxford Companion to Philosophy*, pp. 947–948. Oxford: Oxford University Press.

Smart, J. J. C. (1973), 'A Outline of a System of Utilitarian Ethics', in Smart, J. J. C. and Williams, B., *Utilitarianism: For and Against*, pp. 3–74. Cambridge: Cambridge University Press.

Smart, J. J. C. and B. Williams (1973), *Utilitarianism: For and Against*. Cambridge: Cambridge University Press.

Smith, A. (1976[1789]), *An Inquiry into the Nature and Causes of the Wealth of Nations*, ed. Edwin Cannan. Chicago, IL: The University of Chicago Press.

Smith, A. (2002), *The Theory of Moral Sentiments*, ed. Knud Haakonssen. Cambridge: Cambridge University Press.

Smith, V. (1985), 'John Stuart Mill's Famous Distinction Between Production and Distribution', *Economics and Philosophy*, 1, pp. 267–284.

Smith, V. L. (1998), 'Two Faces of Adam Smith', *Southern Economic Journal*, 65, pp. 1–19.

Snowdon, C. (2010), *The Spirit Level Delusion: Fact-checking the Left's New Theory of Everything*. London: Little Dice.

Stephen, J. F. (1993[1874]), *Liberty, Equality, Fraternity*, ed. Stuart D. Warner. Indianapolis, IN: Liberty Fund.

Stiglitz, J. (2012), *The Price of Inequality*. London and New York: Allen Lane.

Stratton-Lake, P. (2002), 'Introduction' in his *Ethical Intuitionism: Re-evaluation*, pp. 1–28. Oxford: Oxford University Press.

Su, H. (2009), 'Is Social Justice For or Against Liberty? On the Philosophical Foundations of Mill and Hayek's Theory of Liberty', *Review of Austrian Economics*, 22:4, pp. 387–414.

Su, H. (2012), 'Beyond the Positive-Normative Dichotomy: Some Remarks on Colander's Lost Art of Economics', *Journal of Economic Methodology*, 19:4, pp. 375–390.

Sugden, R. (2004), 'Living with Unfairness: The Limits of Equal Opportunity in a Market Economy', *Social Choice and Welfare*, 22, pp. 211–236.

Sugden, R. (2006), 'What We Desire, What We Have Reason to Desire, Whatever We Might Desire: Mill and Sen on the Value of Opportunity', *Utilitas*, 18:1, pp. 33–51.

Sumner, L. W. (1979), 'The Good and the Right', in W. E. Cooper, K. Nielsen and S. C. Pattern (eds), *New Essays on John Stuart Mill, Canadian Journal of Philosophy*, suppl. vol. 5, pp. 99–114.

Urmson, J. O. (1953), 'The Interpretation of the Moral Philosophy of J. S. Mill', *The Philosophical Quarterly*, 3:10, pp. 33–39.

Uyl, D. D. and Machan, T. R. (1983), 'Recent Work on the Concept of Happiness', *American Philosophical Quarterly*, 20:2, pp. 115–133.

Varian, H. R. (1990), *Intermediate Microeconomics: A Modern Approach*. New York: W. W. Norton & Company.

West, H. R. (2004), *An Introduction to Mill's Utilitarian Ethics*. Cambridge: Cambridge University Press.

Wilkinson, R. (2005), *The Impact of Inequality: How to Make Sick Societies Healthier*. London: Routledge.

Wilkinson, R. and K. Pickett (2009), *The Spirit Level: Why More Equal Societies Almost Always Do Better*. London: Penguin.

Williams, B. (1973), 'A Critique of Utilitarianism', in Smart, J. J. C. and Williams, B., *Utilitarianism: For and Against*, pp. 77–150. Cambridge: Cambridge University Press.

Williams, B. (1995), *Making Sense of Humanity and Other Philosophical Papers 1982–1993*. Cambridge: Cambridge University Press.

Wilson, F. (1998), 'Mill on Psychology and the Moral Sciences', in John Skorupski (ed.), *The Cambridge Companion to Mill*, pp. 203–254. Cambridge: Cambridge University Press.

Wolff, E. N. (2012), *The Asset Price Meltdown and the Wealth of the Middle Class*. NBER Working Paper 18559. Cambridge, MA: National Bureau of Economic Research

Yeager, L. B. (2001), *Ethics as Social Science: The Moral Philosophy of Social Cooperation*. Cheltenham, UK and Northampton, MA: Edward Elgar.

Index

Page numbers in **bold** denote figures.

ability 121, 124–5, 139, 147, 149; ability-to-pay principle 88, 94–5; different 95, 153; to do things 162; enhanced 44; to exercise power 184, 186; independent 129; natural 193n3; physical and mental 150; respective 94; superior 90
Adler, M.J. 61
Allen, R. 115
Angeles, P.A. 191n8
Anscombe, G.E. 98, 190n8
Aristotle 33, 75, 88, 90, 143, 179; eudemonia 66, 145, 175, 179
Arneson, R. 155
Arrhenius, G. 71
Arrow, K.L. 116
art(s): and science: 13, 30–1, 45, 143, 168 169, 177, 189n5; of life: 30–1, 34, 37–8, 59, 99, 177; moral: 32, 189n4–5, 190n8
association: 15–17, 19–21, 46, 54, 56, 104, 143, 146, 188n3; laws of: 12, 14
autonomy 99–101, 196n7

Backhouse, R.E. 115
benefit 16, 54, 59, 71, 86, 119–20, 122, 133–4, 166, 185, 196n13; benefit-principle 88, 94–5; costs and benefits 52; deprived of 81; from the government 94–5; of the least advantaged 126; material 164; net 37; social economic 122–3
Beitz, C. 154
Bentham, J. 1, 13–14, 16–19, 24, 31, 46, 66, 77, 79–82, 113, 116–18, 129–31, 145, 188n8–9, 190n3, 191n4–7
Berger, F.R. 14, 17, 19, 25, 34–5, 41–3, 46, 50, 53, 64–5, 99–101, 182–3, 189n15, 191n2, 193n1, 197n15
Bergson, A.B. 116
Berker, S. 170
Berridge, K. 67–8, 179
Brandt, R.B. 29, 189n3, 190n10
Brink, D. 190n6
Britain 9, 23, 115; British 98; intuitionism 10, 170, 188n1; tradition 13, 115; *see also* England; English; UK
British Equality and Human Rights Commission (EHRC) 175
Broome, J. 115, 117
Brown, D. 37–8, 51, 53, 56, 61, 99, 142, 190n1, 194n8

capability 95, 121, 124–5, 138, 149, 153–5, 176–7, 196n7; account of justice 138; approach 4–5, 136–41, 146–55, 175; physical and mental 93; set 139, 147, 154–5; of sympathy 58; theory 190n7
capitalist 131; capitalism 162, 165, 192n17; economy 185; personal expenditure 193n3; society 90, 192n17
Carlyle, T. 63
Clark, B.S. 148
Collard, D. 189n10
Comte, A. 34
conduct 18, 29, 101; benevolent 20; ends of 64, 142, 147; human 16–17, 21–2, 64, 86, 88, 144, 146–7, 167, 188n8, 150n3; principles of 31; rational 63; rules of 46, 59, 102, 156; social 164; suppression of 102; wrong 52, 58
conflict 39, 41, 62, 131–2, 149, 151–2, 165, 191n7, 193n1; of liberties 101, 103, 134–5, 161; principles 31, 47, 89, 91, 94; reconciliation 155, 181, 184; of utilities 72, 147; views 90

consequentialism: 136, 140, 147 169–70
Copp, D. 51
Crisp, R. 17, 38–9, 42, 106, 190n6

democratic 127, 164; democracy 81; equality 125; political theorists 151
Dent, N.J.H. 61
De Prycker, V. 177
desert 77, 83, 86, 92, 157–9
development 23, 36, 38, 61, 177, 190n10; bit-by-bit 79; of economics 189n14; of emotivism 189n1; human 175–6; of neuroscience 169; self-development 69, 99; of utilitarianism 115, 136–7
doctrine 10, 54, 99, 136; body of 30; derivative 47, 83; of each for one 82; of ethical naturalism 60; false 11; functional 71; maximization 117; moral 14, 16, 29, 61, 115, 119; of morality 54, 66; of rights of individuality 100; Rawls's 134; secondary 77; teleological 113; utilitarian 14, 16, 78, 106, 146, 172, 177, 189n10, 195n2; of utility 54–5; wages-fund 109, 193n3
Donner, W. 25, 33, 38, 40–2, 44, 50, 68–70, 189n15, 189n5, 191n7
Dryer, D.P. 51

economists 2, 20, 77, 79, 88, 97, 99, 117, 126–8, 136, 139, 154, 192n17; classical 108–9; contemporary 138; English political 23; Italian 115; modern 109; utilitarian 113; welfare 115–116, 151
Edgeworth, F.Y. 113
egalitarian 74, 86, 183; anti-egalitarian 137; demands 165; egalitarianism 77, 107, 196n10; principles 194n4
eighteenth century 9–10, 79–80, 82, 108, 129, 171
Ekelund, B.R. 132, 165
emotion 20, 68, 169; automatic emotional responses 169; emotional capacities 179; emotional constitution 55; emotivism 189n1
empiricism 10; British 13, 134
end of life 46, 66, 144–5, 147, 172
England 129; eighteenth- and nineteenth-century 10, 79–80, 82, 91, 108, 129, 170; twentieth-century 189n1
English 10, 29; empiricism 134; legal system 79–80, 82, 97; people 22, 91; political economists 23
equality 4, 74–7, 81, 83, 90, 93–6, 100, 122, 123–5, 127, 131, 137, 149–50, 163–5, 180, 182–4, 191n2–3, 191n5, 191n7, 193n1, 195n14, 196n7; commitment to 191n2; distributional 82; ex ante 132; in formal justice 97; gender 138; of holdings 157; idea of 149, 196n7; of income or wealth 106; material 159; notion of 79, 83, 86; of opportunities 122, 129, 166; principle 78; requirement of 92
Equality and Human Rights Commission 175, 196n8
Equality Measurement Framework (EMF) 175, 196n7–8
ethical 61, 67; claim 133; criterion 35; intuitionism 9–10, 44, 170–1; intuitionists 55, 170; meta-ethical reflection 42; mistake 137; naturalism 14, 60; questions 102, 147, 194n13; relativism 89, 191n8; standard 25, 34–5; studies 169; theories 114, 172; theorists 2; thinking 29; writings 43, 170
ethics 30, 34, 54–5, 63, 117, 171–2, 178, 189n4, 191n3; applied 44; distributive 78; psychological foundation 60; revolutionary approach 170; virtue ethics 43, 190n8
ethology 22–4, 30
eudemonia (or eudaimonia) 145; eudemonic happiness 66; eudaimonic well-being 175, 179
expediency 2–3, 35–7, 52, 54, 58; inexpediency 72; simple 51, 56–7, 59, 108

fellow-feeling 25, 174
Feser, E. 157, 195n1
first principle: 10, 30, 32, 42, 44–5, 47–9, 66, 77, 79, 83, 88, 98, 90, 120, 135, 142, 169, 177, 179; 107; of all human conduct: 64; of justice: 48, 74, 77–86, 119–23, 127; of life: 65; plurality of: 188n2; proof of: 64, 142; Rawls's: 119–27, 193n2 and secondary principles: 45–6, 90,
Frankena, W.K. 114, 190n6, 190n9
freedom 100–1, 107–8, 123–4, 128, 136–7, 140, 147–51, 153–4, 161–3, 181–2, 187, 196n8; absolute 153, 177, 185; of bequest 166–7; conflicting 103, 184; from corruption 181; economic 105, 161, 180–2, 184–5, 187; equal 98, 122, 129, 186; fiscal 181, 196n13; in the labour market 109; loss of 114, 134; of movement 180; negative 184–5;

neglected 136, 146; from pain 142, 144; personal 2, 124, 161; person's 139–40; of the property right 131; real 4, 161, 167, 182; realization of 106; substantive 5; supporting 113; valuable 176
Friedman, M. 182, 186
Fromm, E. 178–9
Fuchs, A. 38–40, 42–4, 190n10

Galbraith, J.K. 196n10
German: transcendentalists 10; metaphysicians 14; metaphysics 134
government 23, 30, 88, 93, 107, 132, 166, 181, 196n13; bad 183; coalition 192n16; commitment 165; dictatorial power 186; functions of 95; good 107, 123; interference 109, 128–9, 157; law enforcement 164; power of taxing 131, 133; protection 94; representative 81, 99; transfer of resources 155
Government Equalities Office (GEO) 175
Gray, J. 36, 41–2, 51, 65, 99–103, 162, 168, 190n11, 191n2, 193n1, 196n8–9, 197n15
Greene, J. 169–72, 196n2
Griffin, J. 71, 178

Halevy, E. 188n7
Hamilton, W. 9
Hammond, P.J. 152
happiness 3–6, 10, 14, 19, 21–2, 25, 37; as the end of all human conduct 22, 46, 64, 146; Greatest Happiness Principle 39, 46, 48, 50, 63, 66, 76, 77, 79–83, 85, 88–9, 117–18, 129, 144; index 175; promoting 31, 39, 51, 177
Hare, R.M. 39, 47, 89, 191n9
Harrison, J. 36
Harrod, R.F. 29, 36, 189n3
Harsanyi, J.C. 115–17, 189n3
Hart, H.L.A. 36, 77–8, 134–5
Hayek, F.A. 3–5, 156–67, 180, 182, 185, 190n11, 192n15, 195n1–3, 196n8–10, 197n17
Held, V. 106–7
Heritage Foundation 180–1, 196n12–13
Hicks, J. 115
Hicks–Kaldor criterion 126
Hoag, R.W. 193n1
Hobbes, T. 61
Hoffman, E. 189n12
Holdsworth, W. 80
Hollander, S. 160–1
Holtz-Eakin, D. 194n6
Hudson, W.D. 188n1
human 15–19, 21–2, 24–5, 46, 64, 86, 102, 147, 163, 174–5, 177, 179; beings 63, 65, 69, 71, 81–2, 87, 93, 96, 128, 134, 139, 148–51, 171, 173, 178, 184, 187; character 189n14; race 132; beings 6, 9–10, 33, 54, 58; conduct 31, 88, 144, 146, 167, 188n8, 190n3; faculties 13, 66–7, 69; nature 3, 5, 23, 89, 106, 123, 172, 189n10, 190n3; rights 196n8
Human Development Index (HDI) 175–6
human mind 9–10, 13, 16, 21–2, 24; Analysis of the Phenomena of the Human Mind 14, 56
Hume, D. 1, 9, 12–14, 32–3

illiberal 1, 152–3
impartiality 75, 85, 195n14
income 92–3, 95–6, 122, 124–5, 139, 148, 150, 153–4, 192n15–16; control 196n13; cut-off 108; distribution 131, 157, 159, 183, 196n9; gross national 176; income and happiness 173–4; maximization 126; for subsistence 176, 192n16; tax 47, 87, 90, 94, 98, 127, 148, 167; unearned 166–7; unequal 6, 106, 123
income and wealth 122–4, 139, 196n13; distribution 6, 125, 131, 157, 159; equality 93, 183; maximization 126
individual 22, 91, 94, 101, 128, 130, 133, 158; control over 186; happiness 176; liberty of the majority 184
individuality 99–102, 145–6, 153
inequality 124, 126, 149–50, 164–5, 196n7; economic 106–7; of income 106; of opportunities 93, 107, 123, 127, 129, 132, 165; unmerited 90; of utilities 137; of wealth distribution 180
inheritance 194n6; acquire by 133, 166; collateral 130; law 167, 195n14; protecting 166; right of 130–2; tax rate 165
inheritance taxation 127, 129–30, 192n15, 196n10; heavy 131–3; modern laws on 167; power to impose 166; progressive 133, 165
injustice 36, 55–7, 59, 86, 106, 127, 132, 138, 157, 185, 192n16; economic 98
institutionalization 175, 177
institutions 48, 80–1, 83, 123, 127–8, 136, 183, 191n11; bad 11; economic 3, 96, 99, 126, 151; human 89, 158, 195n5; just 90, 124; legal 125; modern 22;

institutions *continued*
political 3, 184; property 48, 88, 91–2, 165; social 5, 22, 24–5, 48, 91–2, 113, 119–20, 163, 167; taxation 95, 166
interests 17, 35, 94; conflicting 135; essential 177; human 191n7; long-term 128; other-regarding 18–19; others' 25, 64, 103, 151; own 18–19, 24, 101, 103; permanent 102, 147–8, 194n13; satisfaction of 103, 114; selfish 174; self-regarding 18; vested 81; vital 40
interpretation 3–5, 37, 67, 69–72, 75, 82, 85, 95, 98, 104, 115, 120, 125–6, 137, 142, 144, 152, 160, 189n5, 194n4; act- and rule-utilitarian 29, 36–8, 41, 44, 50; Berger's 25, 42, 100; Brown's 53, 190n1; Crisp's 39; dominant 127; Donner's 40; first 69; Hart's 77–8; Hayek's 159, 161; internal sanction 53; Lyons' 51, 53, 57; proportionality criterion 51; punishability 51, 56; revisionary 99–100; second 69, 85; Sen's 124, 149, 194n4; standard 78; traditional 31; unsympathetic 79; Urmson's 37; West's 43
intuitionism 29, 55, 61, 189n1; British 188n1; ethical 9–10, 44, 170–1; epistemological 10, 188n2; methodological 10
intuitionists 13, 171; British 10; ethical 55, 170

Johnston, D. 157
justice 1–6, 16, 35–6, 39–40, 45, 52, 55, 57, 60, 71, 74–6, 80, 83–4, 86–93, 97–8, 100–1, 104–6, 121, 123–5, 127, 151; commutative 87–8, 120–1, 193n1; conceptions of 75–7, 95, 120–1, 127, 196n7; distributive 1–2, 4–5, **48**, 54, 95–6, 103, 107, 109, 114, 119–20, 131, 133, 150, 153–6, 158–9, 161, 193n1, 194n2; economic 3–4, 183; formal 75–6, 124; principle of 191n10, 193n3; principles of 4, 47, 49, 94, 116, 118, 122, 126, 149, 193n1, 194n4; sentiment of 16, 58–9, 188n4; substantive 149–50, 164–5; taxation 95; utilitarian account 1, 74, 89, 140
justification 11, 81, 128, 148, 166; of the claim to protection 84; of individual liberty 102–3; moral 59; of rules 61, 64; of universal suffrage 80

Kahneman, D. 196n1
Kamm, F.M. 170, 195n16
Kant, I. 58–9; moral theory 9–10
Kelly, P.J. 81, 188n7, 191n7
knowledge 22, 58, 157, 169, 178, 196n8; access to 176; basic 122; fountains of 175; human 11; means of 128; moral 10–11, 171, 196n2; of political economy 130; scientific 30, 179; set of 32; system of 5–6, 30, 168, 177; theory of 188n3
Kreider, S.E. 194n9
Kringelbach, M. 67–8, 179
Kymlicka, W. 85

labour 21, 93, 106; force 194n6; freedom 181; fruits of 2, 92, 131–2, 165, 185; market 108–9; remuneration of 129; theory of value 97
labourers 90, 108–9; landless 137; moral rights 193n4; skilled 129
labouring classes 108–9, 118, 193n3
Lachmann.L.M. 195n3
laissez-faire 98–9; principle 105–6, 128
Lambert, P.J. 126
Larmore, C. 190n8
law 12–13, 33, 51, 56–7, 59, 76, 84, 104, 129, 131, 161, 164–5, 178, 188n8; administration of 124; of association 12, 14; elementary 12; emotional constitution 55; enforcement 192n17; English 79–80, 97; equality before the law 75, 123–4, 156, 163–5; of escheat 130, 133; on inheritance 132, 167, 195n14; known 58; mechanical 12; of mind 11–12, 22–3, 160; minimum-wage 108–9; physical 161; of production and distribution 158–61, 195n2; of property 2; rule of law 156, 167, 180–1; sociological 23; universal 22
Layard, R. 196n3
legal 82, 175; entitlement 75; freedom 101; minimum wage 108; reform 79–80, 82, 129; right 57, 125; rules 47, **48**; security 176; system 79
Légé, P. 157–8, 195n2
legislation 1, 17, 35, 81, 93, 107, 123, 132, 157, 165, 184; minimum-wage 108–9
legitimate 43, 61, 103, 131, 178; legitimacy 74
liberal 98, 153; activist 168; element 127; equality 125; justice 100; Paretian Liberal Paradox 151–2; policy 166; society 6; thinkers 5
liberalism 99, 101, 168; neo-liberalism 186
liberty 3, 5–6, 84, 99–107, 113–14, 118,

124, 129, 134–5, 138, 149–50, 157, 161–3, 165, 167–8, 179, 182, 185, 187; basic 121; economic 108, 180; equal 1–2, 4, 122, 126; individual 2, 4, 111, 151–3, 156, 159, 164, 180–1, 184; love of 186; natural 125; negative 196n8; personal 2, 142
Lukes, S. 157
Lyons, D. 36–7, 51–4, 57, 99

McCloskey, H.J. 78–9, 84
MacIntyre, A. 189n1, 190n8
McRae, R.F. 188n3
Mack, E. 156
MacLeod, A.M. 157
majority 40, 46; liberty threatened 184, 186; neglected 79, 129; sacrifice of the few 79, 81; tyranny of 82
Marx, K. 192n17
Mill, James 12–15, 17, 21 46, 54, 56, 60
Mill, J.S. 1–6, 9–19, 21–5, 29–79, 82–109, 113–20, 122, 127–34, 137–8, 141–7, 149–51, 156–63, 165–6, 168, 170–7, 179–80, 183–7, 188n3–9, 189n11–13, 190n8–10, 190n2–3, 190n6, 191n2, 191n10, 193n1–4, 194n13, 195n14, 195n2, 195n5, 196n7
Miller, D. 51, 53
Millgram, E. 190n6
Moore, G.E. 29, 189n1
morality 3, 13, 16, 30, 35–6, 40, 51, 54–9, 61–2, 64, 74, 144, 153, 171–2, 177–9, 189n4, 190n8, 191n8; a priori view of 10–11, 14; customary 39; doctrine of 54, 66; first principle 2–3, 10, 37, 44, 135, 169; Mill's 43–4, 50, 52–3, 189n4, 190n8; personal 138; practical 163; rules of 160; standard of 34, 91, 137; theory of 4, 29, 31, 38, 49–50, 136, 142, 146, 170, 194n10; ultimate principle 31; utilitarian 9, 25, 33, 47, 189n10
moral knowledge 196n2; a priori 10–11, 171
moral philosophy 1, 5, 115, 117, 133, 153, 185, 189n4, 194n10; first principle 179; Mill's 3, 6, 9, 30, 36, 43–4, 168, 175, 177; modern 190n8; system 5, 9, 30, 36, 50, 141, 146; utilitarian 3, 9, 21–2, 141, 186; Western 178
moral principles 6, 45, 48, 52, 87; secondary 32, 46, 90
moral reasoning 42, 90; consequentialist 170; Mill's 45, **48**, 50; practical 42, 61; rules of 32; three-level structure 39; utilitarian 3, 30, 43, 188n5
moral sciences 9, 23
moral sense 10, 13–14, 64, 68–9, 171, 188n1, 196n2
moral sentiments 16, 24–5, 54, 189n15; origin of 9, 13, 15, 53, 58, 60, 188n4; theory of 14
moral theory 2–3, 6, 9, 13, 17, 32, 34–6, 38, 54, 57, 58, 66, 78, 115, 136, 138, 147, 171; Bentham's 188n9; comprehensive 24, 119, 135; Kantian 9–10; Mill's 10, 24, 29–30, 37, 39–44, 50–3, 61, 68, 89; right-based 53; teleological 86, 114; utilitarian 22, 63, 83, 117, 144, 174
Morgenstern, O. 115–16
motivation 19, 53, 136, 142; of doers 34–5; Mill's 53–4, 82
motives 14, 18–21, 23, 25, 134, 159; base 189n11; of conduct 16–17, 188n8, 190n3; spontaneous 15
Mueller, D.C. 126, 134
Musgrave, R.A. 126, 192n12
Myers, D.G. 175

Nathanson, S. 162
needs, basic: 108, 125, 174, 182–3, 192n16
neo-liberals 5, 186
Neumann, J.von 115–16
neuroscience 67, 172; neuroactivities 68; neuropsychology 171; neuroscientific 6, 169–70
nineteenth century 9–10, 23, 54, 79, 80, 82, 91, 100, 108, 129, 150, 170–1; late 4, 115
non-hedonists 46; non-hedonistic 99
Nussbaum, M.C. 145, 153

objections 53, 55, 69, 78, 149, 159, 161; to utilitarianism 35, 54, 172, 178, 190n7
Okun, A.M. 194n4
On Liberty 100–1, 103–4, 145, 153, 161, 177, 186
other-regarding 100; interests 18; matters 101, 103; motives 19

pain 14, 17–21, 47, 63, 65–7, 143, 145–6, 178–9; freedom from 142, 144; painful feelings 60
Paretian Liberal Paradox 151–2
Pareto improvement 126; optimality 152
Pareto, V. 115
paternalism 152–3, 172, 177
Pattanaik, P.K. 116
Perelman, C. 75–6, 90, 92, 95, 124

Phelps, E.S. 87–8
Pigou, A.C. 113, 115
philosophers 1–2, 181; philosophy 149; reform 81–2, 168, 170; theorists 99, 151
pleasure(s): 15–21, 47, 51, 59, 63, 65–6, 104, 137, 141–8, 179; higher and lower: 66–73, 102, 118, 172–6, 190n6, 192n14
political 23, 99, 119, 135, 175, 179, 186; agenda 177; debate 180–1, 192n16; economic writings 88; economy 30, 130, 149, 159–61; ethology 22, 24; institutions 3, 125–6, 184; liberty 124; order 5; policy 148; theory 138, 182, 187
political and moral philosophy 1, 55, 133
politics 11, 30, 175, 186; of happiness 6, 177
Postema, G.J. 81–2, 191n7
post-utilitarian paradigm 79, 82, 84, 119
Prichard, H.A. 189n1
principle 30, 45, 47–8, 74, 89–91, 94–5, 97–9, 105, 107, 114, 118–19, 121–4, 126–7; conflict 31, 39; of distributive justice 101, 125; of economic justice 76, 88; first 120, 188n2; moral 6, 32, 46, 52, 87; practical 83; of right 134; of sanctions 44; secondary 49
Principle of Political Economy 94, 97, 105, 130, 160, 163, 192n13
principle of utility 30–2, 36, 44–5, 48, 52, 62, 65, 77–8, 82–3, 87, 89, 107, 118, 121, 142, 145, 147, 153, 179, 184; Bentham's 79–80; Brown's 194n8; first 42, 46–7, 49, 90; Mill's 2, 4, 37–8, 41, 50, 64–5, 76, 85, 98–9, 103, 113, 120, 193n1
principles of justice 4, 47, 49, 60, 74, 76, 84, 97–8, 116, 118, 120–7, 149, 193n1, 194n4; conflicting 94; for remuneration 98; secondary 89–90
property 15, 61, 63, 68, 106, 130, 133, 185; accumulation of 125; escheat 130, 133; inequalities 93, 131, 165; institutions 88, 92; laws of 2; moral 13; ownership 105, 180; private 48, 90–2, 131–2, 165–6; protection 94; right 129, 131–2, 166, 180–1; security 183; unearned 133
proportionality 42, 50–51, 92
psychological analyses 12, 14; characteristic 25; crisis 46; egoism 17–19; experiments 171; fact 55; features 121; foundations 3, 6, 9, 11, 60, 172; hedonism 17; state 141; study 175; theory 171
psychology 11–13, 22, 30, 67, 72, 168, 172, 189n13; associationist 16, 21, 104, 146; moral 61, 169–70; neuropsychology 171; phenomena of mind 12, 189n13
punishability 41–2, 50–1, 53, 56

Qizilbash, M. 152–3, 195n16
Quinn, M. 81–2, 191n4, 191n7

Rabinowicz, W. 71
Rae, D. 75
Raphael, D.D. 14
Rawls, J. 1–5, 9, 60, 87, 103, 114, 116, 120–8, 134–5, 137–8, 149, 152, 156, 180, 191n6, 191n11, 193n2–3, 194n5; *A Theory of Justice* 1, 100, 113, 115, 117–19, 133, 194n2
reward 15, 129, 165; in accordance 92, 166; *ex post* 93; of labour 97, 167, 183
Ricardo, D. 193n2
right 31, 35–6, 42, 50–1, 62, 92, 114, 122, 131, 190n9, 194n13, 196n4; of bequest 127, 130–2, 166; concept of 42, 51, 122, 131; of inheritance 130–2; the right and the good 4, 61, 118, 133–4 ; right and wrong 10, 29, 31, 39, 42, 44, 51–4, 60–1, 72, 142, 146, 171, 194n8
rightness 2, 42, 50–1, 146, 171; moral 41; rightness and wrongness 13, 24, 34–5, 37–8, 42, 50–1, 53, 60, 118, 190n7
rights 39, 43, 57, 122, 130, 137, 147, 191n11; accepted 40; assigned 120; basic 117, 119, 124, 134; of bequest 127; equal 2, 4; human 175, 177; individual 152; legal 125; of liberty 100, 129; natural 80; neglecting 136, 146; personal 59, 104; property 181; proprietary 132; slave 86; violation of 114; voting 81; women's 168
Riley, J. 53, 70–2, 102, 190n6, 194n7
Robson, J.M. 52, 63
Rosen, F. 78–9, 81, 119
Ross, W.D. 189n1
Ryan, A. 10, 31, 37, 78, 99
Ryff, C.D. 175

Sally, D. 189n12
sanctions 44, 60; internal or external 53
Saunders, B. 191n7
Sawyers, R.B. 194n6
Scarre, G. 14, 189n1–2
Schaller, W.E. 53, 190n1
Schmidt-Petri, C. 72, 191n7

Schofield, P. 79–82
Schwartz, P. 197n17
science 6, 9, 11, 13, 22–3, 30, 45, 68, 169, 173, 175, 179, 189n5; advances in 168; cognitive 171–2; experimental 189n13; of happiness 68, 177–8; of man 174; moral 16, 32, 189n5; neuroscience 67, 169–70, 172; physical 188n3; of psychology 12; social 115
Sedgwick, A. 9, 62, 171
self-regarding 100; actions 102; area 103; interests 17–18; matters 101; motives 19
Seligman, M. 175
Sen, A. 2–5, 116–17, 124–5, 136–42, 146–56, 175, 178, 180, 190n7, 191n3, 194n4, 194n2–4, 194n12, 195n16
sex or gender 138, 150
Sidgwick, H. 113
slaves 86, 124, 178; slavery 160, 178
Slote, M. 190n8, 190n12
Smart, J.J.C. 78, 190n12
Smith, A. 1, 19–20, 33, 94, 108, 152, 189n4
Smith, V. 160, 189n12, 195n5, 196n6
Snowdon, C. 196n11
social 2, 4–5, 18, 23–5, 36, 47, 87–9, 91, 93, 116–17, 120–5, 127, 150–1, 156, 163–4, 183–4; arrangements 148, 191n3; climate 194n12; encroachment 153; feelings 189n10, 189n15; improvement 102; inequalities 126, 193n2; institutions 22, 48, 113, 119, 167; justice 1, 3, 90, 111, 157–9, 161, 180, 182, 187, 190n14, 195n2; mobility 166; motive 19; pressure 33; product 195n5; reform 82, 129, 168, 170; rules 41, 52; states 86; sympathies 58; utility 59, 71, 74, 84, 94, 100, 103–4, 134, 194n7; welfare 115
socialist 130, 182; ideal 165; ideas 159; mentality 5; socialism 90–1, 132, 157–8, 162
society 10, 22 –5, 36, 40, 45, 48, 59, 65, 76, 79, 83–5, 87–9, 92, 101–4; capitalist 90, 192n17; human 58, 91, 184; members 94, 185; modern 106–7, 130, 176, 185; structure of 24, 87, 120
social choice theory 116–17, 151
Stephen J.F. 100
Stiglitz, J. 196n10
Stoics 63
Stratton-Lake, P. 188n2
Su, H. 190n6, 192n15
subsistence 81–2, 109, 191n7, 193n4; income for 96, 148, 176, 192n16; means of 4, 106–8, 123, 129, 133, 148, 150, 163; minimum 107, 150, 163, 174, 182–3, 192n16; threats to 101, 105
suffrage 168; universal 80–1, 99, 191n5
Sugden, R. 93, 127, 152–3, 195n16
Sumner, L.W. 44, 51, 194n3
sum-ranking 5, 136–7, 140–1
sympathy: 17–20, 25, 58, 174

tax 76, 94, 193n4; allowances 96, 192n16; base 95, 130; granny tax 192n16; income tax 95–6, 127, 167; inheritance 131, 166; rate 95, 130, 165, 167; rate structure 95–6, 192n16; system 96, 192n16
taxation 88; income 87, 90, 94, 96, 98, 148; inheritance 127, 129–33, 165–7, 192n15, 196n10; justice 95; principles of 88, 94–5; proportional 96
tax rate 95, 130, 165; progressive 167; proportional 96, 167; structure 95–6, 192n16
teleology 4–5, 61–2, 64, 86, 114–15, 133–5, 147, 169
theory of life: 70–1, 142, 145
transcendentalism 44; German transcendentalists 10
twentieth century 5, 29, 36, 55, 75, 82, 98, 115, 117, 119, 140, 158; early 9, 29, 189n1, 194n5; mid 4, 9, 78, 99

UK 185; parliament 192n16
unhappiness 65, 80, 178–9
United Nations Development Programme (UNDP) 175–6
United States (USA) 23, 182, 184–5, 187, 197n16
Urmson, J.O. 36–7
utilitarianism 1–6, 9–11, 16, 24, 29; act-utilitarianism 3, 29–30, 36–7, 41–4, 84, 99, 140, 189n3; multilevel act-utilitarianism 38; rule-utilitarianism 3, 29–30, 36–44, 50–1, 99, 140, 189n2–3, 190n10; ideal moral code rule-utilitarianism 38–40, 190n10;
utilitarian theory of justice 3, 44, 74, 113, 138, 156, 196n7
utility 4, 16, 41, 50, 78, 81, 87, 90, 103, 113, 118, 184; Bentham's principle of 77, 79–80; first principle of 42, 46, 49; general 25, 59–60, 71; marginal 96; maximizing 1, 51, 99, 116–17; Mill's principle of 2, 37–8, 64–5, 76, 85, 98–9,

utility *continued*
120, 145, 193n1; principle of 30–2, 36–8, 44, 48, 52, 62, 82–3, 89, 107, 121, 142, 147, 153, 179, 194n8; social 74, 84, 91, 94, 100, 134, 194n7
Uyl, D.D. 194n9

Varian, H.R. 126–7
violation 1, 105; of a common good 36; of free will 107; of distributive justice 131; of liberty 113, 122, 142, 154; of moral obligations 52; of rights 59, 114, 127; of principles 31; of rules 32, 35–6, 38, 40, 60; spirit of private property 165
virtue: 16, 22, 25, 63, 104, 119, 145–6; virtues and morality 32–5, 40, 43, 188n9; virtue ethics, 43, 190n8

welfare aggregate 77, 116; economics 78, 115–17, 140, 147–8, 194n5; economists 115–16, 151; general 77, 103; social 115–17, 127, 151; total welfare increase 126
welfarism 5, 136, 140, 146, 152
well-being 5, 33, 99, 138, 140, 150–1, 172, 196n7; aspect 154; eudaimonic 175, 179; hedonic 179; human 60, 139, 175, 178; individual 136; loss of 137; measure of 176; subjective 68, 173, 175; transfer primary goods into 124
West, H.R. 41, 43–4, 66–7, 71
Whewell, W. 9, 55, 171
Wilkinson, R. 196n 10–11
Williams, B. 2, 10, 78, 152, 188n2, 190n12
Wilson, F. 13
Wolff, E. 197n16

Yeager, L.B. 191n8